METALLICA
FLEETWOOD MAC
RUMOURS
DOORS
DIO
NIRVANA
NEVERMIND
Cream
DAVID BOWIE
HUNKY DORY
JETHRO TULL
JUDGES DISQUALIFY "LITTLE MILTON" IN LAST MINUTE RUMPUS
LATE EXTRA
RUSH
2112
IRON MAIDEN
GUNS N' ROSES
(pronounced 'leh-nerd 'skin-nerd)
AEROSMITH
ROCKS
RED BLOOD

sona
BOOKS

First published in the UK 2020 by Sona Books
an imprint of Danann Publishing Ltd.



All Images courtesy of;
Getty Images
Atlas Icons/Neil Zlozower
Chris Walter/Getty images
K & K Ulf Kruger OHG/Redferns/Getty images
Fin Costello/Getty images
Andre Csillag/REX/Shutterstock/rex
Atlas Icons/Neil Zlozower
Ron Pownall Photography
Michael Putland/Getty images
Peter Still/Getty images
Express/Getty images
Jeffrey Mayer/Getty images



CAT NO: **SON0480**
ISBN: **978-1-912918-32-4**

**Made in UAE.**

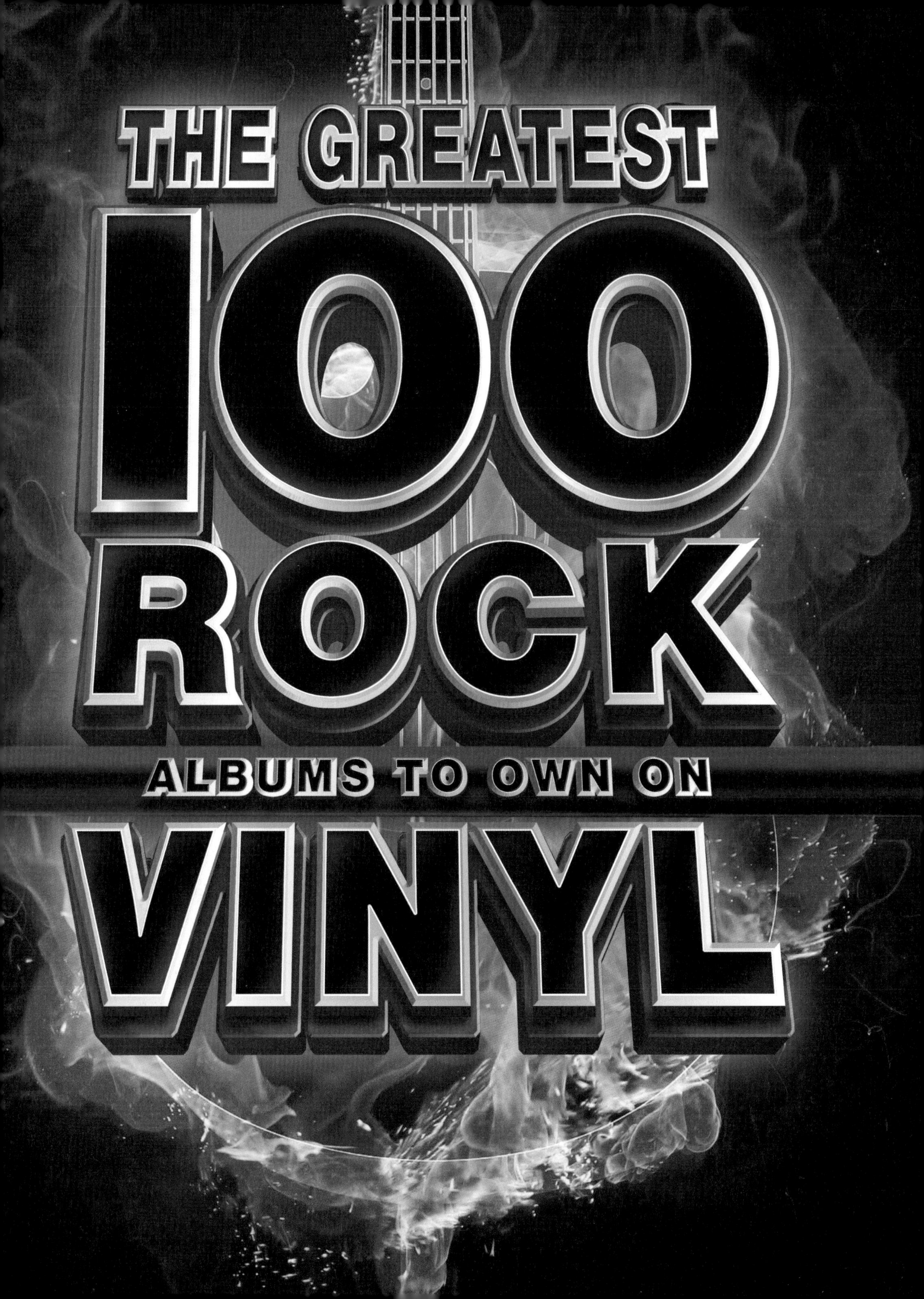

# THE GREATEST 100 ROCK ALBUMS TO OWN ON VINYL

# CONTENTS

**8-11 Bubbling Under**
The albums that didn't quite make the top 100.

**12-23 100-90**
From Foreigner 4 to Blood Sugar Sex Magik, via Tres Hombres and more.

**24-34 89-80**
Classic albums from Kiss, David Bowie, Bob Dylan, Queensrÿche, Ramones and more.

**34-45 79-70**
From Radiohead's prog classic to classic live double Strangers In The Night (UFO), via killer albums from Iron Maiden, Bon Jovi, Dire Straits and more.

**46-59 69-60**
Axis: Bold As Love, Live At Leeds, Live And Dangerous, Layla, Let There Be Rock and some other albums that don't begin with 'L'.

**59-69 59-50**
Prog classics In The Court Of The Crimson King and Aqualung, plus classic long players from Prince, Priest and the Pistols.

**70-81 49-40**
The countdown of the 50 greatest albums starts here. Let It Bleed, London Calling, Bat Out Of Hell and more.

**82-95 39-30**
In to the top 40, with LA Woman, Exile On Main St., Moving Pictures and the classic debut from Boston...

**95-105 29-20**
How Metallica upped their game on The Black Album, the revolving bedroom doors of Rumours, the Doors' dark debut, the birth of heavy metal and many more.

**106-117 19-11**
The countdown to the top continues with classic albums from Rush, The Beatles, David Bowie, Queen and more.

**118** *Led Zeppelin* – **Led Zeppelin**
The story behind their game-changing debut album.

**120** *Highway To Hell* – **AC/DC**
Their last album with Bon Scott was also their big breakthrough moment.

**122** *Abbey Road* – **The Beatles**
The last album recorded by The Beatles may be their finest statement and hardest rocking record.

**124** *Back In Black* – **AC/DC**
Death, rebirth and divine inspiration: the story behind the best-selling rock album of all time.

**126** *Appetite For Destruction* – **Guns N' Roses**
The biggest-selling debut album of all time is also the youngest album in the top 10.

**128** *Wish You Were Here* – **Pink Floyd**
How Floyd's loose concept album about absence and lost friends coincided with the band falling apart.

**130** *Sgt. Pepper's* – **The Beatles**
In praise of one of the best-loved albums in any genre.

**132** *Led Zeppelin II* – **Led Zeppelin**
Zep's second album set the template for the hard-rocking 70s. It's just beaten by it's younger brother.

**134** *Led Zeppelin IV* – **Led Zeppelin**
Stairway To Heaven, Black Dog, Rock And Roll, When The Levee Breaks – just four reasons why Zep's 'Four Symbols' will always be their best loved album.

**136** *The Dark Side of the Moon* – **Pink Floyd**
The album voted the greatest of all time.

**138 The making of The Dark Side Of The Moon**
The full unexpurgated story behind the making of the Greatest Rock Album Ever

# Bubbling Under

The albums that didn't quite make the top 100.

### Unleashed In The East
***Judas Priest***

The Metal Gods, live in Tokyo and hell bent for leather in '79.

...Like Clockwork – ***Queens Of The Stone Age***
Out of the Cellar – ***Ratt***
Too Fast For Love – ***Mötley Crüe***
Love It To Death – ***Alice Cooper***
Script For A Jester's Tear – ***Marillion***
Six – ***Mansun***
Trash – ***Alice Cooper***
Permission To Land – ***The Darkness***
The Man Who Sold The World – ***David Bowie***
Surfer Rosa – ***Pixies***
Goo – ***Sonic Youth***
Freak Out – ***The Mothers Of Invention***
Plastic Surgery Disasters – ***Dead Kennedys***
Texas Flood – ***Stevie Ray Vaughan***
Eat 'Em and Smile – ***Dave Lee Roth***
Electric – ***The Cult***
Blackbird – ***Alter Bridge***

### Tapestry
***Carole King***

A multi-million-selling songwriting masterclass.

To Our Children's Children's Children – ***The Moody Blues***
Glory Road – ***Gillan***
Kill 'Em All – ***Metallica***
Songs For The Deaf – ***QOTSA***
Woodstock Soundtrack – ***Various***
Harvest – ***Neil Young***
Full Moon Fever – ***Tom Petty***
Beck, Bogart & Appice – ***Beck, Bogart & Appice***
Bringing It All Back Home – ***Bob Dylan***
Band On The Run – ***Wings***
All Things Must Pass – ***George Harrison***
Blind Faith – ***Blind Faith***

Skid Row – ***Skid Row***
Roger The Engineer – ***The Yardbirds***
Hero And Heroine – ***The Strawbs***
Crime Of The Century – ***Supertramp***
Sweet Baby James – ***James Taylor***
L.A. Guns – ***L.A. Guns***
Slave To The Grind – ***Skid Row***
Diary Of A Madman – ***Ozzy Osbourne***
Kingdom Of Desire – ***Toto***
Leftoverture – ***Kansas***

### Script For A Jester's Tear
***Marillion***

The 1983 debut album from a new force in prog.

Tim – ***The Replacements***
The Modern Lovers – ***The Modern Lovers***
Battering Ram – ***Saxon***
Violator – ***Depeche Mode***
Dookie – ***Green Day***
All Mod Cons – ***The Jam***
Script Of The Bridge – ***The Chameleons***
Blast Tyrant – ***Clutch***
One More For The Road – ***Lynyrd Skynyrd***
Leave Home – ***Ramones***
Foxtrot – ***Genesis***
Blow By Blow – ***Jeff Beck***
Day for Night – ***The Tragically Hip***
One Hot Minute – ***Red Hot Chili Peppers***
Surfing With The Alien – ***Joe Satriani***
Captain Beyond – ***Captain Beyond***

### Fresh Cream – *Cream*

Expectations for Cream's first album at the end of 1966 were high. Eric Clapton had already been proclaimed God while both Ginger Baker and Jack Bruce had unimpeachable musical credentials. Fresh Cream fully justified Clapton's description of the group as "blues ancient and modern". There was nothing purist about Cream's approach to the blues. Bruce and Baker's jazzy rhythms and Clapton's panoply of guitar tones and controlled feedback took the blues to another level, vividly illustrated by their epic version of Howlin' Wolf's two-and-a-half-minute Spoonful.

## Rubber Soul – *The Beatles*

Having run out of steam on the lukewarm Help!, and with one eye on the evolving work of Bob Dylan, Rubber Soul found The Beatles tackling deeper subject matter and broadening their musical horizons beyond the 'work songs' that had previously been their stock-in-trade. Certainly the four personalities were starting to flavour the music, with Lennon and McCartney laying themselves bare on Nowhere Man and You Won't See Me, Harrison debuting his sitar obsession - for better or worse - on Norwegian Wood, and Ringo picking up his first co-writer credit for What Goes On.

Mellon Collie And The Infinite Sadness – ***Smashing Pumpkins***
Rubber Soul – ***The Beatles***
Vol. 4 – ***Black Sabbath***
A Bit Of What You Fancy – ***Quireboys***

## Presence
## ***Led Zeppelin***

Their difficult 7th album still has the power to blow minds.

Piledriver – ***Status Quo***
Sabbath Bloody Sabbath – ***Black Sabbath***
Who Are You – ***The Who***
Graceland – ***Paul Simon***
Some Girls – ***The Rolling Stones***
Next – ***The Sensational Alex Harvey Band***
Scenes From A Memory – ***Dream Theater***
A Day At The Races – ***Queen***
Caravanserai – ***Santana***
Definitely Maybe – ***Oasis***
My Aim Is True – ***Elvis Costello***
Stained Class – ***Judas Priest***
Moving Waves – ***Focus***
Violator – ***Depeche Mode***
Wind And Wuthering – ***Genesis***
Blackwater Park – ***Opeth***
Powertrip – ***Monster Magnet***
Hand. Cannot. Erase – ***Steven Wilson***
Eye Of The Tiger – ***Survivor***
Bridge Of Sighs – ***Robin Trower***
Slash – ***Slash***
Black Rose – ***Thin Lizzy***
High Voltage – ***AC/DC***
Wings Over America – ***Wings***
Synchronicity – ***The Police***
Teaser – ***Tommy Bolin***
Wheels of Steel – ***Saxon***
Fear Of A Blank Planet – ***Steven Wilson***

Cosmo's Factory – ***Creedence Clearwater Revival***
Alchemy – ***Dire Straits***
Night Moves – ***Bob Seger***
A Nod's As Good As A Wink To A Blind Horse – ***Faces***
Meddle – ***Pink Floyd***
Live Full House – ***J. Geils Band***
Passion And Warfare – ***Steve Vai***
Ride The Lightning – ***Metallica***
Texas Flood – ***Stevie Ray Vaughan***

## Angel Dust
## ***Faith No More***

Their 4th album was Mike Patton's real songwriting debut.

On A Storyteller's Night – ***Magnum***
Overkill – ***Motörhead***
Live – ***Status Quo***
Welcome To My Nightmare – ***Alice Cooper***
Heroes – ***David Bowie***
Hunky Dory – ***David Bowie***
Free – ***Free***
Out Of The Blue – ***ELO***
Goodbye Yellow Brick Road – ***Elton John***
Damn The Torpedoes – ***Tom Petty and Heartbreakers.***
Come Taste The Band – ***Deep Purple***
Village Green Preservation Society – ***Kinks***
Skylarking – ***XTC***
Repeater – ***Fugazi***
Bridge of Sighs – ***Robin Trower***

## Sheer Heart Attack
## ***Queen***

A move away from the batshit prog of their first two albums.

Operation: Mindcrime – ***Queensryche***

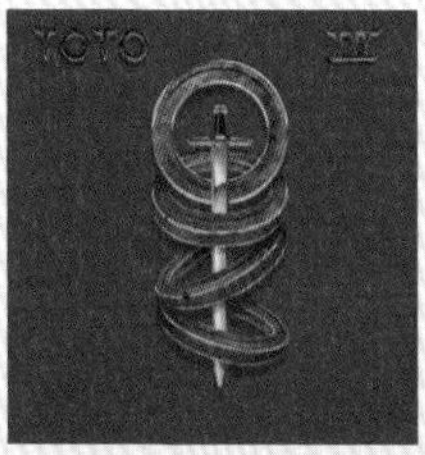

## Toto IV – *Toto*

Toto IV's slick sound - an immaculately crafted blend of AOR, progressive rock, light funk and soul - was slammed by Rolling Stone magazine as the epitome of corporate rock. But it went on to sell five million copies in the US, yielding the No.1 single Africa and the No.2 hit Rosanna. Africa was an unlikely hit song, with its unorthodox rhythmic structure, built around a drum loop from Jeff Porcaro, and with a convoluted, quasi-mystical lyric from David Paich, typified by the famous line: 'Kilimanjaro rises like Olympus above the Serengeti.'

## Animals – *Pink Floyd*

Animals shuns the widescreen musical soundscapes of Dark Side and Wish You Were Here and instead updates George Orwell's Animal Farm for a bleak, withering look at humanity. Roger Waters' lyrical vitriol drips all over the greedy, conniving Dogs, the self-righteous Pigs (Three Different Ones) and the downtrodden but finally rebellious Sheep. These three epic tracks are book-ended by the disarming two-part acoustic love song Pigs On The Wing. The prevailing musical atmosphere is sparse and menacing. It's not a pretty album but then it's not really meant to be.

***Throwing Cooper – Live***
Tago Mago – ***Can***
Low – ***David Bowie***
Days Of Future Passed – ***The Moody Blues***
Diary Of A Madman – ***Ozzy Osbourne***
Idlewild South – ***Allman Brothers***
Selling England by The Pound – ***Genesis***
Camembert Electrique – ***Gong***
Irish Tour '74 – ***Rory Gallagher***
John Barleycorn Must Die – ***Traffic***
The River – ***Bruce Springsteen***
Moondance – ***Van Morrison***

## Thick As A Brick ***Jethro Tull***

The ultimate concept album/parody of a concept album.

Leftoverture – ***Kansas***
Automatic For The People – ***REM***
News Of The World – ***Queen***
Images and Words – ***Dream Theater***
Contraband – ***Velvet Revolver***
Use Your Illusion I&II – ***Guns N' Roses***
Darkness On The Edge of Town – ***Bruce Springsteen & The E Street Band***
Fair Warning – ***Van Halen***
The Final Cut – ***Pink Floyd***
Brain Salad Surgery – ***ELP***
Argus – ***Wishbone Ash***
Montrose – ***Montrose***
Houses of The Holy – ***Led Zeppelin***
Frampton Comes Alive – ***Peter Frampton***
Moving Waves – ***Focus***
Heaven And Hell – ***Black Sabbath***
Queen II – ***Queen***
Weezer – ***Weezer***
Close To The Edge – ***Yes***
Last Decade Dead Century – ***Warrior Soul***
Loveless – ***My Bloody Valentine***

## Generation Terrorists ***Manic Street Preachers***

Like Appetite For Destruction, if it was made by brainy Welsh punks.

Burn My Eyes – ***Machine Head***
In Color – ***Cheap Trick***
The Crossing – ***Big Country***
Berlin – ***Lou Reed***

## Antichrist Superstar ***Marilyn Manson***

Where the parent-troubling star first hit big.

Sweetheart Of The Rodeo – ***The Byrds***
Psychocandy – ***The Jesus & Mary Chain***
Vivid – ***Living Colour***
In Search Of Space – ***Hawkwind***
Force It – ***UFO***
Trout Mask Replica – ***Captain Beefheart And His Magic Band***
Undertow – ***Tool***
Doolittle – ***Pixies***
Blue – ***Joni Mitchell***
Secret Treaties – ***Blue Oyster Cult***
Out of the Silent Planet – ***Kings X***
Odessey And Oracle – ***The Zombies***
The Holy Bible – ***Manic Street Preachers***
Truth – ***The Jeff Beck Group***
For Your Pleasure – ***Roxy Music***
The Polite Force – ***Egg***
Pretty Hate Machine – ***Nine Inch Nails***
Mott – ***Mott The Hoople***
Korn – ***Korn***
Cat Scratch Fever – ***Ted Nugent***
Peter Gabriel – ***Peter Gabriel***
Rated R – ***Queens Of The Stone Age***
Born Under a Bad Sign – ***Albert King***
Siamese Dream – ***Smashing Pumpkins***

## Made In Japan – *Deep Purple*

One of the all-time great live rock albums, and a great summation of Purple's career to date (in 1972), *Made In Japan* should really have made it into the top 100. When it was released in 1972, it was a revelation. There had been momentous live albums before (*Get Yer Ya-Ya's Out!* by the Stones, *Live At Leeds* by The Who) - but these were single LPs, glorified stop-gaps. *Made In Japan*, however, was the first time a truly international heavy hitter had made such a bold musical statement, just as its star was reaching the apex of its commercial ascendancy.

## Powerslave – *Iron Maiden*

Maiden's greatest album according to Classic Rock's website, Powerslave is the album that sent Maiden around the world on the legendary World Slavery tour, turning them into global megastars in the process. It is both the definitive record of the band's first decade and the album with the best artwork of all time. If you could prove such things scientifically, there would be no room for argument: Aces High, 2 Minutes To Midnight, Powerslave (featuring Dave Murray's greatest ever solo), the mighty Rime Of The Ancient Mariner... Everything else sounds a bit half-arsed in comparison.

The Downward Spiral – ***Nine Inch Nails***
Horses – ***Patti Smith Group***
Reckless – ***Bryan Adams***
Nebraska – ***Bruce Springsteen***
Unknown Pleasures – ***Joy Division***
Second Helping – ***Lynyrd Skynyrd***
Cheap Thrills – ***Big Brother & The Holding Company***
The Pretenders – ***The Pretenders***
Sonic Temple – ***The Cult***
Pearl – ***Janis Joplin***
Tarkus – ***Emerson, Lake & Palmer***

## Kick Out The Jams
## ***MC5***

1969 live debut that was a massive influence on punk.

Hybrid Theory – ***Linkin Park***
Marquee Moon – ***Television***
Piece s of Eight – ***Styx***
The Stone Roses – ***The Stone Roses***
Nothing's Shocking - ***Jane's Addiction***
Heart – ***Heart***
Back Street Symphony – ***Thunder***
The Bends – ***Radiohead***
Astral Weeks – ***Van Morrison***
So – ***Peter Gabriel***
Grace – ***Jeff Buckley***
The Real Thing – ***Faith No More***
Earth vs. The Wildhearts – ***The Wildhearts***
Clutching At Straws – ***Marillion***
Asia – ***Asia***
Electric Warrior – ***T.Rex***

## Transformer
## ***Lou Reed***

David Bowie produced and Mick Ronson arranged. Aces.

Surrealistic Pillow – ***Jefferson Airplane***
New Jersey – ***Bon Jovi***
American Beauty – ***The Grateful Dead***
Demons and Wizards – ***Uriah Heep***
Pump – ***Aerosmith***
Seasons In The Abyss – ***Slayer***
Outlandos d'Amour – ***The Police***
The Southern Harmony And Musical Companion – ***Black Crowes***
Raw Power – ***Iggy Pop & The Stooges***
Escape – ***Journey***
Permanent Vacation – ***Aerosmith***
Shake Your Money Maker – ***Black Crowes***
American Idiot – ***Green Day***
Fire and Water – ***Free***
Wheels Of Fire – ***Cream***
Badmotorfinger – ***Soundgarden***
Déjà Vu – ***Crosby, Stills, Nash & Yong***
The Band – ***The Band***
Blackout – ***Scorpions***
Blood On The Tracks – ***Bob Dylan***

## Dirt
## ***Alice In Chains***

Dark grungers' 1992 breakthrough album.

Eliminator – ***ZZ Top***
Abraxas – ***Santana***
Every Picture Tells A Story – ***Rod Stewart***
In The Land Of Grey And Pink – ***Caravan***
(What's The Story) Morning Glory? – ***Oasis***
Achtung Baby – ***U2***
Harvest – ***Neil Young***
No SleepTil Hammersmith – ***Motörhead***
Vulgar Display of Power – ***Pantera***
Aja – ***Steely Dan***
The Velvet Underground & Nico – ***The Velvet Underground***
Blues Breakers – ***John Mayall With Eric Clapton***
The Rotter's Club – ***Hatfield And The North***
Smash – ***The Offspring***

## The Clash – *The Clash*

An album about people in boring jobs, with annoying bosses, in a world going to shit - a London burning with boredom, where everyone sits around watching American cop shows on the TV, (because killers in America work seven days a week). A world where you get hassled in the street by cops and pressured to take a shit job down the Job Centre, 'hate and war' has replaced 'peace and love' and the world is full of cheats and junkies. Sounds joyless? It's only half the picture. The Clash is full of defiance and dark humour and plenty of cheap thrills.

# 100 *Foreigner* 4

The statistics for Foreigner's *4* prove that all the hours, days, weeks and months in the studio, all the deadlines missed, all the budgets broken, were ultimately worth it.

The album enjoyed 10 weeks (in three spells) at No.1 in the Billboard charts, starting on August 22, 1981 and ending February 11, 1982. American sales exceeded six million. It remains the band's best seller in the UK, reaching No.5, and earning a gold disc, while it also made No.4 in Germany. Of the six songs released as singles in the US, only the last - Luanne, in 1982 - failed to go Top 30.

Perhaps most importantly of all, 30 years later all 10 of these songs still resonate strongly. *4*, Foreigner's fourth album, is their masterpiece. Co-produced by Mick Jones and 'Mutt' Lange - the latter on a hot streak having done AC/DC's *Back In Black* - *4* had a state-of-the-art arena rock sound that made it a US No.1.

There was heavy rock'n'roll in *Nightlife* and *Juke Box Hero*, and a raunchy R&B vibe in *Urgent*, which featured a wild sax solo from Motown legend Jr. Walker. And in *Waiting For A Girl Like You* there was sophistication in its subtle, drifting synthesiser textures, and an extraordinary emotional depth in Lou Gramm's vocal. Justin Hawkins of The Darkness calls it "the greatest rock ballad of all time".

So time and money are relative. As is failure.

A bit of context is needed. Foreigner were a success right out of the box: Stateside, their self-titled debut of 1977 sold five million copies and reached No.4. A year later, their second effort, *Double Vision*, made No.3 in the US - even climbing to No.32 in the UK - and shifted seven million copies. So when third album *Head Games*, released in 1979, stalled at No.5 on the Billboard chart and only went quintuple platinum, something was deemed to have gone wrong.

"That did start the thinking," says guitarist Mick Jones, "that we needed to be positive about our identity for the fourth album... I think on *Head Games* we really went into 'excessive mode'. The drugs came into the picture a bit too much there. So we kind of had a massive hangover after that album [laughs]. I look back on it and think it wasn't quite focused. We tried to toughen the image of the band up with *Dirty White Boy* and *Head Games* itself, but that's where the question about where we were going originated..."

Guitarist and band-leader Rick Wills was more concerned that the demands of keyboard player Al Greenwood and ex-King Crimson multi-instrumentalist Ian McDonald to be included in the songwriting process would weaken the band. Greenwood was dismissed first, McDonald followed soon after.

Jones: "It was a tough time, emotionally. Ian was a close friend, but Lou [Gramm, singer] and I

year released
**1976**

producer
**Denny Cordell**

Tom Petty was been many things during his lengthy career - but never a sitting target. His gumption rose to the surface defiantly when he withheld his fourth album, *Hard Promises*, from label MCA, who wanted to put it into the shops at $9.98, a dollar higher than most records retailed for. Petty threatened to rename the record *The $8.98 Album*, before the men in suits finally relented.

That was in 1981. Four years earlier, only great reviews in the UK had convinced the label to persevere with his debut album *Tom Petty & The Heartbreakers*. The record had actually been released 12 months earlier, but the US only caught on to Petty with the re-release of previous flop single *Breakdown*, which proved to be a slow-burner commercially.

"I wrote *Breakdown* on a break from recording at Shelter Studio in Hollywood," Petty reflected, years later. "I think we took a break because we had recorded everything we had. And I made up *Breakdown*. I wrote it on piano. I still have that piano. I

year released
1981

producer
Mutt Lange and Mick Jones

just felt we had hit our stride writing together and we wanted to really start to maximise on that. We talked at length about it and had a fairly clear vision of where we wanted to go, so it was a question of being a bit ruthless. We felt we wanted to focus."

One of the songs that was helping them focus was a ballad, *Waiting For A Girl Like You*. "Mick tended to write most of the songs on a piano, using mostly the black notes, so everything was in sharps and flats, and little bit weird when it came time to transpose them to the guitar... As I recall, it was fairly bitty at first, but the one song he did have completely finished was *Waiting For A Girl Like You*. The first time they played it to me, I said, 'Well if that isn't a hit, I don't know what is!'" Wills recalls.

Asked to reflect on the success of *4* today, Jones says. "It was definitely the sum of what I thought we'd been building towards. When I look back on it I know it's my favourite album. But looking back it's the one I always say I'm probably the most proud of."

# 99 *Tom Petty And The Heartbreakers*

# Tom Petty And The Heartbreakers

bought it. [Laughs].

"Many years later it's sitting in my living room. I wrote it very quickly. I played it to them [his band] and they really dug it and we made the record. I think we got that drum beat from a Beatles record, *All I Got To Do*. We just varied it. That was the idea, to have that kind of broken rhythm on the hi-hat."

As the western world prepared to go incendiary over punk, Petty stepped out of the shadows with a stripped-back record that combined the best bits of the mid-70s musical melting pot.

Driven by understated guitar chimes and Benmont Tench's organ swirls, the impact of his eponymous debut may not have been instant, but the early Springsteen backing vocals of *Breakdown* and call-to-arms battle cry *Anything That's Rock 'N' Roll* helped make certain it would become an enduring classic. The record's best-known anthem is *American Girl* – the guitar riff of which was later filched in its entirety by The Strokes [for *Last Nite*, taken from the New York band's 2001 debut *Is This It*].

Age didn't blunt the man from Gainesville, Florida, either. In 2002 Petty took the brave step of releasing a record (*The Last DJ*) which aimed stinging bile at what he saw as the homogenisation of the US's network of independent radio stations.

In interviews, too, he was never backward in coming forward; a music TV channel was blasted for removing ''n'roll' from 'rock'n'roll', and promoting the likes of Latin chanteuse Shakira as 'rock' artists.

He may once have proclaimed himself "incredibly lazy", but Petty kept many irons in the fire.

"It always makes me laugh when people say my music is simple," he claimed. "Because if you think it's simple, try to do it. It's not simple. There's a lot of nuance. And light and shade. It's not a simple thing. I was in a music store, and this guy tried to impress me by playing all our licks... And he had every one wrong. He had the right root of the chord, but we use a lot of variations. And this guy was playing everything straight."

It's an approach that won him critical praise and scores of devoted fans over the years, including famous ones.

"Tom Petty represents all the things you love about Americana and rock'n'roll," says Juliette Lewis, "but there's an understated-ness to the sound that makes it feel very real – like you're there in the room with him."

Ultimately, Tom Petty was that rare breed of rocker who enjoyed enormous commercial and critical success, both with The Heartbreakers and as a solo artist – and for a very long time. To this day he continues to create music that is fresh and dynamic.

# 98 *Megadeth*
# Peace Sells...But Who's Buying?

With the mercurial Dave Mustaine steering them, LA's Megadeth brought an element of explosive volatility to thrash. If Metallica were the scene's party-loving kingpins, Slayer its cartoon Satanists and Anthrax its court jesters, then Megadeth were its feral delinquents.

That they managed to make one of the defining albums of the thrash era in *Peace Sells...* – and one of its most immortal songs in the classic title track – is some achievement. That they managed to do it without killing each other or themselves is nothing short of miraculous.

"Dave and I were in a position where there was no Plan B," says Dave Ellefson. "There was no escape hatch. There was no: 'If this doesn't work we'll go do that.' That backs-against-the-wall commitment is what drove us to make *Peace Sells.*"

*Peace Sells* remains one of the most iconic tracks of the thrash era. With its instantly recognisable bass line and rolling groove, it set Megadeth apart from the thrash pack. Lyrically, too, its jaundiced view of government and religion dispensed with metal's traditional swords 'n' sorcery approach in favour of a more realistic world view. When Mustaine sang: 'What do you mean, I don't support your system? I go to court when I have to,' he meant it. This was CNN as filtered through the eyes of a street punk.

The album did occasionally stray into standard-issue heavy metal horror territory, though. *Bad Omen* was based on a 1972 supernatural novel by Thomas Tyron that Mustaine remembered reading at school, while *The Conjuring* is an occult ritual set to music, supposedly with a partial hex embedded in the lyrics (the band stopped playing the song in the 2000s because it clashed with the frontman's Christian beliefs).

Corniest of all is the serial-killer fantasy *Good Mourning/Black Friday*, although its tale of a 'bloodthirsty demon stalking the streets' has been undercut in recent years by fans posting memes featuring the song's lyrics on Twitter on the US shopping day Black Friday.

*Peace Sells... But Who's Buying?* was released on September 19, 1986, six months after Metallica's *Master Of Puppets* and a month before Slayer's *Reign In Blood*. Thrash metal was undergoing a transformation. No longer was it seen as heavy metal's feral offspring, but as a legitimate musical movement, a changing of the guard.

This new-found respect was reflected in the media's reaction. Where Megadeth had previously been confined to the underground metal press, they were now being written about by the likes of the *NME* and *Rolling Stone*. "I remember *Rolling Stone* saying I was the new Stevie Ray Vaughan," says Mustaine. "I was like, 'Get the fuck out.' Cos I love Stevie Ray Vaughan."

Like punk before it, thrash metal was a break with

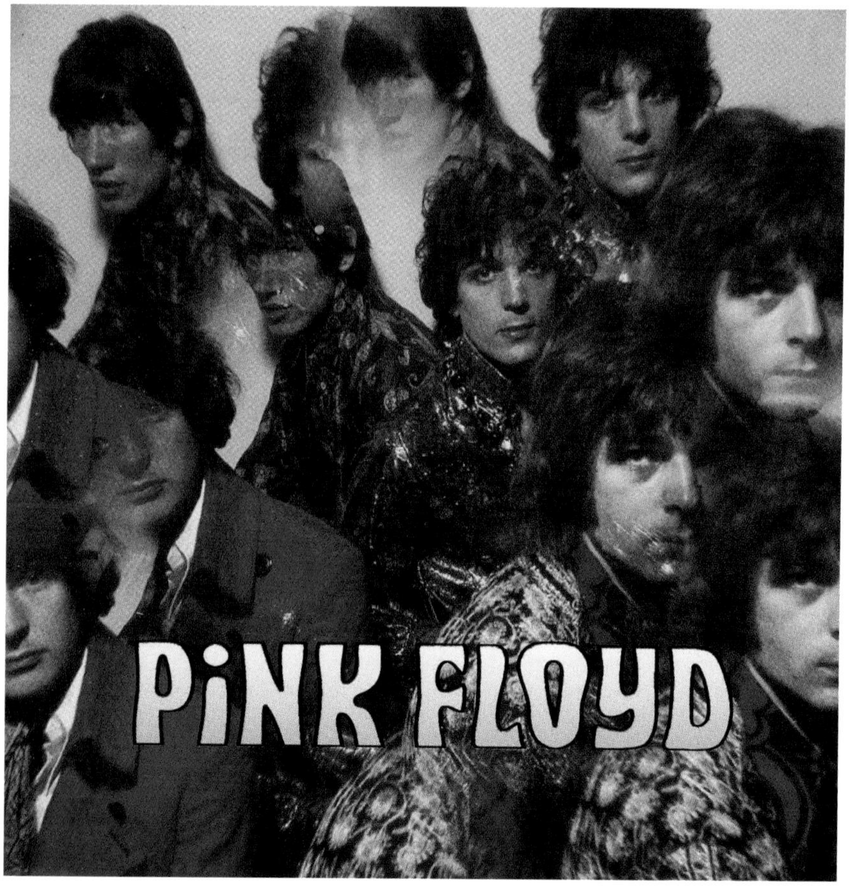


year released
**1967**

producer
**Norman Smith**

This was the first full album from Pink Floyd and a sparkling testament to the genius of Syd Barrett who wrote virtually the whole of this psychedelic masterpiece off the top of his head, so to speak.

Liberated by LSD, Barrett's songs take flight on a magic carpet of cosmic philosophy (*Astronomy Domine, Chapter 24*), surreal whimsy (*Matilda Mother, Flaming*), and sublime nursery rhyme lyrics (*The Gnome, Scarecrow, Bike*), bolstered by trippy, technicolour instrumentals (*Interstellar Overdrive, Pow R Toc H*). The rest of the band are willing and able fellow travellers.

The album was immediately pronounced sacred by the small cult of flower children and it remains the musical Mecca for British psychedelia. Sadly for Syd it was a brief flowering followed by a nervous breakdown. But his spirit has hovered over the band ever since.

It's difficult to explain to anyone who wasn't there at the time, the impact made when *The Piper At The Gates Of Dawn* appeared on the musical landscape of 1967.

year released
**1986**

producer
**Dave Mustaine and Randy Burns**

the past. Metal's old guard didn't understand its velocity and realism, its lack of dragons and rainbows. Megadeth's audience wasn't just the denim and leather crowd, it also pulled in skate punks and surf rats, kids who grew up listening to Black Flag rather than Black Sabbath. Influential skate mags such as *Thrasher* latched on to the likes of Megadeth, giving them an air of edginess that the previous generation lacked.

More than 30 years on, *Peace Sells...* remains one of the benchmark records of the 1980s. Megadeth themselves arguably bettered it with *Rust In Peace*, an album that benefitted from their newfound sobriety, but even that can't match the sheer youthful rush of *Peace Sells*.

More significantly, *Peace Sells... But Who's Buying?* – along with Metallica's *Master Of Puppets*, Slayer's *Reign In Blood* and, a year later, Anthrax's *Among The Living* – was one corner of the foundations for the Big Four. Thrash metal had grown out of its adolescence and was hurtling full-tilt towards adulthood. The guard had changed, and things would never be the same again.

# 97 *Pink Floyd* The Piper At The Gates Of Dawn

In a year when the singles chart was swaying to the likes of crooner Engelbert Humperdinck's *Please Release Me* and the album chart was in the vice-like grip of The Beatles' *Sgt. Pepper* and *The Sound Of Music* soundtrack album, and cod-psychedelia was all over everything like a fluro-pimpled rash, *The Piper At The Gates Of Dawn* came arcing in from a different orbit altogether.

It's certainly a schizophrenic record, with Barrett's whimsical, sometimes almost childlike lyrics and bouncy, nursery-rhyme melodies (*Bike, The Gnome*), sharing the same head-space as psychedelic experimentalism and pioneering space rock exploration (*Astronomy Domine, Take Up Thy Stethoscope And Walk*, and the expansive but popular *Interstellar Overdrive*).

But for all the schizophrenia and some seemingly disparate elements, the different, potentially clashing musical personalities end up being remarkably well-balanced.

Ground-breaking, unique and influential, *The Piper At The Gates Of Dawn* was not an 'easy' first listen in 1967 and it still isn't today. The fact that it spent several weeks in the UK Top 10 probably had as much to do with the consumption of acid by people who bought it as by those who recorded it.

In retrospect, looking back on their whole career, it's difficult to overstate the influence of Pink Floyd as a defining force in rock culture. And it's not just about the number of records they've sold. You can reel off pages of statistics concerned with the success of *Dark Side Of The Moon*, but that doesn't tell you why that album – both the music and the album sleeve itself – from 1973 became an icon for a generation. Or why Pink Floyd became a phenomenon that has affected every generation since. The answer is that they have made some of the most amazing, most singular music in rock.

The punks may have hated the band and what they often (wrongly) perceived they stood for, but Pink Floyd's bile against the system was often as venomous as anything the punks could spit out.

And through the 80s and 90s, angst-ridden teenagers, including legions who later would also make an impact with their own music – from Axl Rose to Trent Reznor to Billy Corgan to Noel Gallagher – grew up listening to The Wall. Pink Floyd had an impact on them all.

"For me, the joy of Pink Floyd was going backwards and discovering what they did before," Pink Floyd fan and Soundgarden frontman Chris Cornell told us in 2016. "And the important thing about *The Piper At The Gates Of Dawn* was the music's strange juxtaposition – sometimes whimsical and pastoral, but simultaneously desperate and sad. I don't think I ever found another record which that type of dichotomy worked so well. With Syd Barrett, it never felt like an invention."

# 96 *Soundgarden* Superunknown

The Seattle band, one of the first to record for Sub Pop, had already, with 1991's *Badmotorfinger*, established themselves as the leading lights of the new alternative rock scene alongside Nirvana and Pearl Jam.

But this was the one that propelled them into the stratosphere, selling nine million copies worldwide and earning critical raves that positioned *Superunknown* in the classic pantheon.

That's "classic" in the broadest sense. *Superunknown* stands out as a key release of its period, but you could just as easily play it back to back with the greats from an earlier era. Chris Cornell's piercing blues wail nods to Robert Plant while Kim Thayil's riffs at their sludgiest have the heavy torpor of Tony Iommi's for Black Sabbath.

Soundgarden had not formed overnight (the band originally started in 1984), and they played unrequited metal – albeit metal melded with deranged humour on their debut 1988 album *Ultramega OK*. And even then, with the psychedelic metal pulse of their early albums, and the mighty agitation of *Hands All Over* from 1989's turbulent, genre-reinventing *Louder Than Love*, Soundgarden seemed more serious somehow, more focused. Blues, not punk.

Essentially, *Superunknown* is the Soundgarden album that blew everyone away. At heart it's unadulterated, unrequited, unapologetic metal. Pure and beautiful. Listen to *The Day I Tried To Live*, with its heart-clenching vocal performance, and try telling me that it's not an equal of Sabbath or Zeppelin. Listen to the era-defining *Black Hole Sun* (era-defining, at the time of Kurt Cobain's death) and try convincing anyone that this is not metal shot through and through.

The primal blues, moved on through distortion and time.

As drummer Matt Cameron termed *Superunknown* to me in '94, "It grooves and it rocks and everything is where it should be. I can listen to it. Normally, rock songs are about certain things – chicks, cars and dicks. But the lyrics to Superunknown are very introspective, very dark. They're saying a whole different thing. Basically it's a big 'fuck you' to the world, a plea to leave us alone!"

Back then, only Metallica could equal Soundgarden for emotional range, and they fell away fast. (Metallica themselves acknowledge Soundgarden's status – guitarist Kirk Hammett told *Rolling Stone* magazine in 2008 that *Enter Sandman* might never have existed if it hadn't been for the "big, heavy riffs" on Soundgarden's second album, 1989's Louder Than Love)

And yet, where early-'70s hard rock was exultant, its early-'90s variant was consumed with ennui. If Superunknown's title suggests a vast, bleak, empty cosmos, the album – every last one of its dense, immense 70 minutes – explore the

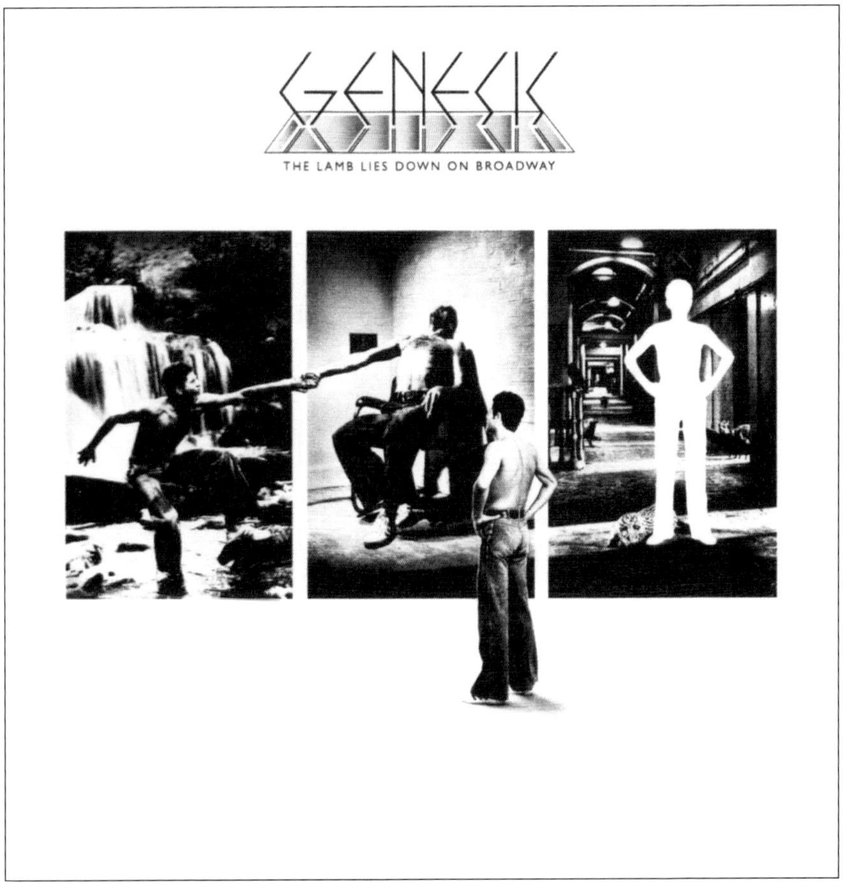


year released
**1974**

producer
**John Burns and Genesis**

After *Supper's Ready* [the epic, 23-minute centrepiece of 1972's *Foxtrot*], I think we'd always had the idea of one long piece that could carry a whole album," says Genesis keyboardist and founding member Tony Banks. "You could call *The Lamb Lies Down On Broadway* a concept album, except that it's such a dirty word these days," he adds cryptically.

In which case 'lamb' is perhaps a four-letter word. Because along with The Who's *Tommy* and *Quadrophenia*, David Bowie's *The Rise & Fall Of Ziggy Stardust & The Spiders From Mars*, Jethro Tull's *Thick As A Brick* and Pink Floyd's *The Wall*, Genesis's *The Lamb...* is one of a handful of releases that defined the concept album genre.

*The Lamb...* has been an essential touchstone for those who've developed the style over the last 30 years: Rush, Styx, Queensrÿche, Iron Maiden, Marillion, Marilyn Manson, Fear Factory and (despite their denials) Radiohead. You can find websites that offer a line-by-line analysis of Genesis's lyrics and more

year released
**1994**

producer
**Michael Beinhorn**

equally supermassive black hole that is the human soul in an attempt to explain the unknowable.

And if the results scream "downer", it was probably deliberate. "I write songs best when I'm depressed," as Cornell said at the time.

As those nine million fans can attest, however, Cornell's sorrow was our pleasure, starting with the compressed thrills of opener *Let Me Drown*. The titles – *Fell On Black Days, Head Down, The Day I Tried To Live*, Like Suicide – chimed almost too perfectly with the zeitgeist (Cobain killed himself a month following its release), and Mailman's 'I know I'm headed for the bottom' almost reads like a parody of alt rock angst.

Nevertheless, *Superunknown* is a dark joy-ride, from the shrieking fervour of Spoonman's amped-up blues to *Black Hole Sun*'s beauteous grungeadelia which rivals the best of Nirvana for Beatles-meets-Sabbath noisy melodicism. More poignant than ever since Cornell's tragic passing, *Superunknown* remains a pitch-black delight.

# 95 *Genesis*
# The Lamb Lies Down On Broadway

theories and meanings than you can throw a colony of Slippermen at.

Not that it as greeted that way when it was released in late 1974. The story of a Puerto Rican New York punk and his surreal adventures in the underworld, as told by a bunch of English public schoolboys, did not exactly set critical pulses racing. The dense plot, sprawled across a double album, was impenetrable to many reviewers who decided it was simply pretentious.

"It got a pretty mixed response in terms of reviews – and from the fans, initially," Banks remembers. "People tend to look back and see it as the culmination of the early era of the band, but it wasn't seen that way at the time. It was darker than our earlier albums, and being a double album it took people longer to get into."

It didn't even seem that impressive to the band at the time, either. The six months Genesis spent making the album stretched the band to breaking point – and, briefly, beyond. The experience changed them irrevocably, not least when singer Peter Gabriel left the group at the end of a six-month tour of America and Europe to promote the record.

"When it was done I just remember thinking: 'Phew'," guitarist Steve Hackett recalls. "Some albums are a natural birth. This one was definitely a breech birth. It came out kicking and screaming, rather than in the tranquility of a birthing pool in your living room."

The Lamb tour, which opened in America in November 1974 was Genesis' most elaborate stage show so far, incorporating a slide show featuring 1,100 slides, special effects and multiple costume changes for Peter Gabriel including the infamous Slipperman outfit with testicles hanging everywhere.

"There were an awful lot of props," recalls Banks. "It was a very theatrical show, but a lot of things went wrong. I don't think there was a single show when all the slides worked perfectly."

"The stage effects were amazing," adds Phil Collins. It wasn't a particularly expensive show to put on, but mic cables would get caught or Peter would be struggling to get the microphone into his Slipperman costume."

The band also found playing the whole of *The Lamb* quite restricting. "It was the least enjoyable of all the shows we've played. It was very rigid. You couldn't change the set. The other problem was that the first half of the show was better than the second half."

The band also found themselves relegated to backing musicians as all the attention was on Gabriel. "People would come in afterwards and steam past Tony, Steve, Mike and I and go straight up to Peter and say, 'You're fantastic,' said Collins. "It was becoming a one-man show to the audience." Of all which made the outlook for the rest of them even grimmer when Peter decided to leave after the tour.

# 94 *Black Sabbath* Sabotage

Black Sabbath were responsible for many things: they were malevolent devil worshippers; they were evil incarnate; they turned generations of morbid teenagers into ghastly vampires; they practised black magic and got quite good at it.

Or maybe not. The truth is, the Sabs began in Aston, Birmingham at the tail-end of the 1960s as a band called Polka Tulk (after a local Indian clothing emporium). By early '69 they had wisely changed their name to Earth. Some commentators say they were originally a blues band; others claim they were a jazz-fusion outfit. What is for sure is that their Zapata-moustachioed six-stringer once played in Jethro Tull for three weeks or so.

How the four band members – singer John Michael Osbourne, guitarist Anthony Frank Iommi, bassist Terence Michael Butler and drummer William Thomas Ward – stumbled on to the unique, doom-laden, bludgeoning sound of Black Sabbath has, in my view, never been satisfactorily explained. Jim Simpson, who ran a midlands club called Henry's Blues House and became Sabbath's manager, once claimed the group were influenced by Kansas City swingers, The Count Basie Orchestra. It seemed as likely a clarification as any.

The Sabs were also responsible for introducing me to heavy metal. I remember it vividly. I was visiting my aunt and uncle in Maidstone, Kent and went shopping one late summer's afternoon in 1971. Gazing into a record-shop window, a rather prosaic purple-and-black-coloured album sleeve with swirly writing on it caught my attention. I don't know why, but it seemed to beckon me like the twisted fingers of a wicked witch's hand. It turned out to be a record called *Master Of Reality* – and for whatever reason, I knew I had to purchase it. Immediately, instantly and without further delay.

I wasn't at all familiar with Sabbath's music. As I handed over my precious shillings-and-pence to the store proprietor, little did I realise that a never-ending spiral down into the murky depths of metaldom had begun. I was just 16 years old. There was no turning back.

There was black humour in the title of Sabbath's fifth album, made while they were in litigation with their former manager Patrick Meehan. But in a time of crisis, the band created another classic. Sabotage was conceived as a back-to-basics album, a return to what Bill Ward called "the iron-clad sound of Black Sabbath".

This much was evident in the bludgeoning riffs of *Symptom Of The Universe* and *The Writ*, the latter a stinging riposte to Meehan. But as a whole, *Sabotage* was as expansive as *Sabbath Bloody Sabbath* – its most leftfield track, Supertzar, featuring a choir, and described by Ward as "a demonic chant". It was the last great album from Sabbath's golden age with Ozzy.

Iommi's heavy riffing is the dominant tone on

year released
**1978**

producer
**Cheap Trick**

Dateline 1979. Cheap Trick mania had hit the world. After years of slogging it out on the road playing every ratty dive in the States or opening for the likes of Kansas, Santana, Kiss and Be-Bop Deluxe, Cheap Trick had finally arrived.

They'd achieved what only a few years prior had seemed to be a near impossibility – superstardom. Their 1979 live album, *Cheap Trick At Budokan* was an international sensation and its follow-up studio release, *Dream Police*, was tearing up the US charts on the heels of the Beatlesque ballad *Voices* and the epic title track.

However, just prior to this massive success, the Rockford, Illinois quartet's prospects for a prosperous music career were looking decidedly bleak. "If it weren't for ...*Budokan*," says Robin Zander," it might have been the end for us. We were in debt by about a million dollars. That album saved us from probable obscurity."

Rewind to early 1978, and despite a series of critically acclaimed records and an endless slate of punishing road work, the band were in trouble. Meanwhile,

year released
*1975*

producer
**Black Sabbath and Mike Butcher**

*Sabotage*, not least on the song chosen as the album's opening track, *Hole In The Sky*, which begins with the hum of amplifiers set at maximum volume and a scream of "Attack!" The scream was an in-joke, delivered by Mike Butcher. "Sabbath had a supporting act (live on tour) who had a manager who would stand behind them on stage shouting, 'Attack! Attack!'" says the producer. "So that's what I shouted from the control room through the Tannoy."

Even heavier was *Symptom Of The Universe*, *Sabotage*'s most famous and influential song. Its bludgeoning, staccato riff would provide the template for Metallica and countless other metal bands, but it was more than a one-note head-banger. It ended in a funky coda, created by the band jamming while recording the track and subsequently overdubbed with acoustic guitar.

There were more left turns throughout the album. And, ironically, it was Iommi who created the most bizarre and unorthodox song ever to feature on a Black Sabbath album: *Supertzar*. ❶

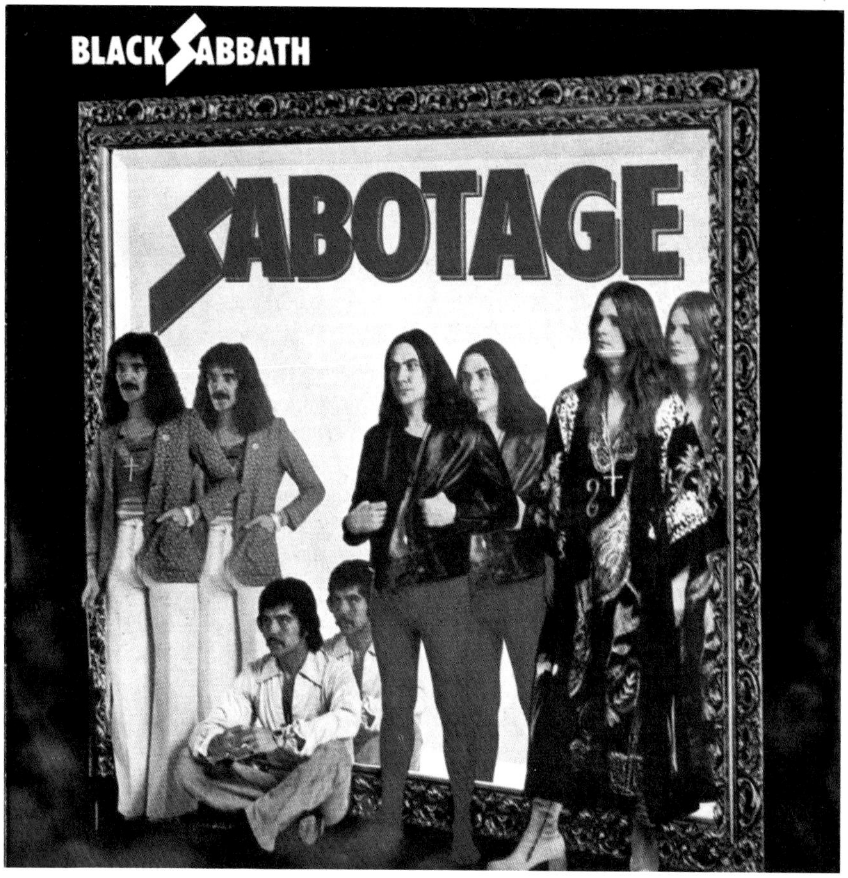


# 93 *Cheap Trick*
# Cheap Trick At Budokan

unexpectedly, and thousands of miles from their hometown, Cheap Trick had broken the Japanese market, racking up three Gold albums and a string of Top 10 hits, for singles such as *Clock Strikes Ten*, *I Want You To Want Me* and *Surrender*.

By late April 1978 Cheap Trick were heading to the Orient for their first Japanese tour, primed to revel in the glory of their newly acquired fame. Landing in Japan, 5,000 screaming fans greeted them at the airport. Rick Nielsen laughingly recalls, "We rode coach on the way there and first class on the way back."

Throughout their stay, the band would experience the same uncontrollable mania that their spiritual musical forefathers, The Beatles, had witnessed just 12 years earlier on their last world tour.

The band were slated to perform shows on April 27 in Osaka and on April 28 and 29 at Tokyo's Budokan, a 14,000-seat arena which had previously hosted performances by the likes of The Beatles and Led Zeppelin. The idea to record a live album didn't come from the band, though; it was a decision made by the suits.

"In Japan, CBS/Sony was splitting into two companies," explains Bun E Carlos. "They decided that every time a band on Epic or Columbia came over they'd record their show and put out a series of Live At Budokan albums. Bob Dylan and Cheap Trick were the first albums they released."

Their incendiary shows in Japan captured a band at the height of their live powers. Onstage, lead guitarist Rick Nielsen was a cartoon character run amok, a tsunami of wild, distorted power chords and demented showmanship, who'd routinely bombard the audience with a hailstorm of guitar picks.

Zander's between-song patter could seemingly incite the primarily female audience into a frenzy at will. Drenched in rapturous applause and punctuated by the riotous screaming of thousands of devoted fans, the insane audience reaction made an indelible impression on the Rockford, Illinois quartet.

Masterfully straddling the delicate divide between tight and loose, the record sees the band power-drive through pop-rock classic after pop-rock classic. To this day, the winning combination of brilliant, simple tunes, confident musicianship and crowd hysteria is a reminder as to why Cheap Trick are among the elite artists in hard rock history. And as a direct consequence of the album's success, Cheap Trick's live status was transformed from opening act to headliner.

"It was four guys from the Midwest just doing what they do best – playing live," shrugs Rick Nielsen with hindsight. "The songs still stand up. We made the Budokan famous and the Budokan made us famous." ❶

# 92 *The Rolling Stones*
# Beggars Banquet

In 1968, an awareness of heritage was the new leap forward: John Lennon sang *Yer Blues*, The Band made *Music From Big Pink*, Bob Dylan simplified matters on his eighth album John Wesley Harding, even The Beach Boys wanted to *Do It Again* - all restatements of first principles.

But if the Stones went back to basics on the Jimmy Miller-helmed *Beggars Banquet*, it remains a far more sophisticated take on roots music than their crudely rampaging early efforts.

It's a classic amalgamation of country, blues, country-blues and Americana - not bad for a bunch of oiks from Dartford and the surrounding environs - although Jagger plays both musicologist and pasticheur, his stylised drawl on *Dear Doctor* and *Prodigal Son* suggesting an ironic distance that he would make up on *Sticky Fingers' Wild Horses*.

As for *Stray Cat Blues*, well, it might cause more than passing consternation at Yewtree HQ - this shocking tale of debauchery and lust is brought vividly to life by Jagger's leering vocal delivery. *'There'll be a feast if you just come upstairs - it's no hanging matter, it's no capital crime'* he defiantly sneers, an invitation that groupies around the globe evidently found hard to resist.

And there was *No Expectations*. Written by Mick 'n' Keef, this haunting ballad, released as the b-side to *Street Fighting Man* sounds equal parts blues and country, like a songwriting session between Robert Johnson and Hank Williams. Using the classic lonesome train motif employed by countless delta blues artists the track was subsequently covered by The Man In Black, Johnny Cash.

Still, *Beggars Banquet*, and follow-up *Let It Bleed*, remain defining artefacts of the counterculture, their four best-known tracks - *Sympathy For The Devil, Street Fighting Man, Gimme Shelter* and *Midnight Rambler* - chillingly capturing convulsions at home and abroad and connoting dread more authentically than any death metal.

Though Brian Jones' contributions - tambura here, mellotron there - occasionally haunt proceedings, his narcotic- and paranoia-debilitated state essentially left the band one man down during the *Beggars* sessions.

And yet, with assistance from first-time Stones producer Miller, Keith Richards stepped up to the plate to deliver one of their best albums.

*Beggars Banquet* followed *Satanic Majesties'* unfocused psych with a confident redefinition of all rock could be. From the tribal anti-gospel insistence of *Sympathy For The Devil* (to say that Jagger totally owns this song is an understatement. He literally is the devil incarnate as he unfolds Lucifer's fierce intent with unnerving menace.

It's Jagger's relentless drive that pushes the performance of the whole band to the limit,

year released
**1973**

producer
**Bill Ham**

This was the band's third album, and the one that broke them nationally in the US. And it's not hard to understand why. The record just overflows with great songs: *Jesus Just Left Chicago, Waitin' For The Bus, Beer Drinkers & Hell Raisers, La Grange*... these are among the finest moments of early-70s hard rock, drenched in bluegrass bonhomie.

There's also a filthy snap to the sound that suited ZZ Top perfectly, with the balance just right between running with the songs as if live, while maintaining studio discipline. The vibe is such that this record comes across with a freshness that still cuts deep.

"*Tres Hombres* clearly defined that Texas- built braggadocio," ZZ Top frontman and occasional actor Billy Gibbons told *Classic Rock*. "It has that whole 'it's bigger and better' Texas thang. Meaning: 'I can drink more beers, herd more cattle, drive faster cars, got more hats than anyone' - that whole chink of humour."

Their first Top 10 single, *La Grange*, was recorded as an afterthought, almost by accident. "We were taking a break,

year released
**1968**

producer
**Jimmy Miller**

reaching a breathless demonic like climax), through the Zeitgeist-defining sedition of *Street Fighting Man*, to the libertine salaciousness of *Stray Cat Blues*, *Beggars Banquet* hardened the Stones' bad boy image into a vision of amoral excess that rock'n'roll's been trying to live up/down to ever since.

The reception wasn't always completely positive, however. After writing *Sympathy For The Devil*, Keith Richards was even dubbed a satanist at one point. In retrospect, however, the guitarist wasn't entirely surprised.

"In a way you saw it coming," he told *Classic Rock*. "At the same time, everybody is going to find something about me, or Charlie or Mick, in anything that we do. We're the whipping hounds. It's calmed down a bit now. Now I'm just a wrinkled rocker."

The year after *Beggars Banquet* was released, the band would embark on a landmark US tour that would take their music to even greater crowds and loftier praise. And the rest, as they say, is history.

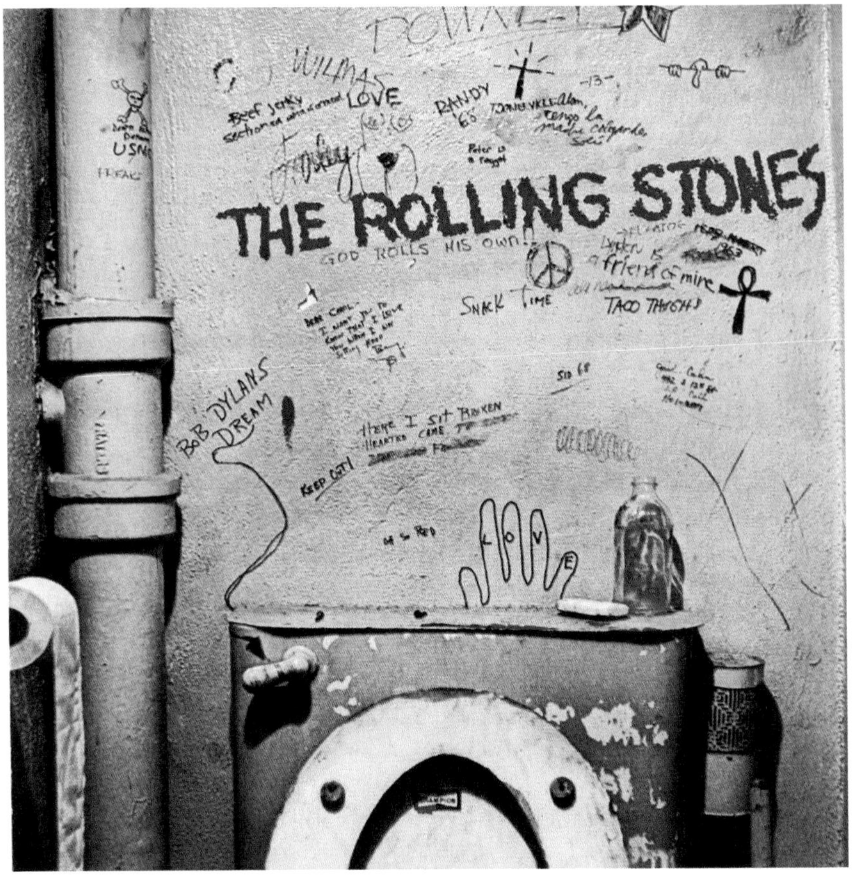


# 91 *ZZ Top*
# Tres Hombres

just relaxing around in the studio, and at that moment... one take! Total boogie, coupled with a sly reference, in the fine ZZ Top tradition, to a seductive and somewhat secretive Texas country club. That one take was the keeper – place that track as our breakthrough release."

Stylistically ZZ were offering nothing new, but *Tres Hombres* convinced you that the band were exploring hitherto uncharted territory – con artists supreme.

"*Tres Hombres* is really one of their two high points," engineer Terry Manning says. "Later on, we went to more modern techniques of recording. I'm talking about *Eliminator*. It wasn't worse: it was a great album, and it sold even more. But it didn't have that togetherness, with everyone really firing it out, in a rock-blues kinda way.

"*Eliminator* was much more Billy and me doing things after hours, kinda overdubbing things, rather than just the band playing. *Tres Hombres* was almost like an incredible live performance. Of course, it wasn't live – they were overdubbing things – but it was much more of the band at their absolute playing-together height.

"So I have two favourites, and I can't choose. *Tres Hombres* being the band at their powerhouse live height. And then *Eliminator,* for their new style, with the machines added and the new production – but still maintaining the blues and rock element. Those two are by far my favourites."

In the UK, ZZ Top remained a cult phenomenon... until 1983's *Eliminator* appeared from out of nowhere and rearranged the charts. The logic was simple: easy-on- the-ear songs, a modern production, and MTV-friendly videos that had a potent mix of sex, laughs and hardware. Suddenly ZZ Top were everywhere. Like Aerosmith and Alice Cooper would do later in the decade, ZZ had reinvented themselves.

Of course, it was never going to last. Within a few years their commercial star was on the wane – at least as far as record sales were concerned. It didn't bother them. They even survived a scare when Hill inadvertently shot himself in the chest while taking off a boot (don't ask). ZZ Top have become a treasured American institution; icons who love to upset the establishment. And they still make great music.

Today, 40 years on, they might have a few more coins in the bank, and Billy Gibbons and Dusty Hill have remained committed to their trademark facial hair – Frank Beard famously hasn't – but they're still the Little Ol' Band From Texas. And it shouldn't come as a surprise that the three amigos who, in the words of Texan radio DJ Redbeard, "spent four decades taking Texas to the world", have stayed faithful to their original line-up.

"We've done this band longer than we've done anything else," says Beard. "We've always stayed true to what we wanted to do: play music and have a good time."

# 90 *Red Hot Chili Peppers*
# Blood Sugar Sex Magik

In many ways *Blood Sugar Sex Magik* is the Chilis' finest hour. It's the link between the hard-nosed funk rock of their early years, and the smoother style that has propelled them to superstar status. The return of guitarist John Frusciante, after a brief, drug-related absence, energised the band like never before. And the songs are uniformly stunning: *Suck My Kiss* and *Under The Bridge* are among the decade's most glorious.

At first, frontman Anthony Kiedis didn't know if he wanted his band to work with infamous producer Rick Rubin on the album. Somehow he felt that the chemistry might not be right.

"We didn't know if he would be able to blend in well, what with Slayer and the boiling goat heads of Danzig and all," Kiedis admitted later, referring to Rubin's previous work. "But he turned out to be a completely open-minded, free-flowing, comforting spirit. If Baron von Munchausen were able to ejaculate the Red Hot Chili Peppers onto a chess board, Rick Rubin would be the perfect player for that game."

Kiedis's reservations were understandable. The tail end of the 80s had hit the band hard – drug addiction, the death of founding member guitarist Hillel Slovak from a heroin overdose and drummer Jack Irons quitting the band – but had resulted in an upturn in their commercial fortunes. With guitarist John Frusciante and drummer Chad Smith now in place, 1989 would be the band's breakthrough year. Their album *Mother's Milk* – featuring Slovak and Irons on a cover of Jimi Hendrix's *Fire* – broke them on MTV in the US with the highly charged videos for *Knock Me Down* and a furious cover of Stevie Wonder's *Higher Ground.*

Famously, Rubin found a mansion, built in 1917, out on Laurel Canyon Boulevard as the place to record the sessions that would make up *Blood Sugar Sex Magik.* Drenched in history, the mansion had played host to gangsters; Hendrix stayed there briefly; The Beatles hung out and partied there...

The Chilis adored their new surroundings and spent seven weeks there in almost total exile, discouraging interruptions from outsiders, and all the while taking comfort from the host of friendly spirits that they said haunted their temporary home. In *Funky Monks*, the group's long-form video of the making of the album, it becomes apparent just how much their recording location had freed them up creatively: at one point Flea plays along with *Mellowship Slinky In B Major* and *Apache Rose Peacock* on two tiny children's pianos; seated at the bottom of the main staircase, the band thrashed along on hubcaps and an empty milk churn for the jangling middle-eight of *Breaking The Girl.* Anything, it seems, went.

"The album had no verbal or intellectual goals," Frusciante elaborated. "We just woke up each morning and played what we felt best to play... making music in the same way that a flower grows. We were just in our own dimension. The rest of the world didn't exist, and we were living in a world of unbridled imagination."

The band recorded 25 songs, of which 22 were originals, and 17 made the final cut. One of these was infamous blues legend Robert Johnson's *They're Red Hot*, which was recorded outside at night, with the sound of cars speeding through the valley below as the band jammed the song playing on a Persian rug laid over the long grass. The sessions also yielded the elegant *Soul To Squeeze*, which, mystifyingly, never made the album but was released as a single in the US in 1993.

The album itself reflected a more refined and mellow Chili Peppers, both musically and lyrically. *I Could Have Lied* and *Breaking The Girl* – with Frusciante's chiming acoustic guitar – gave way to a less relentless band opening up to new new wa ys of translating their groove. They were still capable of bombast and heavy funk, though, with the monstrous *Give It Away* coming out of a Flea-inspired jam that Kiedis was instantly smitten by. The grotesque caricature featured in *Sir Psycho Sexy* had them barracked as sexist and irresponsible, but the lyric is so plainly cartoon-like and fantastical that any criticism seems misguided and reactionary.

*My Lovely Man* was a love letter that Kiedis sent to Hillel: *'Well I'm cryin'/Now my lovely man/Yes I'm cryin'/Now and no one can/Ever fill the hole you left, my man/I'll see you later/My lovely man, if I can...'* He recorded his vocals for the song at night in a makeshift booth set up at a window overlooking the overrun grounds, with a square of candles lit along the walls at his feet.

But it was with *Under The Bridge* that the band struck creative and commercial gold. Kiedis took his enduring love of the band's adopted home city, Los Angeles, personifying it (*'I drive on her streets/'Cause she's my companion/I walk through her hills/'Cause she knows who I am'*) and making it his starting point before reflecting on his downtime there as a heroin addict.

On the band's final day at the house, Frusciante, arms full of clothes and CD cases, remarked that he'd never felt so proud of anything he'd ever done in his life. Flea insisted that as long as the band could keep their love for the music and for one another, then there was no way they could ever fail.

year released
**1991**

producer
**Rick Rubin**

LAKERS

# 89 *Kiss* Destroyer

*Destroyer* was where it all came together for Kiss. With Bob Ezrin pulling the production strings, the band transformed themselves from rehearsal-room hopefuls into multi-platinum gods.

The pressure was on for Paul Stanley, Gene Simmons, Peter Criss and Ace Frehley. Achieving success is one thing, following it up another, and this time around the New Yorkers were following up a corker: *Kiss Alive!* It had gone off like a rocket and rebranded the four as a runaway success.

Kiss couldn't afford to rest on their platforms – they needed to return to the studio (the Record Plant in New York) with more than just a glorified engineer, however good the songs at their disposal. What they needed was a hard man with a plan. Enter producer Bob Ezrin.

*Destroyer* was a concept album, but only in the sense that the concept was Kiss itself. The nine tracks (plus outro passage) allowed the band members to further bond with the fans by both exploring and expounding their individual personas.

"*Kiss Alive!* had all the muscle and the spit," explained Stanley, "but Bob replaced that with a cinematic feel. It was a night-and-day difference to what we'd done before, an altogether larger picture of who we were." And what they were was something special: Gene, the Demon; Paul, the Lover; Ace, the (Urban) Spaceman; and Peter, the Cat. Ezrin realised that turning these rock'n'roll heroes into rock'n' roll superheroes was the key to giving Kiss their biggest record to date.

In grey, grisly, punk-obsessed Great Britain, it's impossible to overestimate the impact opening track *Detroit Rock City* had on the country's beleaguered rock'n'roll populace in 1976. It's a massive cinematic experience that transports you headlong into Motown's seething, heaving bowels, where larger-than-life US rawk rules supreme... and multiple car crashes are commonplace. *King Of The Night Time World* is a great, lumbering menace on the grandest of scales. Like a rusting Iron Giant crashing through a forest of Canadian Redwoods at midnight, and the ultimate Xenon turn-on for any budding headlight queen.

Despite it being so closely associated with Gene Simmons, *God Of Thunder* is actually a Paul Stanley composition. Reminiscent of a stalking, apocalyptic horror movie – and those are Bob Ezrin's kids making the squeaky *Exorcist* noises in the background. The intensity ebbs a little with *Great Expectations* – a massive choral workout bolstered by the wholesome presence of the Brooklyn Boys' Choir, while *Flaming Youth* is a stumblesome anthem made all the more compulsive by the sound of a cheesy, pulsing fairground organ. Who can resist a song that rhymes '*my uniform is leather*' with '*getting it together*'?

Neither Simmons nor Stanley wanted the wafty ballad *Beth* on the album, but thank God they relented because its hit single status rescued

year released
**1971**

producer
**Ken Scott**
**David Bowie**

It is almost impossible to overstate Bowie's influence on, and importance to, popular music.And it takes little more than the names of some of the top-drawer songs on *Hunky Dory* – *Changes, Life On Mars, Oh! You Pretty Things, Andy Warhol, Kooks* – as evidence of how good an album it is. Varied and expansive, it's easily among Bowie's very best.

"In the early 70s it really started to all come together for me as to what it was that I liked doing," Bowie told *Classic Rock*, "and it was a collision of musical styles. I found that I couldn't easily adopt brand loyalty, or genre loyalty. I wasn't an R&B artist, I wasn't a folk artist, and I didn't see the point in trying to be that purist about it. My true style was that I loved the idea of putting Little Richard with Jacques Brel, and the Velvet Underground backing them. 'What would that sound like?' Nobody was doing that, at least not in the same way."

This revelation would help create *Hunky Dory,* the kaleidoscopic pop collection that announced Bowie's arrival and began a streak of landmark albums through the 1970s – from *Ziggy Stardust* to *Aladdin Sane* to *Heroes*.

year released
**1976**

producer
**Bob Ezrin**

*Destroyer* from the doldrums. Originally the B-side of *Detroit Rock City,* the third single from the album, it wasn't long before *Beth* was making a major impact on US radio, with DJs flipping the seven-inch with almost undignified haste. This sleeping beauty had been well and truly roused, charting at No.7 Stateside and dictating that Kiss's fire and brimstone stage show would, for the foreseeable future, be tempered by the giving out of roses and the wafting of orchestral music through the PA...

Time has been kind to *Destroyer,* even the last track – a sonic montage usually referred to as *Rock & Roll Party* – has come to sound like a relevant part of the album, when in fact it was put there purely and simply to soak up some time. Recorded in two separate sessions and showing what can be achieved when the studio gods are grinning away like fools. "I guess 'swagger' is probably the right word," concludes Stanley. "The songs have a truly majestic feel, without coming across as either pompous or contrived. This was one of those records where – from the music right through to the name – the planets were all in perfect alignment."

# 88 *David Bowie* Hunky Dory

Excited about his growing cache of songs and ideas for a new direction, Bowie rang guitarist Mick Ronson. With the promise of recording sessions and a place to crash, Ronson, with drummer Woody Woodmansey and bassist Trevor Bolder in tow, moved into Haddon Hall. Woodmansey, who had played on Bowie's *The Man Who Sold The World* was immediately struck by his new material. "I think he focused more as a writer and managed to keep his unique approach, especially lyrically, while streamlining everything," he said. "The songs were more structured. Honestly, I didn't think he had these songs in him."

Bolder, who'd been playing with Ronson and Woodmansey for about eight months in the band Ronno, was also surprised. "I had an impression of Bowie as a bit of a folkie. I didn't realise how good he was until we started doing *Hunky Dory.*"

Sessions began at Trident Studios in London's Soho in early June 1971. Working from 2pm to midnight, Monday to Saturday, with quick breaks for tea, sandwiches and the occasional bottle of wine, the band were swept up in a colourful world of bipperty bopperty hats, Garbo's eyes and homo superiors (the album's recurring theme of children ch-ch-changing into enlightened beings was influenced by Bowie's love of the occult writings of Aleister Crowley, and sci-fi novels by Arthur C Clarke). Bolder recalled the excitement: "Our approach was very off-the-top-of-our-heads. We'd go in, David would play us a song – often one we hadn't heard – we'd run through it once and then take it. No time to think about what you're going to play, you'd have to do it there and then. In some respects it's nerve-racking, but it gives a certain feel. If you play a song too many times in the studio it can become stale, and I think David wanted to capture the energy of it being on the edge."

From start to finish, the album took two weeks to record and two to mix. Released on December 17, 1971, *Hunky Dory* was hailed by *Melody Maker* as "the most inventive piece of songwriting to have appeared on record in a considerable time". *NME* said it was "Bowie at his brilliant best", while the *New Yorker* dubbed Bowie "the most intelligent person to have chosen rock music as his medium". With a sleeve image suggesting a George Hurell portrait of Veronica Lake, Bowie seemed ready for his close-up. Despite glowing reviews, first-quarter worldwide sales barely reached 5,000. Not that Bowie noticed. The man who'd sung *'I'm much too fast to take that test'* was already back in the studio recording the album that within six months would transform him into worldwide glam rock superstar: *Ziggy Stardust.*

Because of *Ziggy*'s rise and all encompassing effect on Bowie, *Hunky Dory* has remained in its shadow as the quiet, talented brother. "*Hunky Dory* was where David's ability as a songwriter came through," said Woodmansey. "It was the start of David's career, really."

# 87 *Yes*
# Fragile

"It was like an explosion of energy, dreams and ideas," Jon Anderson once said, looking back at *Fragile*. "There was so much harmony within the band. We were getting successful, but it hadn't gone to our heads. We were all committed to creating adventurous music, and given the freedom to do that."

Originally released in late 1971 in the UK, the band's fourth waking dream went Top 10 in both countries and built on the momentum initiated by *The Yes Album*, elevating Yes from the troposphere to the stratosphere.

Eddy Offord's role as engineer-turned-producer should not be undervalued. The instantly involving, now-iconic, backwards piano fade into guitar harmonics that kick-starts the record was his idea. (As indeed was healthy living and vegetarianism, a regime the musicians tried to obey, with limited success.) Everyone knew they had to up their game, both to capitalise on the buzz of *The Yes Album* in the States and to stay in contention at what was a heady period for music. The year 1971 had seen important albums from Pink Floyd, Genesis, ELP and Caravan. Prog (as it wasn't labelled then) was in the ascendant. And nobody was keener on ascension than Anderson, who was urging structural risks ("I was interested in how you get from one idea to the next... and then the next," he said) and buzzing with the potential he'd heard within Frank Zappa, The Mahavishnu Orchestra, King Crimson and world music.

"It was a very happy time, a wonderful era," recalls Rick Wakeman, citing drummer Bill Bruford as being "brilliant at reining everybody in. We'd all bring along bits of the jigsaw, then between us slot the pieces in. In a strange way, gluing it together became my job at rehearsals. Bill said: 'You studied orchestration, we didn't.' I was thrilled though. I'd be left for a few hours to come up with as many different chord progressions as possible. It was nice. That was one area where there were no arguments."

"Sessions were slow," Bruford remembers, "and I was an impatient lad. Making music by committee is not my preferred option - you usually get a camel when you're designing a horse. Jon usually got his own way. But sometimes you all swing together, despite yourselves. *Roundabout* was the hit that opened the floodgates, though in retrospect I see *Heart Of The Sunrise* as the winner track. On *Five Per Cent For Nothing* I offered a cheap shot at the outgoing manager, for which I apologise. We didn't play happy families, but we were all genuinely interested in getting the best album, sound, ideas; in being the best band."

As for guitarist Steve Howe, he was feeling increasingly at home, and more confident. And Rick Wakeman, brought in to replace the synth-phobic Tony Kaye, was nothing if not game for experiments. It was he who would slot all the ideas together and forge fluidity and sense from them, his orchestration

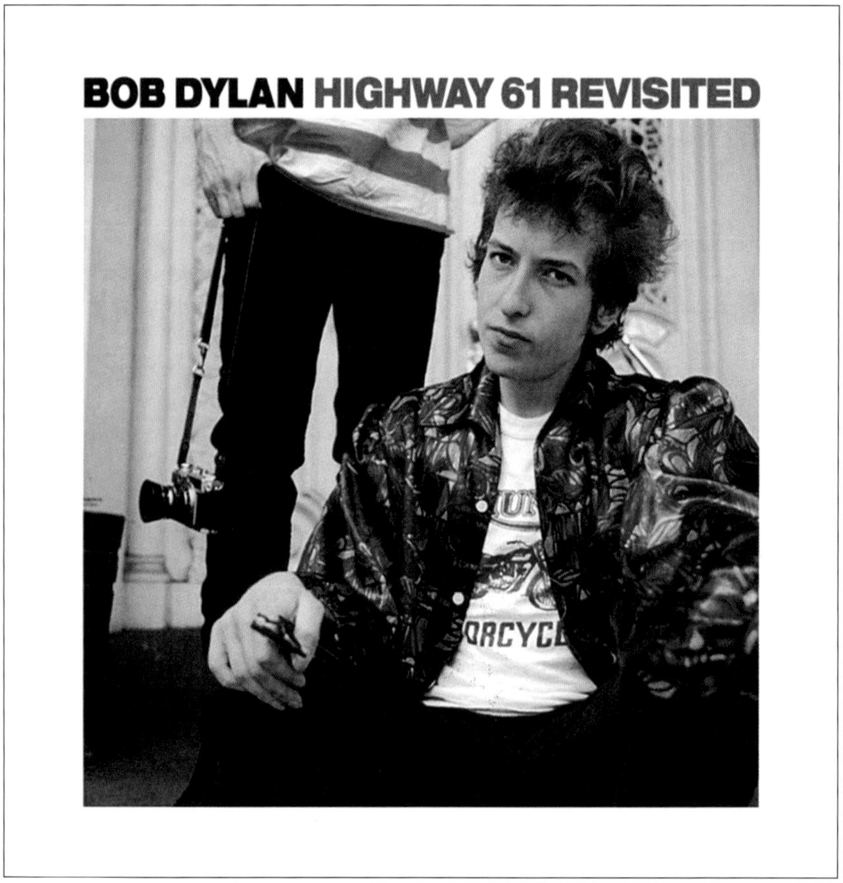


year released
**1965**
label
producer
**Bob Johnston**

The Bob Dylan of 1965 signalled the maturation of rock music. *Like A Rolling Stone* made its live debut at Newport Folk Festival, a six-minute single that challenged the parameters of commercial radio. Either side of the festival, he released two groundbreaking records - the semi-electric *Bringing It All Back Home* and the full-on rock'n'roll of *Highway 61 Revisited*. At a time when albums had yet to achieve the same significance as singles, Dylan had other ideas. Newport served as notice that he'd rather make deliberate artistic choices than merely grab at the brass ring.

The first Dylan album to be recorded entirely with an electric band, *Highway 61 Revisited* was brutally uncompromising. It is just a straight nuclear blast of rock. Dylan has gotten the blend down, and these musicians - Al Kooper, Mike Bloomfield, drummer Bobby Gregg - perform more like a group. The propulsive momentum, especially on *Highway 61 Revisited* itself, with its opening slide whistle, is pure punk. *On Ballad Of A Thin Man*, with its Halloween music and bone-chilling lyrics, you're just glad

year released
**1971**

producer
**Eddy Offord**
**Yes**

skills described by Bill Bruford as "Rick's job".

So *Roundabout* - edited, much to the band's chagrin, for a US hit - whirled in with exuberance. *South Side Of The Sky* is perhaps the most underrated of the big numbers, its riffs gutsy and its dreamy mid-section and return a peak among pinnacles. *Long Distance Runaround* skitters and charms, and of course monumental finale *Heart Of The Sunrise* interlaces a blueprint for thrash-rock and a contrasting choirboy purity.

Then there are the solo cameos, studding the album's starry sky. Anderson sings divinely, Wakeman (contractually blocked from writing credits) reboots Brahms, Howe goes fervent flamenco, Bruford takes a swipe at a former manager and, of course Squire, on *The Fish*, takes the bass into outer space.

*Fragile* also introduced the art of Roger Dean and his now iconic Yes logo, fanning the flames of the music's mystique and other-worldliness. New doors were opened in music and mountains came out of the sky...

# 86 *Bob Dylan*
# Highway 61 Revisited

Bob isn't talking about you. The album ends with *Desolation Row*, a reference to Kerouac's novel *Desolation Angels*.

There's quite a bit of displaced blues poetry on *Highway 61 Revisited*, because that's the highway that runs from Minnesota to New Orleans. It's ghostly because of the blues and because it intersects with the crossroads where the Devil taught delta shaman Robert Johnson to play the blues. But the blues on the album aren't particularly haunted. *It Takes A Lot To Laugh, It Takes A Train To Cry* is a pastiche of blues lines, that would naturally involve more trains. Each verse just hangs there waiting for a song to come along. *Outlaw Blues* uses Southside Chicago blues to hang Dylan's quirky nonsense lyrics on.

Dylan's road manager/confidante Bob Neuwirth challenged him to use the line *'when you're lost in the rain in Juarez and its Eastertime too'* in a song, and he did just that on *Just Like Tom Thumb's Blues*. There never was a weirder opening line to a song, or better advice if you ever find yourself embroiled in this noir-ish tale of misspent youth: *'And your gravity fails, and negativity don't pull you through/Don't put on any airs, when you're down on Rue Morgue Avenue/They got some hungry women there, and they really make a mess outta you...'*

On *Like A Rolling Stone* his voice has a swirling current as he leans on the words *'Howwww does it feeeeeel?'* with those howling vowels you can feel in your bones. *Like A Rolling Stone* was something new and strange delivered with a laid-back hipster's disdain. The implication was that the world doesn't have to be the way we inherited it. On the contrary, it can be like this. Let me show you some pictures. A sense of magic transformation projected a new age of infinite possibility and oddness. You heard *Like A Rolling Stone* and you were in it. It was as if you'd fallen through the rabbit hole. The cast of characters is straight out of a Fellini movie: *'the mystery tramp... the diplomat with his Siamese cat... Napoleon in rags...'* It's about whoever and what they did, but none of this matters. You'd never heard anything like it before.

And the sound. The fusion of music and words that Dylan conjured up out of this tuning fork in his head. Anyway, he doesn't really want to demonstrate too literally what he's thinking. It's better that the players follow whatever lead he gives them and that they try to approximate it. He doesn't want the perfection of the studio musician, and to mix it up he brings in a guitar player from Chicago (Mike Bloomfield), and a guitar player (Al Kooper) to play the organ. When people tell him Kooper's not there to play the organ, he replies: "I'll decide about that." The musicians are trying to tune into Dylan's wavelength, and the tension in that created a certain suspense in the delivery of the song. But eventually they all get contact highs. Kooper later described Dylan's recording methods as "the road map to hell!".

# 85 *Queensrÿche*
# Operation: Mindcrime

This first-rate concept album tells the story of a genius, a junkie and a street girl and their alienation from 80s society. Layered guitars, operatic vocals and Michael Kamen's orchestrations lend the whole thing a grand, epic feel, but this is a rare beast: an 80s metal album that puts the song – or, more specifically, the story – first and lets everything else take a back seat.

"Making a full-blown concept album was viewed as a radical thing for us to have done," recalled drummer Scott Rockenfield, "but we've never been known as a band to go with the flow." In fact, the seeds of what eventually became *Operation: Mindcrime* came to singer Geoff Tate quite unexpectedly. At the time, he was living in Canada, and in friendly contact with members of a political activist group. "I wasn't part of their organisation, but I was sorta guilty by association," he acknowledged. He initially worked alone on the basic storyline of what would later be described as a "thematic album about manipulation through drugs and the media", before selling it to the rest of the band. But guitarist Chris DeGarmo was the only other band member to share the singer's enthusiasm and Tate had to persuade each of the other three on a one-on-one basis.

Among the first songs to be written were *Eyes Of A Stranger* and *The Mission*, while the military-flavoured opening clarion call *Anarchy X* was developed from an idea already worked up for *Rage For Order* but then abandoned. Slowly but surely, the concept fell into place. The central character of the storyline was Nikki, a street kid left to fend for himself who ends up bitter and strung out on heroin. Enter the sinister Dr X, who moulds the anger of his young protégé to his own revolutionary ends, getting him to assassinate the city's political and religious leaders. Sister Mary, a former hooker-turned-nun, then joins the plot. She's been hired by Dr X to be Nikki's conscience, thereby enabling his killing spree to continue.Inevitably, Nikki and Mary become lovers. But when Dr X realises Mary's usefulness is over he orders Nikki to kill her.

In the best storytelling style, Queensrÿche leave the listener to make up his own mind about the conclusion. But we are at least given a few final clues: Nikki refuses to kill Mary; he finds her hanged by her own rosary. By that time Nikki has already been committed to State Hospital and is being detained under extreme security; meanwhile he struggles to piece together his muddled memories: did he really kill Sister Mary, or did Dr X indoctrinate somebody else to do it? Just to complicate matters further, Queensrÿche opt to tell the tale in flashback form, Nikki kicking things off with the dramatic proclamation: '*I remember now...*'

"Geoff had wanted to write about the moral decay of society," guitarist Michael Wilton explained. "It could easily have backfired on us if we'd done a sloppy job. We didn't record it in the sequence you

year released
**1992**

producer
**Garth Richardson**
**RATM**

Fuck you, I won't do what you tell me!' So fumed Zack De La Rocha on this, RATM's debut album. His indignant, effortlessly chantable lyrics married to Tom Morello's scarily innovative guitar work was like nothing we'd ever heard before. *Killing In The Name*, *Bombtrack* and *Bullet In The Head* gave us a perfect excuse to rage (ha!), and discover that it's perfect stuff to piss off your parents with.

Even now, a quarter of a century after it exploded like a car bomb under the hood of mainstream culture, *Rage Against The Machine* has lost none of its power, impact or provocative fervour. It was the sound of Public Enemy yoked to Black Flag, of Dr Martin Luther King and Mal colm X set to a soundtrack of cutting-edge metal.

Rage arrived as the gloriously shallow, MTV-driven rock scene of the 1980s was flat on the canvas with bluebirds fluttering around its head, laid out by the emergent grunge movement. In America, a new generation of hip hop bands was providing a vital social commentary, marrying the gritty reality of the streets with the violent glamour of a

year released
**1988**

producer
**Peter Collins**

hear it on the album, so we had to make sure the songs fitted together correctly. It was like reading a movie script."

Looking back, the band say that they experienced moments of inspiration and frustration during the making of the record. "Some parts were easy, others... were not necessarily difficult, more time-consuming," Tate says. "Communication-wise, we were on a roll. The segues between the songs, for instance, required quite a lot of planning, but you don't mind that when you're enjoying your work."

*Operation: Mindcrime* is the album that briefly crystallized the previously wandering artistic visions of Queensrÿche into something exciting and challenging. An almost flawless collection of songs, it went against the grain by proving that a heavy metal band was capable of displaying intelligence in their music.

Their next album, *Empire*, outsold it by some margin, but ...*Mindcrime* is the benchmark against which everything else the band do is measured.

# 84 *Rage Against The Machine*
# Rage Against The Machine

Hollywood crime blockbuster. All this was happening against a backdrop of global turmoil, racial tension and the threat of war in the Middle East. In hindsight, their timing was perfect.

In reality, it was purely accidental. Vocalist Zack de la Rocha, guitarist Tom Morello, bassist Timmy C (aka Tim Commerford) and drummer Brad Wilk had been in various low-level LA bands, including hardcore firebrands Inside Out (Zack) and Lock Up. "I had been in a band that had a record deal, I had already had my grab at the brass ring," says Morello. "The band got dropped and I thought that was it. I thought, 'If I'm not going to be a rock star, or make albums, I'm at least going to play music that I believe in 100%.' And I was fortunate to meet three people who felt very similarly."

Today, the guitarist still expresses bafflement that anyone would want to take a chance on RATM and their political message, let alone a corporate record company. But the band's 12-track demo found its way to Michael Goldstone, the Epic Records A&R hotshot who'd signed Pearl Jam.

"Our only goal was to make music for ourselves and to make our own record – a cassette tape, an elaborate demo tape of the 12 songs we had written," says Morello. "That was our entire goal. We never thought we'd play a show. We never thought we'd make a record."

Rage began recording their debut album with Garth Richardson, a young Canadian studio engineer whose biggest credit came on an album by hair metal B-listers White Lion, in March 1992. Seven of the 12 tracks from the demo tape, including *Killing In The Name, Bomb Track* and *Bullet In The Head*, would appear on the album.

"The songs were probably about 85%-90% there," remembers Richardson. "We made a few changes, mostly lyrically. Literally, somebody just had to capture them."

To achieve this, the producer brought in a full concert PA system to get the full impact of the band's live firepower. This was undiluted Rage.

The success of *Rage Against The Machine* took everyone by surprise, not least Rage Against The Machine. They rapidly went from being the outcasts of the Hollywood scene to a lightning rod for the altrock movement. Rather than blunting their political edge, success only sharpened it – most famously in 1993, when they took to the stage at a Lollapallooza festival show in Philadelphia naked, apart from gaffa tape over their mouths, as a protest against censorship.

A quarter of a century after it was released, however, Rage's debut remains a landmark – the point where rap and metal truly came together to deliver a body-blow to the status quo.

"Human strife has not changed. Racism has not changed. Things have actually gone backwards," says Richardson. "Rage Against The Machine wrote an incredible record that was current – and it will be time and time and time again."

# 83 *Whitesnake*
# 1987

With more pomp than the Last Night Of The Proms, *1987* is David Coverdale at his preening, self-important best. A huge success in America, this was Whitesnake at their most stylised; their videos glowed with an iridescent gleam, the light reflecting off the band's teeth enough to scar an unprotected retina.

David was always a looker, although no one could have foreseen the almost eerie transformation that took place between 1984's *Slide It In* and *1987*. In America the album was simply called *Whitesnake* - this, David seemed to be saying is a new beginning. For some Whitesnake fans, however, it was also the end.

"I wanted Whitesnake to be leaner, meaner and more electrifying," Coverdale says. "I felt that we'd done extraordinarily well. We'd made six albums in just a few years. We did fabulously on those albums, but I really felt that we were flogging a dead snake. For me, I felt it was time for a change. I didn't want to stay in the same old traditional blues and pop scenario. It was simply my choice as an artist. I wanted to pursue another direction. That was my whole modus operandi. The reason I invited [guitarist] John Sykes into the band was to actually afford that transition, or someone of that style and it happened to be Sykes. And that was it."

A former member of both NWOBHM stars Tygers Of Pan Tang and the *Thunder And Lightning*-era incarnation of Thin Lizzy, John Sykes was a prodigious six-string maestro and an entirely different kind of guitarist from the musicians that David had worked with previously in Whitesnake.

With a line-up completed by bassist Neil Murray and drummer Aynsley Dunbar, Whitesnake decided to record the new album at Little Mountain Studios in Vancouver, Canada. The recording process was a lengthy and arduous one, not least because David fell ill with a serious sinus infection, which prevented him from singing for long periods and eventually led to a major operation, but the album was slowly pieced together, including the return of *Here I Go Again* and *Crying In The Rain*, both tracks that originally appeared on Whitesnake's 1982 album *Saints And Sinners*. On *1987*, The former was transformed from surly blues rock strut to an impossibly glossy radio-metal anthem, replete with a suitably over-the-top guitar solo from guest musician Adrian Vandenberg, whose own titular band had had a big hit with the ballad *Burning Heart* in the US in 1984.

"Recording *Here I Go Again* for the second time wasn't my idea, to be honest," states Coverdale. "I very rarely like to go back on any level. But on that occasion it paid off, and huge! We had a bunch of hits with that song in different forms. Of course, John Sykes fucking hated it, which is why Adrian was featured on there. He didn't play one of his better solos on there. It was metal meets country and western! There were two guitarists that I really wanted to work with. One was Michael Schenker, and Adrian, of course, who I'd met. It was our destiny to work together."

Released in the first week of April, *1987* was an instant and massive success. Primarily in the US where Whitesnake swiftly became a regular fixture on nascent music television channel MTV with the glossy, high-budget promo clips for the album's biggest songs, *Still Of The Night*, *Here I Go Again* and the ultimate power ballad *Is This Love*, all of which featured David's wife-to-be Tawny Kitaen. Chiming perfectly with the glamour and bombast that seemed to be universally popular during the 80s, Whitesnake's music and endearingly unsubtle visual approach led to sales for *1987* of over eight million copies in the US alone.

With the sound and the look, Coverdale had hit on something. It was loud and powerful, suggestive of the classic vibes of Led Zeppelin and Deep Purple (*Crying In The Rain* and *Still Of The Night*), but it was also soulful and chart-friendly (*Is This Love* and the dusted-off *Here I Go Again*). It was an album for its time, packaged and produced and just-so, but also organic and meaningful. It even took its title from the year of release, so well did it capture the zeitgeist. After a 15-year hiatus, David Coverdale was once again in the right place at the right time.

Despite his plans to head onwards and upwards, Coverdale was in no way prepared for such a phenomenal level of success.

"We had a plan but, Jesus Christ, are you kidding?" he laughs, looking back. "My whole plan was to hopefully make an album that sells a bit more than the last one and hopefully I'll sing a bit better, it all sounds a bit better and we'll get to the point quicker in the lyrics. We already had a fabulous relationship with radio after we'd laid the foundation with the *Slide It In* record, but MTV was an entirety new kettle of fish and they just took to the band hugely. I guess we had all the elements that they wanted. So we had a five-year, unbelievable relationship with MTV and it worked out very, very well for us and in essence it helped us to make that transition that I wanted and then it all became astonishingly successful."

year released
**1987**

producer
**Mike Stone**
**Keith Olsen**

# 82 *Deep Purple*
# Burn

Out went Gillan and Glover, in came Coverdale and Hughes. While the world waited for them to crumble, the new Purple line-up solidified, and the first fruits of their labours, *Burn*, sold by the rackful. "There was a collective sigh of relief that we'd maintained the success level by making the change from Mark II to Mark III," Coverdale admitted.

As much as *Burn* was/is a showcase for Purple's then new boys, lead singer David Coverdale and bassist/vocalist Glenn Hughes, it remains overwhelmingly guitarist Ritchie Blackmore's album. Marvelling at it today, two things stand out straight away. Firstly, Coverdale and Hughes's contributions are absolutely top-notch, and their interplay is second to none. Coverdale, bristling with raw enthusiasm, barks like a hound, while Hughes's singing provides a shrill counterbalance. The two play off each other superbly, and it sounds like they've been doing their dual lead-vocal schtick for years. The ghost of Ian Gillan well and truly vanquished. Secondly, Blackmore, as intimated earlier, is the true star of *Burn*. His riffs - particularly on the title track and *Mistreated* - are deceptively simple, astonishingly fluid and oh-so dexterously executed. The tone of his guitar is meaty and magnificent, and his solos - feel your jaw hit the floor as he builds repetitive blues variations at the tail-end of *Lay Down Stay Down*, for example - are out of this bloody world.

Coverdale joined as an unknown (having given up gainful employment in Redcar's Stride In Style menswear boutique to warble with the Purps). Hughes came from Trapeze, who, despite being signed to the Moody Blues' Threshold label in the UK, were a relatively low-profile band. However, Blackmore - once he had actually decided he wanted to carry on with Purple after the acrimonious departures of singer Ian Gillan and bassist Roger Glover - clearly had a vision for what would become the Mark III line-up of the group.

The guitarist desperately wanted Paul Rodgers, of Free/Bad Company fame, as his new vocalist - but he couldn't get him. So a supremely soulful soundalike, Coverdale, was brought in instead. The singer immediately recognised something was afoot: "I quickly found out that Ritchie was the principal composer in Purple," he recalled. "Blackmore had been very busy. His ideas were fresh and exciting, and quite a departure from the more formulaic recent Purple I had been hearing when I was doing my 'research' on the band.

"I wrote about half a dozen sets of lyrics for *Burn* [the song] - I was that keen," remembered Coverdale. "The final words to *Burn* came about because I was just trying to please Ritchie, I guess. These lyrics aren't the stuff I would normally write; I looked upon them as science-fiction poems."

Glenn Hughes, meanwhile, arrived with a forceful personality, a silvery throat, and a slaphappy, funk-

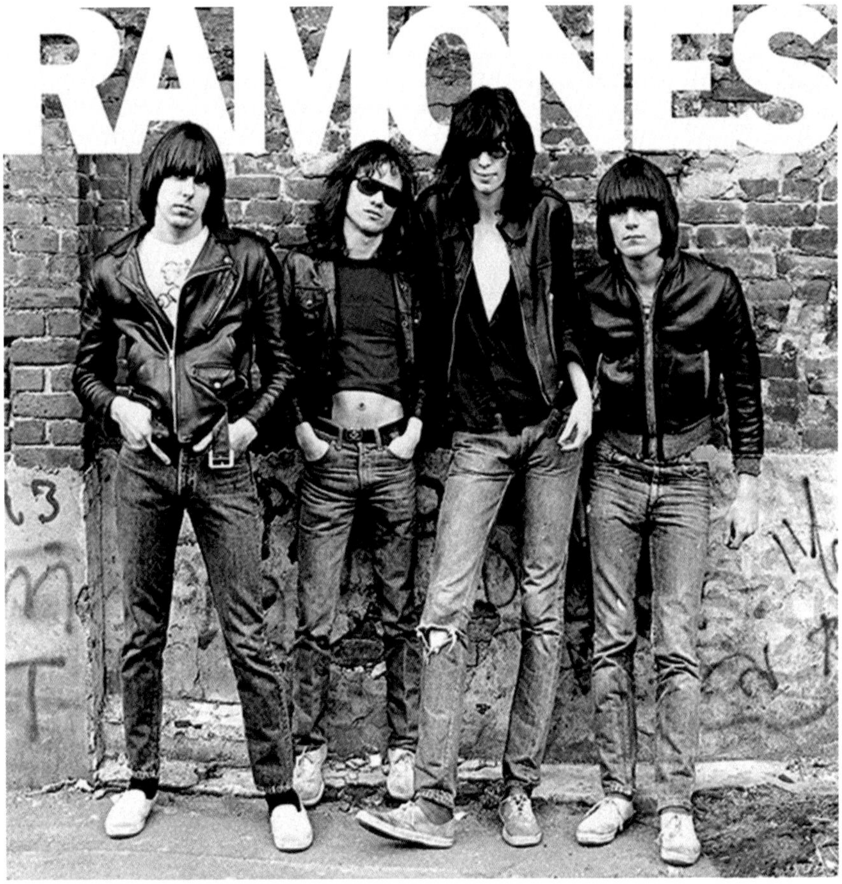


year released
**1976**

producer
**Tommy Ramone**
**Craig Leon**

*Hey ho, let's go! Hey ho, let's go!*' And thus the Ramones announced their be-denimed and leather jacketed arrival in the world.

Heralding the onset of the New York punk scene, the Ramones' debut - with its infectious three chord opening bombast of *Blitzkreig Bop* - bludgeoned us over the head with more than a dozen two-minute songs.

Too many albums are cited as influential, but in this case, notwithstanding its meagre performance at the box office, it could be reasonably argued that virtually every one of *Ramones's* original 6,000 sales were courtesy of key or burgeoning musicians, journalists and creative types, catalysing the birth of an entire movement. Put simply, the Sex Pistols played the Marquee on February 12, 1976, Ramones' debut album was released on April 23, and then punk happened. Overnight, songs got shorter and music got faster and more furious.

But it's a misconception, even a myth, that Ramones were doyens of dumb who just turned up, plugged in and somehow magicked their live set into a 14-track long-player.

year released
**1974**

producer
**Deep Purple**

oriented bass-playing style that Purple drummer Ian Paice would instantly embrace, thus reinvigorating the band rhythmically – at least in the short term.

For stand-out track, the monstrous, brooding *Mistreated*, the two 'new boys' recorded a booming choral section that failed to appear on the final version of the song. Blackmore complained that his guitar was being swamped and had Coverdale and Hughes's work wiped.

Ultimately, *Mistreated* became the only song on *Burn* to feature Coverdale singing lead vocals on his own. "I felt *Mistreated* was a super direction and Ritchie really got his teeth into it. Glenn and myself did our big vocal thing and it just sounded spectacular. It was epic. But Ritchie was absolutely correct that you couldn't hear the guitar if you had the voices too featured."

In the end, though, it wasn't the voices, but the funk factor that would prove to be Blackmore's undoing, and the guitarist would record only one more studio album with the Mark III version of Deep Purple, *Stormbringer*, before quitting.

# 81 *Ramones*
# Ramones

"We were trying to emulate their live sound, but we were also trying to enhance it," producer Craig Leon says, stressing that studio trickery – overdubs, double-tracked vocals – as well as pipe organs to tubular bells were deployed on *Ramones*: it took sophisticated techniques to sound this primitive and raw.

Listening to the album today, you have to wade through 40 years of hype before you can make your mind up. Even if you'd never heard it before, virtually every note, of Side One at least, is recognisable: the language of cartoon mayhem – *Blitzkrieg Bop, Beat On The Brat, Now I Wanna Sniff Some Glue, Chain Saw* – and Joey Ramone's pretty-vacant vocals, the *'Hey ho, let's go!'* and *'Wun-tew-free-faw!'* chants, Dee Dee's pummelling bass, Johnny's sped-up dentist-drill guitars and Tommy's double-time glam beat. As with *Taxi Driver*, that other significant 1976 arty-fact, you could pause it anywhere and 'freeze-frame' an iconic moment.

It's quite an achievement that after four decades of extre me metal and hip hop, the references to *The Texas Chainsaw Massacre* (on *Chain Saw*), male prostitution (*53rd & 3rd*) and Nazis (on LP closer *Today Your Love, Tomorrow The World*) still have the power to disconcert, if not outright disturb.

But for all its air of new-era violence, what surprises is how in hock to history it is, and how tame many of its sentiments are. Ramones is equal parts homage and sabotage, as much of a launchpad for future generations as it is a love letter to the 50s and 60s. The controversial exhortations (*Beat On The Brat, Now I Wanna Sniff Some Glue*) are balanced out by embarrassingly timid demurrals (the reason they *Don't Wanna Go Down To The Basement* is because they're scared!), that employ arcane beatnik argot (*'Hey, daddio'*). *I Don't Wanna Walk Around With You* (*'I don't wanna walk around with you/So why you wanna walk around with me?'*) sounds less cruel and nihilistic than childishly churlish, while on *I Wanna Be Your Boyfriend*, Ramones play the part of the submissive, insecure male, in a state of longing (*'Do you love me babe?/What do you say?'*), which hardly suited the punk credo of 'no feeling'.

*Ramones* is often described as a masterpiece of brevity, shorn of excess, but at two minutes and 33 seconds, *Beat On The Brat*, the longest track, could have done with losing 45 seconds. There's another paradox about Ramones: for such a monument to iconoclasm, it feels sacrilegious to be even faintly criticising it. Still, it also occurs that by *Judy Is A Punk*, Ramones have said everything, espoused their philosophy with such consummate precision that they could have ended it there, with what would have been a blistering three-track EP.

Ramones didn't run out of ideas over the distance of their debut album because they weren't about ideas plural, but The Idea, singular – that the world is absurd, dangerous but full of opportunities for mischief and fun, which they rammed home with ruthless relentlessness.

# 80 *Alice Cooper* Billion Dollar Babies

Having not had even a sniff of the charts with their first two albums, Alice Cooper signed to Warner Brothers Records and, with Canadian whiz-kid producer Bob Ezrin at the controls, hit the peak of their form with three albums released in rapid succession: June '71's *Love It To Death* (the album that shocked America), December '71's *Killer* (the album that conquered America) and July '72's *School's Out* (the album that conquered the world). Bolstered by the huge success of *School's Out*'s anthemic title track and a frenzied tabloid press virtually foaming at the mouth, Alice Cooper became the most newsworthy and controversial band on the planet.

But then came the difficult bit. In the face of blanket condemnation from the great, the good, the humourless, the band needed to consolidate their position. Specifically, they needed to make the greatest album of their career: an over-inflated masterpiece; an ostentatiously offensive, flashy, crass record guaranteed to expand the generation gap to Grand Canyon proportions. In short, they needed to make *Billion Dollar Babies*.

Following *School's Out* was always going to be a daunting task, but with band morale at an all-time high no one involved harboured a shred of doubt that they could not only do it, but also do it in style. "I knew we had a great team," Alice said, "and when you're that age you think you're indestructible. We were really flying by the seat of our pants back then."

Reflecting the dogged buoyancy and inner confidence that kept their spirits high in the face of blanket media condemnation, the band elected to celebrate their newly elevated status in the album's title itself. "The *Billion Dollar Babies* concept was simply making fun of ourselves," Alice says. "Here was a band nobody would touch three years ago, and now we're the biggest band in the world. We'd look at each other and go: 'We're like billion dollar babies.'

*Billion Dollar Babies* marked the apex of Alice's creativity. Expectations were high, and Cooper, at the peak of his tabloid notoriety, delivered. *Elected, No More Mr Nice Guy* and *I Love The Dead* ooze malevolent class. Hit single *No More Mister Nice Guy*, a relatively straight (by Alice standards) FM rock nugget, propelled the album into the charts and turned Alice Cooper into the least likely rock superstars of 1973.

While recording in London the band were photographed by David Bailey for the album's inner sleeve. It presented yet another golden opportunity to gleefully taunt their legion of apoplectic detractors, and the band rose manfully to the challenge. Dressed in diaphanous white silk and surrounded by literally stacks of cash, the musicians casually caress albino bunny rabbits, as their singer presents to the camera a live human baby which is naked except for a splattering of trademark Alice

year released
**1997**

producer
**Nigel Godrich**

These days always close to the top of any list of the best albums of all time, *OK Computer* is the album that took Radiohead far into the mainstream, while retaining rockist cred. Combining prog with alternative influences, they came up with a style that was supple, subtle and sensuous. This wasn't Pink Floyd for the end of the millennium, it was original, visionary and brilliant. Songs like *Paranoid Android* and *Karma Police* cast a spell that propelled Radiohead into the stadium league.

An epochal album that called time on the narrow colloquial nostalgia of Britpop, sold millions and turned Radiohead into global angst-rock superstars, *OK Computer* remains both revered critical milestone and oft-mocked symbol of pretentious overreach.

With hindsight, knowing how deeply Radiohead would delve into artfully deconstructed jazztronica on later albums, it is striking now just how much of a guitar-centric rock unit they still were in 1997, from Jonny Greenwood's wrenching avant-punk convulsions on *Paranoid Android* to

year released
**1973**

producer
**Bob Ezrin**

Cooper eye make-up.

"It was our most decadent album. It was reflecting the decadence of a time when we were living from limousine to penthouse to the finest of everything including... well, the finest of everything. We couldn't believe people were actually paying us to do this. We would have done it for free, because we were just a garage band who happened to be at the right place at the right time."

"It's a statement about American culture," producer Bob Ezrin says of the album. "I always said that Alice Cooper held the fun-house mirror up to society. And that's what I think *Billion Dollar Babies* was. You look in that mirror and there's a bigger, fatter, more excessive, more selfish version of yourself. I feel like the writing got more sophisticated, particularly when you look at something like *Generation Landslide* – one of the great songs of all time. It belongs up there with Bob Dylan's writing as social commentary. I think Alice took a major leap forward into becoming a generational poet and expressing the views of a whole generation."

# 79 *Radiohead*
# OK Computer

the luminous filigree arpeggios that shimmer through *No Surprises*. *Electioneering* and *Climbing Up The Walls*, a couple of more conventional guitar-bloated tracks, have not aged too gracefully. But otherwise *OK Computer* is a pristine 53-minute song cycle, and arguably one of the last great examples of an album as a coherent end-to-end listening experience.

Marking its 20th anniversary, in 2017 the album was reissued, digitally remastered from original analogue master tapes and with new material, including three previously unreleased tracks and reams of extra artwork. Blazing guitars also feature prominently among the reissue's additional non-album tracks and B-sides, notably *Pearly*, which lays down the blueprint for Muse at their most bombastic, and *Palo Alto*, a sci-fi social commentary powered by scorching Pixies-style shotgun riffs.

But of course the main event of the expanded edition is the trio of newly unearthed tracks, all road tested live in the mid-90s but shelved during the *OK Computer* sessions.

In an impressive testament to Radiohead's lofty quality standards, all three are prime-grade cuts. *I Promise*, set to a martial beat and metronomic guitar strum, opens like Nirvana's *All Apologies* before Thom Yorke's soaring falsetto sweeps it aloft to towering Roy Orbison heights. *Man Of War*, previously called *Big Boots (Man-o-War)*, is a dramatic guitar anthem that the band first recorded in 1998 but disliked the results. This version sounds great, all surging riffs and windswept James Bond grandeur. *Lift* is a plaintive power ballad with a sinewy jazzy tempo that builds into an emotionally charged, bittersweet epic. All three are worthy additions to the Radiohead canon, enhancing and enriching an all-time classic album rather than diluting it.

Thom Yorke has revealed that he believes he was haunted during the sessions for *OK Computer*. The album was recorded in the 10th-century English mansion St Catherine's Court, which at the time was owned by actress Jane Seymour, and had its own traditional haunted stories. He told *Rolling Stone*: "Ghosts would talk to me while I was asleep. There was one point when I got up in the morning after a night of hearing voices and decided I had to cut my hair."

He went at himself with the scissor blade of a multi-tool. "I cut myself a few times," he recalls. "It got messy. I came downstairs and everyone was like: 'Er, are you alright?' I was like: 'What's wrong?'

He also reflected that it had been "really, really mental going back into where my head was at" when he looked through old notebooks to gather material for the 20th-anniversary reissue.

Today Radiohead's compendium of pre-millennial tension is not quite the flawless masterpiece of fond folklore, but it holds up extremely well. It still sounds rich, beautiful, mysterious, romantic, anguished, baroque and thrillingly experimental.

# 78 *Iron Maiden* Seventh Son Of A Seventh Son

It's more than 40 years since Iron Maiden barged their way out of London's East End onto the stages of the world, and 37 since their landmark debut album helped usher in a new era for metal. It would not be long before they became the biggest metal band on the planet, selling millions of records around the globe.

For many Maiden fans, *Seventh Son Of A Seventh Son*, their seventh studio album, released in 1988, is the greatest record the band ever recorded. Others will disagree, of course, but even they would accept that it's one of the most sparkling jewels in the band's vast catalogue that includes a wealth of gems. It's the icing on the cake of an eight-album run, beginning with their self-titled debut in 1988, that has still yet to be bettered in heavy music history, and very probably never will.

Unusually for a band used to writing songs that told complex and gripping stories, *Seventh Son Of A Seventh Son* was an entire album dedicated to a single tale. It was all-out prog rock with keyboards introduced into the Maiden sound for the first time.

*Seventh Son Of A Seventh* kicks off with *Moonchild*, an occult epic bristling with primal screams, and massively creepy lyrics about ritual infant murder (an onslaught of goosebumps is guaranteed) and continues through what now reads like a list of platinum-plated Maiden classics, ranging from immaculate singles *Can I Play With Madness* and *The Evil That Men Do* through to the fervent proggery of the title track and the otherworldly squall of *The Prophecy*.

Among them you've got the title track. Even though it's bloody long, and proggy as fuck, it still gallops along like only Maiden can do. Enhanced by keyboards and narration and employing deft changes of tempo, at almost 10 minutes long it offers a persuasive microcosm of its style.

*The Clairvoyant* is bursting at the seams with outlandish mischief, gliding along a gleaming, multilayered verse before melting into a thunderous chorus that was tailor-made for pogoing festival crowds. *Infinite Dreams* ponders along musings of consciousness and the afterlife, bubbling away on a soft opening guitar line before reaching an almighty, urgent crescendo. *Can I Play With Madness* is simply awesome.

In one of the more perverse decisions of their career, not only did Maiden choose to close the *Seventh Son Of A Seventh Son* album with the rampantly commercial *Only The Good Die Young*, they also decided not to release it as a single. Where much of *Seventh Son* is epic and complex, *Only The Good Die Young* is more direct: stirring, soaring and in possession of a hell of a chorus.

"A lot of thought went into it," bassist and band leader Steve Harris says of the album. "It was a good change for us and I think it worked really well.

"It was a new challenge for us, making a concept album. I've always loved prog – Yes, Genesis, ELP – and this album's title track was a powerful song with that prog element to it.

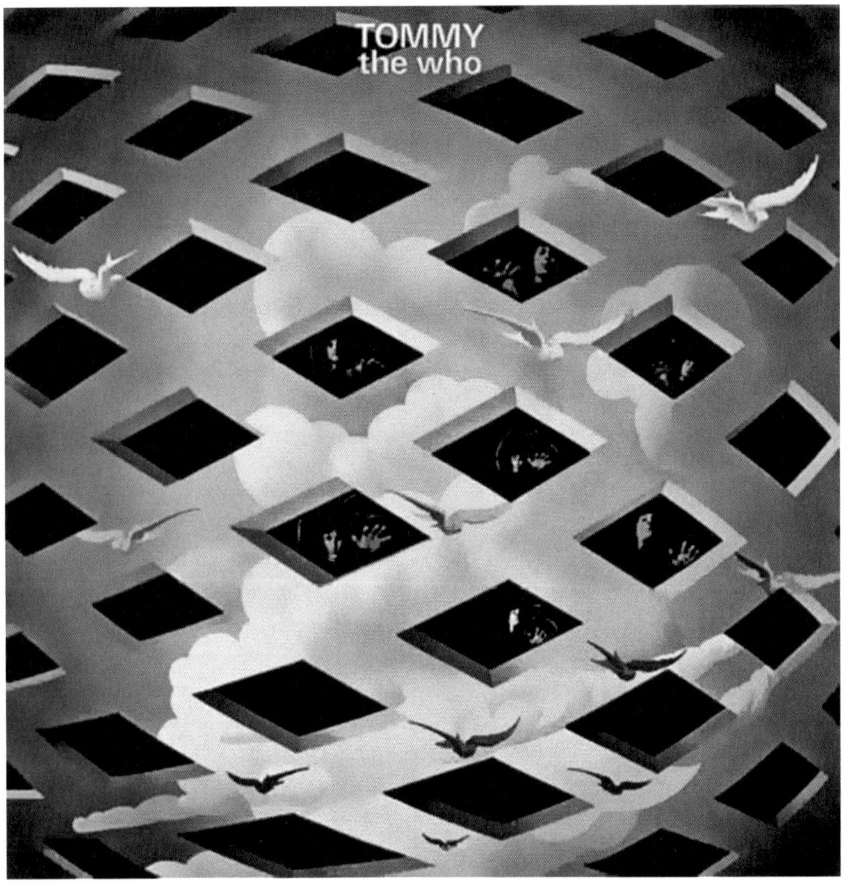


year released
**1969**
label
producer
**Kit Lambert**

*Tommy* was The Who's entry into the world of rock heroism. They had always been a singles group, and they would continue to put out excellent singles, but from now on they would function primarily as an albums band. This made a world of difference, both in how they would proceed with their music and in how they would be assessed, respected and adored.

It was also a pioneering release. It wasn't the first ever rock opera (the Pretty Things had beaten them to it with *S.F. Sorrow* in 1968), but it was the one that swept an ambitious format into the mainstream, setting an astonishing precedent as it streaked to No.2 in the UK albums chart in the early summer of 1969, and then to No.4 in the US.

Townshend had written some of the songs earlier, earmarking them only generally for a possible later use and not necessarily to be part of his masterwork. However, *Welcome*, *We're Not Gonna Take It*, *Underture* and *Sensation* happened to suit the general atmosphere of *Tommy* as it came together, and were easily incorporated.

year released
*1988*

producer
**Martin Birch**

"Not everyone liked the album at the time," Harris admits. "Bruce [Dickinson, singer] even said to me that Queensrÿche had made a better concept album than ours with *Operation: Mindcrime*. I said: 'That's a really good album, but ours is a fucking *great* album!'"

The release of the *Seventh Son Of A Seventh Son* album, in April '88, was somewhat overshadowed by that of Queensrÿche's critically highly acclaimed *Operation: Mindcrime* just a few weeks before, and Maiden's appearance at the ultimately tragic Donington that summer marked the end of Adrian Smith's first stint with the band.

In hindsight it's difficult to see how Maiden could have taken their style further than they did on the *Seventh Son* album, and *Infinite Dreams*, *The Clairvoyant* and *Can I Play With Madness* are up their among the best tracks Maiden's have ever recorded, and some others on this album are not far behind.

After *Seventh Son*, Smith said goodbye, in came his replacement Janick Gers, and things for Iron Maiden were changed irrevocably.

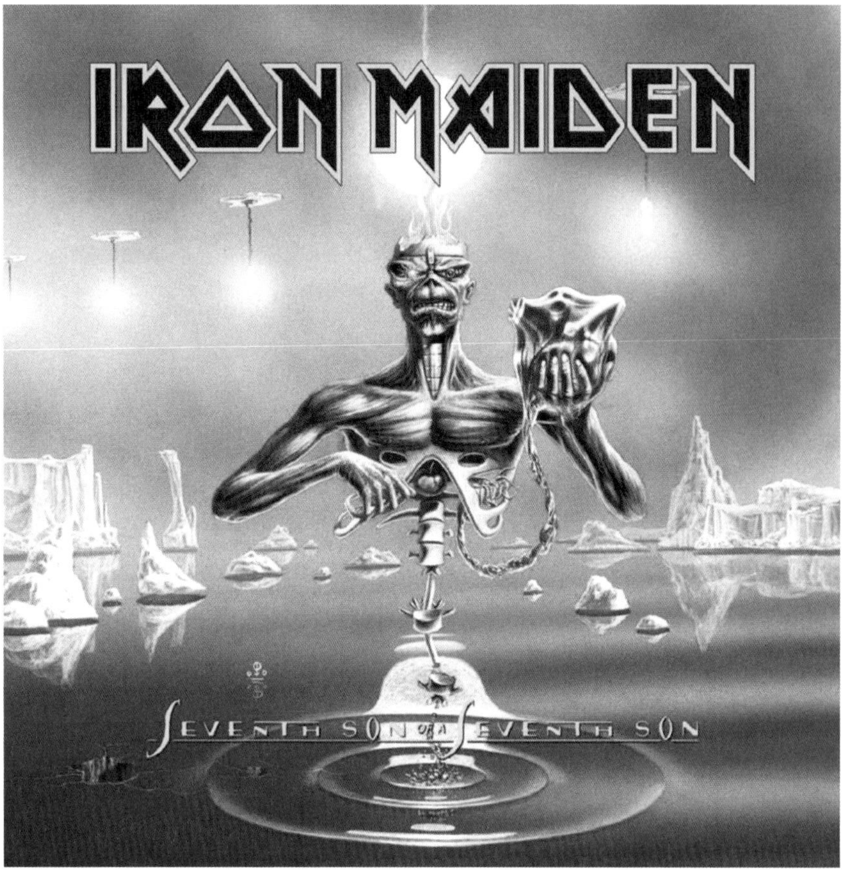


# 77 *The Who*
# Tommy

Other tracks were, of course, written specifically to tell the story of the deaf, dumb and blind kid, Tommy, who can interpret the activities of the people and the things around him only through vibrations – or music. As a result of Tommy's extreme sensitivity, he's able to achieve heroic status and invoke religious fervour as the champion of the pinball machine.

Tommy, a normal child traumatised (by witnessing a murder) into his state of extreme disability, has also been subjected to LSD (*The Acid Queen*) and abused by his wicked Uncle Ernie (*Fiddle About*) – which would seemingly support Townshend's recent contention that he has for many years been concerned about the effects of child abuse, having himself been a victim. But that's a whole other subject.

The story of Tommy is allegorical. On one level it aimed to reflect the rise, the glory and the subsequent fall of a pop star. On another it represents the spiritual quest of a young man – reputedly Townshend himself. The guitarist had been in and out of the psychedelic experience, enduring a terrifying STP trip during a flight in 1967. Asserting that mind-altering drugs could rip a personality apart without any guarantee of putting it back together, Townshend had taken refuge and comfort in the teachings of Eastern guru Meher Baba, and was determined to chart this personal journey in his writing.

If *Tommy*, a double album, was a massive confessional for Townshend, it meant just as much to Roger Daltrey, who later revealed that it enabled him, finally, to find a real voice in The Who. And what he found was a rock voice, one that still ranks among the finest ever committed to vinyl.

The Who were working on *Tommy* throughout the second half of 1968, and their excitement, their true commitment to the music the group were making, resulted in an unusually harmonious working atmosphere. It emerged as an album of contrasts, of light and shade, with enormous power chords ringing out in urgent contrast to moments of fragility and calm, all fitting together perfectly. At the time, it was big and it was clever.

Even if curiosities such as *Fiddle About* and *Cousin Kevin* may now sound less than sensational, they were perceived at the time to serve a practical function as part of the narrative drive, and those two songs have never detracted from the triumphalism of *Pinball Wizard* (the first single to be taken from the album), the climactic drama of the *See Me, Feel Me/ Listening To You* sequence, the exhilaration of *I'm Free* or the rampant anger of *We're Not Gonna Take It*, with Tommy's disciples finally turning on their messiah.

The Who were back. They were bad, beautiful and as brash as they had ever been – but now more colourful. Once again, they were contenders. And when they took *Tommy* out on tour in Europe and America they were just unstoppable, and rose quickly into the realms of rock royalty.

# 76 *Bon Jovi* Slippery When Wet

One of the biggest-selling studio albums of all time, with more than 28 million copies sold worldwide, *Slippery When Wet* is an 80s arena-rock classic to rival Def Leppard's *Hysteria*. Moreover, it rescued Bon Jovi's career after their disappointing 'flop' second album, *7800° Fahrenheit*. The band's first two albums both made the US Top 50, but it was with their next one, 1986's *Slippery*, that Bon Jovi became one of the biggest bands in the world, going on to sell more than 130 million albums in a career of almost 35 years to date.

Their saviour was songwriter Desmond Child, whose commercial instincts proved invaluable on the two breakthrough hits he wrote for the album with mainman Jon Bon Jovi and guitarist Richie Sambora: *You Give Love A Bad Name* and *Livin' On A Prayer*, both US No.1 hit singles.

"To some extent it was our choice," JBJ said of bringing in an outside writer for the first time, talking a few months after the release of *Slippery*. "I liked what Bryan Adams had done with Tina Turner [their duet on Adams's *It's Only Love*], so I suggested we do something similar – I write a song for someone like her, and then we do the song together. But that got changed, and our A&R guy came up with Desmond's name.

"We're growing as songwriters, learning things. What's wrong with collaborating with people like him, who can help to give us the extra ten per cent out of a song? Actually, he's involved with only three tracks on *Slippery* – *Livin' On A Prayer, You Give Love A Bad Name* and *Without Love* – and in each case he hasn't tried to change what we are, but to refine it slightly, to suggest extra ways that we could wring a bit more out of what we had."

The story that fired the seminal *Wanted Dead Or Alive* went back to the band's exhaustive tour in support of *7800° Fahrenheit*.

"I was on the tour bus and couldn't sleep, and was staring out of the window, thinking: 'This is great, but it's an odd existence.' You don't know where you are. You're living in truck stops, sleeping on the bus, showering at a gig. We were thinking of songs like *Turn The Page* by Bob Seger, and how those songs were storytellers doing their best storytelling. I talked to Richie about the concept, he worked up the riff almost on the spot and we knocked it out in two or three hours."

*Livin' On A Prayer*, meanwhile, is locked into the working-class ethic around which Jon grew up.

"I am really proud of that one, because it goes back to the storytelling roots that I was talking about. It deals with the way that two kids – Tommy and Gina – face life's struggles, and how their love and ambitions get them through the bad times. It's working class and it's real. That's what most of our fans can relate to, not the limos and groupies. Tommy and Gina aren't two specific people, they represent a lifestyle.

The third crucial commercial element of the album was *You Give Love A Bad Name*, the second song

year released
**1985**

producer
**Neil Dorfsman/ Mark Knopfler**

After the albums *Making Movies* and *Love Over Gold* saw Dire Straits' slow ascent into the big league, their next one made them unlikely megastars.

In November 1984, Dire Straits arrived at Air Studios on the Caribbean island of Monserrat to make their fifth studio record. The result was *Brothers In Arms*. Released on May 13, 1985, it proved to be a cast-iron phenomenon.

Shrewdly recorded digitally to capitalise on the burgeoning CD market, its breezily cynical toe-tappers (*Money For Nothing, Walk Of Life*), brooding mood pieces (eight-minute epics *Tunnel Of Love* and *Why Worry*) and supper-club jazz (*Your Latest Trick*) together somehow became a global phenomenon. The album topped the charts around the world and went on to win two Grammys and a Brit Award. To date it has sold more than 30 million copies. Not bad going for an album launched by a video of a cartoon fat bloke moaning about MTV and rock stars getting *'money for nothing and chicks for free'*.

year released
**1986**

producer
**Bruce Fairbairn**

written with Desmond Child.

"He came down to the Sambora basement, and the second song was we wrote was *You Give Love A Bad Name*. We demoed it, liked what we heard, but never thought it would be a hit. We'd never had one of those before, so didn't know what to expect."

There was little glitz about the process that shaped one of the most important albums of the era, more a lot of guts, grit and grease.

Twenty years on, *Slippery When Wet* has become iconic, selling more than 13 million copies. It is still, by some distance, Bon Jovi's best album, and seems to be the standard by which everything the band have subsequently released is judged.

In many ways it's the point at which America took on board the lessons Def Leppard had taught with 1983's *Pyromania*. *Slippery* took these rules and ran with them. And the world noticed. Not just hard-rock afficionados, but also casual radio listeners and pop fans. *Slippery* has survived and prospered because it is a record with depth, clarity and no little sincerity.

# 75 *Dire Straits*
# Brothers In Arms

"We spent a lot of time in rehearsals playing around with different ideas," says bassist John Illsley, "so we were quite prepared by the time we went to Monserrat to start recording. Then we had a problem with the tape machine after three weeks of being there. Overnight, the digital tape machine decided to wipe something like seventy percent of all the stuff we'd recorded. This was the early days of digital and we had to start recording all over again."

"At that time, Monserrat was like Shangri-La," says keyboard player Alan Clark. "It was the most beautiful, peaceful place you could possibly wish to visit.

"We ended up getting Omar Hakim [David Bowie, Sting, Madonna, Kate Bush, Miles Davis] in on drums for that album and we cut the backing tracks in about a week. Mark [Knopfler, guitarist/vocalist] wanted to listen to the drum track first and then we'd build the rest of the song up from there. *Ride Across The River* and *Why Worry* were both done like that. We had a sense that *Money For Nothing* was going to be a classic guitar riff from the first time Mark played it.

"In the run-up to *Brothers In Arms,* Mark was making the soundtrack to the film *Cal,* Dire Straits' manager Ed Bicknell remembers: "We were driving up to the studio one day and got stuck in traffic. He turned to me and asked me to ring the guys up because he'd got some songs together.

I remember going down to rehearsals and hearing *Money For Nothing* for the first time. When I was an agent I'd done a tour with ZZ Top and I was a big fan of that kind of fuzzy guitar tone that Billy Gibbons uses. I might be wrong, but I have a feeling Mark might have been listening to a bit of ZZ Top. I thought the song itself might be a bit of a hit, but no one could have foreseen what would happen with that album.

"I also remember hearing *Your Latest Trick* out in Monserrat, which is the only song of theirs that I ever had any musical input on. It was originally played liked a bee-pop jazz number and wasn't working, there was no groove. I suggested to Mark he try it as a bossa nova and take one of the beats out, which is what they did.

"*Walk Of Life* was not going to be on the record. I walked into the studio in New York when Mark and [producer] Neil Dorfsman were remixing the track, and I hadn't heard it. Mark said it was a B-side. I told him it was a hit song on a B-side and it should be on the album. It was actually a bigger-selling single worldwide than *Money For Nothing*. Mark was a big fan of the Animals when he was a kid and he used to go and see them at Newcastle City Hall. Alan Price used to play a Farfisa organ, and Mark was looking to re-create the sound of that on the front end of *Walk Of Life*."

"The *Brothers In Arms* tour was a big one that's for sure," Illsley remembers. "It was a realisation that the band had reached a point that was fairly unique. We did the song *Brothers In Arms* as an encore and I got a shiver down my spine every night as we played it."

# 74 *AC/DC*
# Powerage

Put simply, *Powerage* is arguably the best rock album of the 70s. But, sandwiched between two of the band's other peaks, *Let There Be Rock* and *Highway To Hell*, AC/DC's fourth international release, it didn't immediately stake a claim as their best album.

That *Powerage* is the only AC/DC album title not to feature in a chorus of one of their songs speaks about one of the record's key virtues: subtlety. Granted, there's little that's subtle about the throttling riffs on *Riff Raff* or the crunching *Kicked In The Teeth*, but elsewhere – on the beautifully lachrymose *Down Payment Blues*, the playful *What's Next To The Moon*, the plaintive, in-the-pocket *Gone Shootin'* – AC/DC display a discipline, control and restrained power that only the most mature and confident of players can attain.

Emphatically, it's late frontman Bon Scott's album. Much of the beauty of *Powerage* comes from Scott's wonderfully sketched portraits of disappointed, desperate men pushed beyond breaking point by lost love and empty pockets. As cocksure as he could be, Scott always had an affinity for the broken and bruised; that guy with holes in his shoes, holes in his teeth and patches on the patches on his old blue jeans, and *Powerage* is a celebration of fortitude in the face of soul-crushing setbacks. Crucially, though, at the heart of the album there is always hope, always a glimpse of blue skies for those knocked in the gutter, as evinced by *Sin City*, a glorious 'fuck you' to the fates, a defiant last hurrah in the face of cruelly stacked odds. After *Powerage*, AC/DC would get louder, slicker and bigger, but they would never again display this much heart, soul and humanity.

Although its predecessor *Let There Be Rock* was the first AC/DC album not to crack the Top 10 in Australia (in the UK it reached No.17, in the US it didn't even make the Hot 100), it remains one of their best – the first truly classic, no-duds-allowed AC/DC album.

For a while, the chances of them making an equally good follow-up seemed slim. Prior to recording *Let There Be Rock* Mark Evans had been given the boot and replaced by Englishman Cliff Williams – who couldn't get a visa to perform in Australia. Atlantic, their label in New York, would have liked the group to now give Bon the boot too, blaming his vocals for the band's lack of radio play. But again guitarists the Young brothers decided to knuckle down and prove everybody wrong. Which they did, quite spectacularly, with *Powerage*.

By the time they were ready to go back into the studio in January 1978, they knew that this time they would have to do more than go in empty-handed, throwing it all together as best they could in a fusillade of alcohol and fags and making-it-up-as-you-go-along Aussie spunk. The next record would have to be their heaviest record yet, and also their most musical. It would need to show what AC/DC could do, demonstrating the one thing critics had got into the habit of expecting them not to achieve: growth.

"*Powerage* was where Malcolm, in particular, really wanted to show they were good musicians too," recalls their then manager Michael Browning.

As a result, *Powerage* took longer to record than previous AC/DC albums, with ad-hoc sessions spread across several weeks at the start of the year. Experiencing fully for the first time the intensity of AC/DC in the studio, bassist Cliff Williams, for one, was convinced that *Powerage* was special. When they started work in the studio "we got there and got down, and did the long-hour days," he said. "It was really a tremendous experience."

Conceived as a showcase that would place AC/DC up there with the American superstars they were now sharing stages with, *Powerage* was split between yet more ton-up AC/DC classics such as *Down Payment Blues*, and more elliptical tracks such as *What's Next To The Moon*. The latter, with its circular guitar figure replacing the juddering block chords of yore, was the most transcendent moment on any AC/DC album yet.

Whether intentional or not, the album had the same yo-yoing dynamic throughout its nine tracks: one moment a perfect-10 rock monster like *Riff Raff*, the next moment another mid-paced stroller built around an almost pop guitar figure: *Gone Shootin*.

Of the remaining tracks, the lines between old-school, go get-'em AC/DC and new, more measured, see-what-we-can-do AC/DC are pleasingly blurred. *Sin City* begins like classic AC/DC – towering intro, all-guns-blazing riff *Gimme A Bullet*, with its low-slung guitars and chugging drums, sounds more like the Lynyrd Skynyrd number it almost steals its title from than anything AC/DC had put down on vinyl before.

The final two tracks, *Up To My Neck In You* and *Kicked In The Teeth*, date back to earlier *Powerage* sessions of six months before.

One other track, *Cold Hearted Man*, only made it to the very earliest vinyl editions of the album released in Britain. The band genuinely hated it. For the rest of us it was simply one more catchy tune.

**year released**
**1978**

**producer**
**Harry Vanda/ George Young**

# 73 *Bruce Springsteen*
# Born In The USA

*Born In The USA* is Bruce Springsteen's biggest-selling album, a multimillion-seller that made him a superstar. Odd, then, perhaps, that it may be the easiest Springsteen album to dislike, even for his fans, because it was so overplayed in '84 and '85, with five Top 10 singles from it. Still, *No Surrender*, *I'm On Fire* and certainly *Downbound Train* had a simmering underside, while the title track may be one of the most misunderstood songs in pop history; Springsteen wrote it with sarcasm and defeatism, but the chorus became a battle cry for a patriotism he never intended.

*Born In The USA* had come along right on the heels of a dark period in both Springsteen's own life and for Americans in general. The years immediately preceding its release had seen the US economy slump, jobs vanish, and out in the heartlands these were the worst times folks could recall since the days of the Great Depression of the 1930s. Springsteen, who was susceptible to his own depressions, had for his part sunk into an existential crisis following the tour to promote his fifth album, *The River*, and with which he had kicked off the new decade. He articulated as much on his next record, 1982's *Nebraska*, a stark, solemn collection of songs that he recorded apart from the E Street Band.

Filtered through the returning E Street Band, the *Born In The USA* album was instead rousing, uplifting, as slick and sleek-sounding as a sports car, and balm to tend the battered psyches of millions of Americans. It proved to be a commercial juggernaut, mined for multiple hit singles, and going on to sell over 30 million copies.

In September 1983, Springsteen again rounded up the E Street Band to start recording. The subsequent sessions were given impetus by a surging, R&B-flavoured rocker he had just written, although the upbeat musical backdrop to *Bobby Jean* was also concealing a hurt. Written as a bittersweet farewell to a lover, it was in fact aimed at least in part at his guitarist Steven Van Zandt, who had told Springsteen back in the spring that he meant to go off and have his own career. In spite of his long-time friend's departure, Springsteen moulded the *Born In The USA* album into shape. The title track and another left over from the *Nebraska* tapes, *Downbound Train*, were dusted down and put alongside other held-over songs plus fresh material that included *Bobby Jean*, *No Surrender* and *Glory Days*.

By the following March, 15 completed songs were up for inclusion on the record, but Springsteen's manager John Landau still felt they were missing a signature hit and told Springsteen as much.

That night, back at the hotel where he was staying, Springsteen picked up his acoustic guitar and wrote *Dancing In The Dark* in the hours before dawn. He recorded it with the band in the studio the next evening, completing an album that was chock-full of songs as instant and accessible as *Hungry Heart*, the breakthrough hit he had meant to give up.

year released
**1967**
label
producer
**Felix Pappalardi**

If ever a record stood at the crossroads of rock, it was *Disraeli Gears*, the second album by Cream. Written, recorded and released in the watershed year of 1967, it was a collection that linked the legacy of the blues to the onward rush of psychedelia. Made in America, yet unmistakably British in sound and sensibility, it was a diverse collection that saw some of guitarist Eric Clapton's best playing collide with some of bassist/vocalist Jack Bruce's best songs. While their debut was largely based in Delta blues, this was bolder and more open-minded. *Disraeli Gears* sounded effortless; unhurried without being indulgent.

With its iconic cover artwork by Martin Sharp, featuring the granite-faced trio staring out across a garish red and pink dreamscape of irradiated flowers, peacocks, galloping horses and amorphous swirls, the album became a touchstone recording of the 1960s counterculture. A massive worldwide hit, it propelled Cream to international stardom and remains the trio's finest hour.

Among the album's highlights is opener *Strange Brew*,

year released
*1984*

producer
**Jon Landau/Chuck Plotkin**
**Bruce Springsteen/Steven Van Zandt**

He had no such reservations regarding *Born In The USA*. In fact, quite the opposite was true this time around. Having until then zealously guarded how his songs were sent out into the world, Springsteen was soon handing over *Dancing In The Dark* and *Cover Me* to New York hip-hop producer Arthur Baker to be remixed as dance tracks, following the example of labelmate Cyndi Lauper.

The album was custom-built to come booming out of car radios and jukeboxes and, most of all, for the shiny new compact disc format. Dancing In The Dark rocketed up the Billboard Hot 100. The just-released album was pulled along in its slipstream, on its way to becoming a 30-million-selling colossus.

*Born In The USA* took on a momentum of its own. 1984 was an election year in the US, and now famously at a campaign stop in Hammonton, New Jersey that September, the incumbent President Reagan tried to hitch himself to Springsteen's bandwagon. "America's future," Reagan announced, "rests in the message of hope in the songs of a man so many young Americans admire – New Jersey's own Bruce Springsteen."

# 72 *Cream*
# Disraeli Gears

which began life as a cover of an old Albert King number called *Lawdy Mama*. Producer Felix Pappalardi (later to form Mountain) took the tape of the backing track home after the first day of recording and returned with it the next day, as Clapton recalled, "having transformed it into a kind of McCartney-esque pop song".

Another is of course *Sunshine Of Your Love*, with its grinding, step-down riff, war-toms drum beat and dynamic vocal interplay between Bruce and Clapton. Arguably the most universally recognised and influential number that Cream ever recorded, it's also the one that launched a generation of heavy rock bands in its wake.

But *Disraeli Gears* was not just about the heavy riffs in life. *World Of Pain*, written by Pappalardi and his wife Gail Collins, was brought in at about the same time as *Strange Brew*. "It is along the lines of some of the more melodic, less bluesy things that I was writing," Bruce says. *Dance The Night Away* is another of the more melodic songs, all soaring harmonies and jangling 12-string guitars. "This was a nod to The Byrds, who I really loved at the time," Bruce says of the song, one of many Cream songs he co-wrote with lyricist/poet Pete Brown, another *Gears* one being the bizarrely titled *SWLABR* (an acronym for *She Was Like A Bearded Rainbow*).

A perhaps lesser-known standout is *We're Going Wrong*, written by Bruce and sung by him in an extraordinary, high-pitched "head" voice ("not falsetto" he says) that was one of the most distinctive elements of Cream's sound.

"Musically, what I always wanted to go for with Cream was really heavy instruments with really light vocals," Bruce explains. "Also I liked the idea of the two voices, both in the same register, so that you can't actually distinguish who is singing what."

The real star of *We're Going Wrong*, however, is drummer Ginger Baker, whose fluid, steadily building, ebb-and-flow playing, using beaters rather than sticks, is masterful and mesmerising.

The album's closer an unlikely performance of *Mother's Lament*, an old music-hall number, sung by Clapton and Baker in a broad cockney accent; Bruce, who speaks with a distinctive Glaswegian brogue, kept clear of the mic on this occasion.

"I think it was just our way of saying: 'This is us. We're not trying to be what we're not.' That was an important part of our attitude. At the time, you had two kinds of people that were playing the blues. You had the John Mayall approach, which was to recreate a Chicago blues sound. But my idea –and I discussed this with Eric quite a lot – was to actually take the blues and apply it to what we were."

But any idea that Cream were blues revivalists was dispelled by the forceful originality of the songwriting elsewhere on the album and the many highly distinctive performances on a collection that has most surely stood the test of time.

"It's nice that people remember that album," Bruce says. "It was a lot of fun."

# 71 *Kiss*
# Alive!

With painted faces, outlandish costumes and seven-inch stack-heeled boots, Kiss arrived in the 70s like superheroes straight out of a comic. They had superhero names: The Starchild, The Demon, The Space Ace, The Catman. In concert the presented The Greatest Show On Earth, with explosions, blood, fire-breathing, a rocket-launching guitar...

At the heart of it was a great all-American rock band. They might have been derided by serious music fans (and, of course, critics) as nothing more than a circus act, but Kiss didn't go on to sell 100 million records by fluke. In the band's vast catalogue are some of the greatest and most influential rock albums of all time. One of those is *Alive!*.

In 1975, Kiss were in deep shit. Their first two studio records (both released in '74) had bombed. The third reached the US Top 40 but didn't have a hit single. A live album was a no-brainer for a band that had built their reputation on stage, but a double album was costly, a high-stakes gamble. But they went for it.

Despite the obvious attractions of the preceding studio album, *Destroyer* (released just a month earlier than *Alive!*), Kiss needed a record that truly captured their on-stage power. And *Alive!*, a thunderous double-live set, delivered in spades. Bristling with gung-ho intensity and feral metal power, it puts you right at the heart of the storm. It's like having bassist Gene Simmons stomping around your living room. Did rock'n'roll ever sound so gigantic? Listen to the mighty *Black Diamond* or the epic *100,000 Years* and the answer has to be: no.

"We're not the best-looking guys in the world," said Gene Simmons. "We're not the best of almost anything in the world. But when we get up on that stage we consider it holy ground, and even when we suck we're spectacular. You can love us or you can hate us, but you'll still walk out of that stadium at the end of the night and say: 'That's the best fucking show I've ever seen."

Released in September 1975, *Alive!*, blasted into the US Top 10, stayed in the US chart for 110 weeks and went quadruple platinum (i.e. it sold gazillions).

It was a tour de force and a coming of age for Kiss as an arena-rock behemoth – as illustrated by their definitive, crowd-pleasing anthem *Rock And Roll All Nite*, which, at last, gave them their first hit single. With *Alive!*'s intro of "You wanted the best, you got the best, the hottest band in the world... Kiss!", the album marked the birth of a legend, turning Kiss into superstars. Not only that, they also became a cultural phenomenon with those four sides of vinyl.

Always a huge live draw, for the recording of *Alive!* they'd brought together all the finest anthems from three previous studio records, and let rip in front of thousands of ecstatic fans. The results sounded utterly compulsive. No wonder generations of kids took to standing in front of the mirror, wearing their mum's make-up and waving clenched fists while hollering

year released
**1979**

producer
**Ron Nevison**

On the road in 1978, UFO's Phil Mogg and Michael Schenker were busy recreating World War 2. Yet they still managed to make one of the greatest live albums ever – *Strangers In The Night*.

"Listen to the album. There are some wrong notes on that song. I hate mistakes." Decades later guitarist Michael Schenker still recalls the straw that broke the camel's back and prompted his exit from UFO. It was 1978, and the band were holed up in New York's Record Plant studios, mixing their double live album *Strangers In The Night*.

Schenker had been at loggerheads with producer Ron Nevison over which version of his showcase song *Rock Bottom* to use on the live album.
The guitarist was unhappy with the producer's choice of take, and insisted that he either change it or let him overdub it. Nevison refused.

"Michael's entitled to believe that there were better takes of *Rock Bottom* that might have been used," Nevison says, "but a guy like Michael Schenker is only

year released
**1975**

producer
**Eddie Kramer**

along to *Rock And Roll All Nite* or *Strutter*. How many of them went on to their own piece of stardom? Probably quite a few. And Anthrax drummer Charlie Benante was one of them.

"The thing that I remember most about it," Benante recalls, "was just staring at the package – it opened out to a gatefold, and there was a huge booklet in it. I just remember staring at it and being like: 'What the hell?!'

"I loved every single track one on that record. I remember just playing it continuously, over and over again. I loved the way side one would kick in – it was like the introduction was the beginning of the show. Then you get to the middle portions – sides two and three – and side four was the big ending; I'll never forget listening to *Black Diamond* and being like, 'What the hell is going on?' The explosions and everything. [The track-list] is a little out of sequence – actually, it's not even a live show; they totally re-recorded it [Simmons refutes this]. But who cares? "I absolutely still listen to *Alive!*. I listen to it sometimes right before we play – it pumps me up, puts me in a different state of mind."

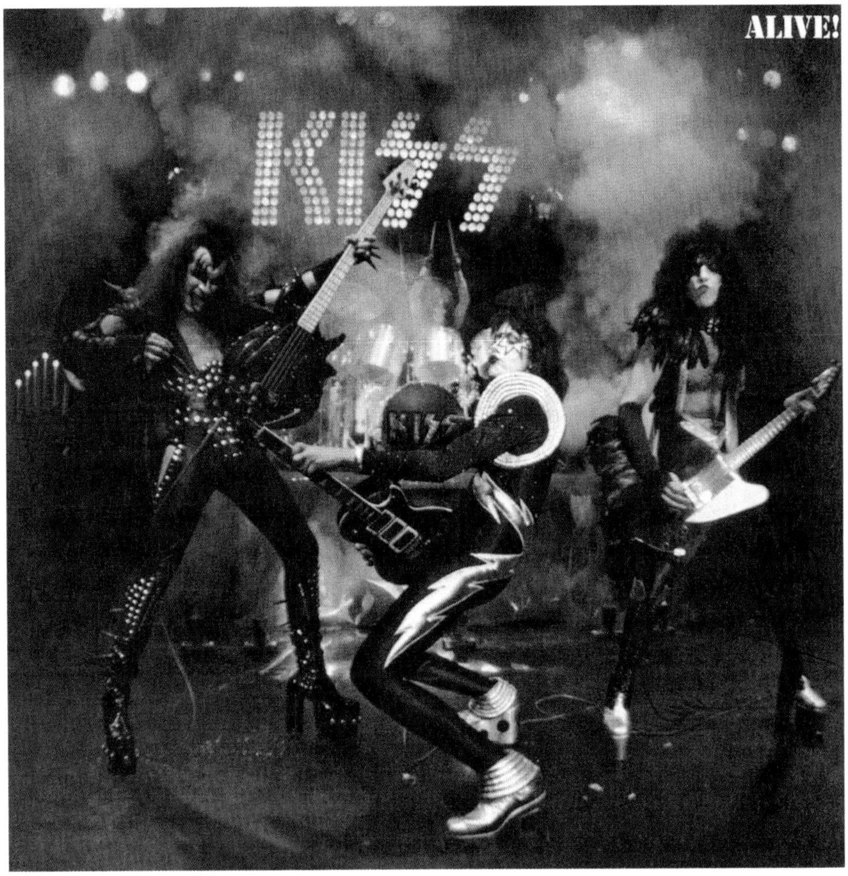


# 70 *UFO* Strangers In The Night

listening for Michael Schenker. As producer I listen to the bigger picture. Michael was never what you'd call a 'band guy'."

For singer Phil Mogg, this flashpoint provided a moment of unintentional comedy. "I can still see Michael, who was becoming more and more distanced from the band, going out of the studio mumbling: 'Poor, poor *Rock Bottom*'," Mogg recalls with a smirk. "And that was the last we saw of him."

The songs that would appear on *Strangers In The Night* were recorded on the US leg of the Obsession tour in Autumn 1978. To minimise potential disaster, the band's label, Chrysalis, hired the Record Plant's remote unit and dispatched Ron Nevison – who had produced UFO's previous two albums – to record six shows on the tour. Despite gravel-voiced stage manager Steve Brooks's opening rallying cry of: "Hello, Chicago. Would you please welcome, from England... U!... F!... O!", the album was eventually pieced together like an audio patchwork quilt.

"There are some things about that record that Mike Clink [who co-manned the mobile truck and would go on to produce Guns N' Roses' *Appetite For Destruction*] and I still can't remember," admits Nevison. "I don't even recall recording the show in Louisville, Kentucky, but apparently we did so. And then, of course, there's also some conjecture over the amount of 'fixing' that was done."

Certain 'fixes' were made. In order to accommodate four sides of vinyl, Nevison was forced to rearrange the running order of the set as it had been played. Two of the songs that appear on the album – *Mother Mary* and *This Kid's* – were also re-recorded in the studio afterwards and overdubbed with crowd noise from the tour.

"Some people will say: 'Oh, then it's not a real live album,'" says drummer Andy Parker. "But we set up the gear like we'd have done at a gig and played the damned songs. It really was as live as you could get."

Nearly forty years on, a surprisingly large number of musicians have spent time as a member of UFO, but it says much about *Strangers In The Night* to note that many of the songs on that album are still in the band's live set.

"Strangers is our best album, and I'm blown away that it's still considered important," says Parker today. "We made some great studio albums, but to understand UFO you always had to see us live. It remains the epitome of what we're about."

"It has a lot of vigour and strut," adds Phil Mogg. "As a doubting Thomas that hadn't wanted to do it, I was very, very wrong."

"Everybody agrees that *Strangers In The Night* is one of the best live albums ever, so I didn't do such a bad job," laughs Nevison. "Whatever complaints Michael Schenker might have, he can stuff them."

And after all these years, even Schenker himself has learned to live with what he calls the album's "mistakes". "Those notes might have been wrong," he concedes, "but they became classic wrong notes."

# 69 *The Jimi Hendrix Experience*
# Axis: Bold As Love

It was Little Richard, Hendrix's previous employer, who managed to sum up Jimi's ethos on life, and his subsequent rise: "He gave it all to you," he enthused. "And that's what you want, isn't it? You want it all."

And all really did mean exactly that, from the incredible, over-the-top stage shows, to completely rewriting the book in terms of sound and what music can be, do and also go on to become. Before the world had even heard the groundbreaking sonic mastery of Hendrix's debut album *Are You Experienced*, he was already writing new material for its follow-up, *Axis: Bold As Love*. It took what he had started on *Are You Experienced* to another level altogether. Hendrix's mastery of the guitar was increasing, and after having been a side man for so long his creativity seemed to know no bounds.

Jimi had been living in the UK for less than two years at this point, under the guidance of his manager, former Animals bassist Chas Chandler. Despite the early start on the new record, Hendrix and his band – drummer Mitch Mitchell and bassist Noel Redding – were due to tour, which would effectively bring their acid-drenched psychedelia to the world. The band did not return to London's Olympic Studios until late in the year, by which time they were slightly older, wiser, and with the experience of well over 150 live shows. They needed to capitalise on the success of their debut album.

By December 1967, *Axis: Bold As Love* was ready to be released on an unsuspecting public. As well as sounding like nothing that had gone before, the record even looked different. Originally released as a gatefold edition, *Axis...* incorporated images of Hendrix, Mitchell and Redding into a shrine. The cover artwork was psychedelic, and so was the music inside. It was said that Hendrix was disappointed by the design. He had supposedly asked for the cover to pay tribute to his Indian heritage (as in Native American – his grandmother was Cherokee), but the British designers assumed he meant India the country.

Hendrix came into his own in terms of the songwriting on *Axis...*; but what made the album so special, so unique, so beguiling, was a combination of the writing, new studio technology, the growing synergy between the musicians and the often underappreciated input of Chas Chandler.

"Chas was definitely in charge of production," producer Eddie Kramer remembered. "Without Chas's help I don't think Jimi could have done what he did. I think Chas was an unsung hero in the whole career of Jimi Hendrix. He really helped Jimi develop. He was the man with the patience and fortitude to help him with his songwriting, to give him books on science-fiction to help fire his imagination, and to sit with him day after day in his apartment and let him be creative. Chas had a vision of what it would take to put Jimi on top, because Chas came from this background of the three minute pop song with The Animals. In a way, that restricted Jimi. But I think it was a good kind of restriction really, because it forced Jimi to think: 'Okay, if my ideas are out here, six feet wide, say, I have to make them three feet wide; gather all that information and compact it into a little three- or four-minute piece.' That produced some really amazing results."

Those sci-fi novels also came in remarkably handy, firing Jimi's imagination – along with the LSD he was ingesting. The opening of the album proper took its inspiration from these very novels: *EXP* had Mitch Mitchell and Jimi engaging in a fake interview, with Jimi playing the role of Paul Carusoe, a fictitious 'expert' on alien life.

However, it was what followed that seemed more extraterrestrial: opener *Up From The Skies*, with its alien sounds, and Hendrix imploring that he wanted to discover the contents of *'the rooms behind your minds'*; the enticing melodies and startling imagery of *Castles Made Of Sand...* The fantasy worlds that Jimi created and portrayed stood out like swirling, Day-Glo colours on a dull grey reality. The songs' far-out lyricism made perfect sense to those who were as tripped out as the band were. The wah-wah pedal, which featured heavily on *Axis...*, was a recent innovation and an effect that Jimi would make his own – even now he's considered its greatest exponent.

But it wasn't all surrealism and taking the guitar to brave new dimensions; there are moments on Axis... where you could be forgiven for thinking there was no experimentation going on, just good oldfashioned, solid musicianship, the best example being the delicate craftsmanship and the truly sublime execution of *Little Wing*, a counterpoint to the cacophony that raged elsewhere on the album. It's here that Hendrix shows off the true depth of his considerable skill as an artist. He knew when to hold back, when it wasn't necessary to try to subvert every musical convention.

Seemingly unaware of the impact that it would go on to have, Jimi gave the sort of self-effacing reply when questioned about how successful Axis... would be to his – now not insubstantial – fanbase: "And if the audience doesn't dig it, well, I don't know, there's nothing else we can do. Music is what it's all about. Oh, I can't explain. You know what it is."

**year released**
***1967***

**producer**
**Chas Chandler**

# 68 *Lynyrd Skynyrd* (Pronounced 'Lĕh-'nérd 'Skin-'nérd')

No band has been cut down in their prime so suddenly, and so horrifically, as Lynyrd Skynyrd. Having risen from humble origins in Jacksonville, Florida, Skynyrd had become major stars by the mid-70s. Their name a joke on their despised former schoolteacher Leonard Skinner.

This, Skynyrd's classic debut, is the quintessential southern rock album and includes the most sacred of all southern rock songs. Founding member guitarist Gary Rossington said of *Free Bird*: "It wasn't anything heavy, just a love song about leavin' town." But this nine-minute epic is Skynyrd's *Stairway To Heaven*, a legendary rock anthem. The album also features two beautiful blues-based songs: *Simple Man* and *Tuesday's Gone*. And on the swinging *Gimme Three Steps*, singer Ronnie Van Zant recalled having a gun pulled on him by the jealous boyfriend of a girl named Linda Lou - the archetypal southern tale.

The oft-told, star-crossed saga of Lynyrd Skynyrd has been portrayed as the convergence of opportunity, preparedness, talent and luck. What were the chances of Dylan associate and producer extraordinaire Al Kooper walking into an Atlanta dive in the summer of 1972 and spotting this band?

Kooper had persuaded MCA records to bankroll his Sounds Of The South label in an effort to compete with Capricorn Records (home of the Allman Brothers). He was bowled over by Skynyrd's professionalism, arrangements, guitar work, and mostly by short and stocky lead singer Van Zant, who showed up in a black T-shirt and droopy jeans.

"At first he annoyed me, because he was a mic stand twirler," says Kooper. "The drum major of Lynyrd Skynyrd, but instead of a baton he had a microphone stand that was, by the way, lightweight aluminium - it only looked like it was heavy. That just got me. Plus I was amused because he left his shoes on the side of the stage. But looks didn't really matter to me. The music was incredible. How can you not respond to the first time you hear *I Ain't The One* or *Free Bird*?"

In Kooper's eyes, Lynyrd Skynyrd were his Allman Brothers - the jewel in the southern rock crown. Skynyrd transcended the genre with their swaggering, dangerous music that conjured the dark fury of betrayal, perfidy or just plain orneriness and hopelessness over the diminished prospects in the rural south. These were guys who never expected anything, but wanted everything. Van Zant's lip would curl into a surly half moon as he spat out the lyrics to *Poison Whiskey* or *Things Goin' On*. You could hear it in the prosaic plea of *Gimme Three Steps*, and the stately requiem of *Free Bird*.

That anthem-turned-albatross began life as a wistful love song about a man who was trying to extricate himself from a claustrophobic relationship. It grew to epic stature when they grafted on a mad combative closing coda that builds and tumbles on itself then doubles back again, making a nine-minute

year released
**1970**

producer
**Kit Lambert, The Who
Jon Astley**

After *Tommy*, The Who were overflowing with confidence when they played the juggernaut live show that provided the material for *Live At Leeds*. Loud, boisterous and in-your-face, the sheer energy and momentum of *Substitute, Magic Bus* and, in particular, the dynamic rendition of Eddie Cochran's *Summertime Blues* more than makes up for the band's sloppy performance and poor sound quality. .

When *Live At Leeds* first appeared, the initial surprise was the packaging. The plain manila folder with the simple 'The Who Live At Leeds' seemingly inked by a rubber stamp looked like a bootleg. When you opened it up there were two pockets. One contained the vinyl record, like a test pressing in a paper sleeve, the other held facsimiles of assorted Who memorabilia from the band's highly chequered past, including Townshend's hand-typed lyrics to the song *My Generation*, a receipt for smoke bombs, disastrous band accounts, a rejection letter from EMI, the contract for Woodstock, and the Maximum R&B poster.

year released
**1973**

producer
**Al Kooper**

sonic edifice that stretches right across the Mason-Dixon line, purloining fills from Duane Allman and travelling all the way to London to sit at the right hand of Jeff Beck, siphoning off his *Beck's Bolero* riffs.

The beginning of the song is almost a power ballad, as Van Zant asks the immortal question *'If I leave here tomorrow, would you still remember me?'* - a line that, after the plane crash that took the lives of Van Zant, Steve and Cassie Gaines and roadie Dean Kilpatrick, took on so much irony and pathos that for years after the reunion of 1987 Johnny Van Zant refused to sing it. The second part of the song is the glorious, almost apocalyptic guitar crescendo. Do we remember him? Hell yeah.

Lynyrd Skynyrd were always more influenced by second wave British invaders (Eric Clapton, Free, and the garagey thud of the Stones, Kinks and Yardbirds) than the jazzy, free-falling improvisation of the Allmans. With their tales of beautiful losers, thwarted romance and dashed ambition, Skynyrd were a more menacing bunch. Peace, love and understanding never made it to Jacksonville.

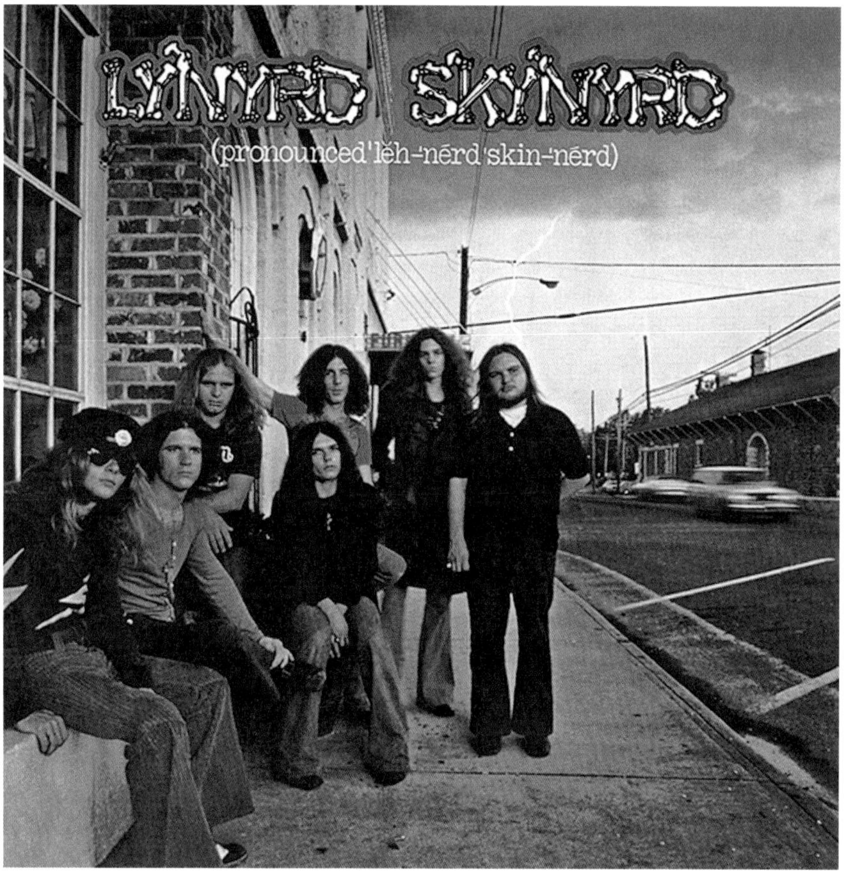


# 67 *The Who*
# Live At Leeds

Coming in the wake of *Tommy*, with its lavish triptych cover by Mike McInnerney that was part psychedelic and part M.C. Escher, seemed to indicate that The Who's sense of humour was asserting itself, and also their love/hate relationship with 20th-century consumerism. The next surprise was the record itself. Its original form consisted of just six tracks, three of which were covers - Johnny Kidd's *Shakin' All Over*, Eddie Cochran's *Summertime Blues* and Mose Allison's *Young Man Blues* - along with *Substitute*, *My Generation* and *Magic Bus*. This is not to say that *Live At Leeds* exactly short-changed the punters in 1970; *My Generation* is a 16-minute medley with snatches of *See Me, Feel Me*, *Listening To You*, *Underture*, *Naked Eye* and *The Seeker*, while *Magic Bus* runs for a riotous seven-and-a-half minutes.

The story at the time was that, after the release of *Tommy* in mid-1969, The Who went on an extended world tour to promote the rock opera with the full intention of coming back with enough material for a live album. Back in England, however, the idea of wading through more than 80 hours of live recordings and selecting the best was just too daunting. Instead, they would go for broke and record just two shows, one at Leeds University and one at Hull City Hall, both in the same weekend of February 14 (Valentine's Day), 1970, and the tour tapes would be physically burned to prevent bootlegging. This seems like a triumph of either demented confidence or shit-or-bust courage.

"I wish this were true," says Townshend. "In fact our sound man, Bob Pridden, did wade through all the tapes. It took about three weeks and we were close to a delivery deadline. A few of the stereo tapes I listened to were great. It was hard to pick one that rose above the rest. The standard was good, and very consistent. So I asked Bob to do the listening. When he'd finished I asked him if any particular show stood out. He said they were all good. I then asked him if I could see his notes. He hadn't made any. The only way we could have made a decision was with a tail pinned on the donkey. In frustration - and I was pretty angry too, I think - I told him to burn the lot to avoid bootlegging, and hire an eight-track rig for the forthcoming weekend of shows in Hull and Leeds and I would mix it at home; I had an eight-track machine there. He swears he burned all the tapes, but he may have kept a few. I hope so! I mixed *Live At Leeds* in my tiny home studio where I had recorded all my demos thus far, Thunderclap Newman and some stuff with the Small Faces. What distinguishes it from most other Who mixes is that the electric guitar is very loud."

Even if the truth is more hit-and-miss than legend, one thing is clear: by the time the band had reached the crucial Valentine's Day weekend they had hit an unstoppably solid groove, and a level of musical integration that was unequalled at the time

# 66 *Bad Company* Bad Company

Headley Grange, Hampshire, spring 1974. Drummer Simon Kirke walks into the run-down, three-storey former poorhouse where Led Zeppelin had recorded parts of *III* and *IV*, and the first thing he claps eyes on is Bonzo's giant drum kit set up in the entrance hall, plastered in its runic symbols. "Fuck me," he thinks. "This is great!"

Call it magic, call it luck, but there was something going on; something smoothing their path, clearing the way. Look at how they got here, after all. Kirke and his pal Paul Rodgers, the 'country boy' (read: not from swinging London), half of the late and not-yet-as-lamented-as-they-would-be Free; Mick Ralphs from Mott The Hoople and ex-King Crimson bassist Boz Burrell. They came together in the kind of semi-planned, semi-fortuitous way that mitigated against the label of 'supergroup' that was quickly applied and still sticks.

They were at the Grange because Zeppelin were supposed to be there but John Paul Jones had come down with the flu and so there were 10 days of expensive studio time lying fallow while Jonesy sorted himself out. And as Bad Company shared a manager with Led Zeppelin, well...

With their material written and ready to go, it wasn't Peter Grant's most difficult decision to pick up the phone and offer them the Grange once Jones went down with that bug.

The band weren't just digging the vibes of the Grange – they were becoming intoxicated by the new chemistry they were creating together. As Simon Kirke told *Classic Rock*'s Mick Wall, "You couldn't have been further away from [Free's] Paul Kossoff than Mick Ralphs. And he brought Rodgers out of his shell. Paul really blossomed with Mick."

They were a perfect creative partnership, and one that fired right away: the first song that Ralphs showed Rodgers was *Can't Get Enough*. The guitarist might have dismissed it, with some misplaced modesty, as "a three-chord bash", but it was exactly the kind of song that Rodgers' unsurpassable voice could fully inhabit. Kirke retained his effortless swing behind the kit and Boz Burrell proved that his playing was as easy-going as he was. Deep within its grooves was the essence of the band to come. Ralphs played Rodgers *Ready For Love*, another of the tunes he'd written – and recorded in this case – with Mott The Hoople. In Rodgers' effortless voice, Ralphs' songs had their ideal interpreter. There's a yearning in the way he sings them that carries across the decades, a sweet sadness that gives the songs the common touch.

*Can't Get Enough* was the first tune the band laid down, and it became a blueprint that would last throughout their career. Any record with those two songs on would have launched a band, but Bad Co had begun recording at the optimum moment. They had more material ready to go, and they were tight, rehearsed, seasoned. They didn't need a producer – they weren't Pink Floyd, after all. *Seagull*, the simple and beautiful acoustic tune that would close the record, had come together when Rodgers' lyric and melody were joined by Ralphs' chorus. The song was completed with Rodgers sitting outside in part of the Grange gardens at night. It was a trick the singer repeated on the album's title song, the epic *Bad Company*, although he channelled other aspects of the night into that one.

The themes of the band ran through the song too. They had battled to keep the name when various marketers had suggested it was too negative for so freewheeling a group, but Rodgers was set on the imagery. He'd picked it up from a recently released Western called Bad Company. The three chords that introduce the song are also in the movie's soundtrack. Rodgers won the fight and the song opened side two of the record. It's odd to think now that it might not have been there.

"Too much clutter makes a record sound small," Mick Ralphs would say many years later, and the rest of *Bad Company* lives by that credo. *Rock Steady*, *Movin' On*, *Don't Let Me Down* – all songs that could be played by any covers band worth their salt, and yet what sets them apart is the chemistry of their originators.

After 10 days of work at the Grange, they had a record. They also had a lot to live up to. Peter Grant had told them to worry about the music and he would take care of the rest. Eschewing the 'no singles' policy that was forging the Zeppelin legend, he led them out with *Can't Get Enough*, a song that rocketed to the top of the US charts and made the album one of the most anticipated of 1974.

When it came, it was dressed in an austere black-and-white sleeve, the band's name (abbreviated to just Bad Co.) running from the bottom left-hand corner to the right-hand top. It contrasted with the excess of the decade that surrounded it. As a suggestion of the band's music, it was perfect, and when the record came out, an audience was waiting. It was Top 5 in the UK right away, and soon it topped the US charts. It was a deserved triumph. Eight songs, tight and chilled, and with some magic inside them somewhere, were enough to clear the decks and give them all a fresh start.

**year released**
**1974**

**producer**
**Bad Company**

# 65 *Thin Lizzy* Live And Dangerous

The double live album with gatefold sleeve had become a dino-rock cliché by 1978. But Thin Lizzy revitalised the tired form with this jawdropping live set, recorded with the classic Brian Roberston/Scott Gorham line-up and blistering renditions of Lizzy classics like *Jailbreak* and *Don't Believe A Word* poured out of speakers all summer. And who can resist Phil Lynott's rogue-ish charm with banter like: "Is there anybody here with any Irish in them? Is there any of the girls who's like a little more Irish in them?"

Many words have been written about *Live And Dangerous*. Was it a live album or a studio one? So much history has been rewritten over the years regarding this iconic album that the true story has become blurred. The genesis for the inevitable Thin Lizzy live album first came during an American tour. The Peter Frampton's *Frampton Comes Alive* album and his single *Show Me The Way* had been taking the States by storm and – let's face it – it was pretty tame stuff. Lizzy felt so too. "I remember sitting in the car with Phil," Gorham remembered. "We've heard it for the billionth time. Phil says 'Fuck – we could do that...' Everybody sat in silence for a second. And that was the moment."

Lizzy had been recording shows in an attempt to harness their powerful live sound. There were four shows from Hammersmith Odeon from the Johnny The Fox tour of '76 "recorded for posterity" (with support band Clover providing harmonica player Huey Lewis for *Baby Drives Me Crazy*); various shows from the Bad Reputation Tour in the Autumn of '77 (with support band Graham Parker And The Rumour lending saxophonist John Earl for *Dancing In The Moonlight*); and two US shows recorded for the famous *King Biscuit Hour*, one at the Tower Theatre in Philadelphia, supporting The Tubes, and another in Toronto.

Now with Tony Visconti in tow, they had a producer who had worked live magic with David Bowie. Visconti was dispatched to do the same for Thin Lizzy – but it wasn't an easy task. So keen were Lizzy to use Visconti for the follow-up to *Bad Reputation* that he was given an option as to what would be released. The choice was a studio album, which would take some time, or a live album, which everyone reckoned would be quickly remixed and released.

"This project started with the question posed by Phil, 'What would you rather do, a regular studio album or a quick live album mix?'" remembers Visconti. "Because I had a new Bowie album scheduled in a few weeks, I opted for the live album. This 'live' album ended up taking six weeks to finish!"

Visconti found that the tapes he was expected to weave his magic on were recorded in many cities and several countries at very different times and different engineers ("None by me," he emphasises). "They were at different speeds, some were 'Dolbied' some were not. This was a big technical problem because if Phil wanted to work on a new song in a different format I'd

year released
**1970**

producer
**Derek and the Dominos**
**Tom Dowd**

If great music comes out of tragedy, then it's little wonder this album is a masterpiece. It was recorded amid drink and drug abuse and undiagnosed schizophrenia. But for all the travails surrounding it, the five musicians involved – Eric Clapton, Duane Allman, Jim Gordon, Carl Radle and Bobby Whitlock – created something passionate and timeless that would stand as arguably the finest album of their respective careers. *Layla* is obviously the most high-profile song, but the likes of *Bell Bottom Blues* and *Tell The Truth* are just as beautifully realised, combining pin-sharp musicianship with earthy spirituality and a true sense of joy. The overall impact is diverse, devastating.

"What I really loved about that album was, nobody knew who we were," says Clapton. "We did a tour of England playing little clubs and there would be nobody there, because nobody knew who we were – so they didn't come! And yet there was this quartet that was one of the most powerful bands I've ever been anywhere near – and I was in it! It was the most pure experience I've ever had in terms of making an album and then

year released
*1978*

producer
**Tony Visconti**
**Thin Lizzy**

have to have a technician to realign the analogue multi-track machines."

And the constant debates about whether *Live And Dangerous* was more studio than live? "Phil originally wanted to fix a few bad notes on the bass. After that was done he felt like he should replace the bass on every song. His excuse was that it was difficult to play bass and sing at the same time. This is harder, for sure, than playing guitar and singing at the same time. The bass plays one melody and the vocal is another. Then he said it would only take a few hours to re-sing all the vocals. It took a few days.

"Then the guitarists got jealous and wanted to replay all their guitar parts. In the end, all we used was the real audience tracks, the drums and the original guitar parts. The subsequent guitar overdubs were ultimately used as a double track.

"No studio recordings were used in the making of *Live And Dangerous;* just the overdubs were done in the studio. By the way, most live albums are 'fixed', so this is no big deal."

# 64 *Derek & The Dominos*
# Layla And Other Assorted Love Songs

promoting it anonymously. It's almost unheard-of."

Most of the songs Clapton wrote for the *Layla* album were co-written with Bobby Whitlock, an American keyboard player who'd recently quit Delaney & Bonnie, a band Clapton had befriended and toured with. But *Layla* itself is credited to Clapton and Dominos dummer Jim Gordon, who came up with the lengthy piano coda.

Whitlock remembers that Clapton already had *Layla* when they started writing together: "He wrote that song by himself at home".

"I'm incredibly proud of that song. To have ownership of something that powerful is something I'll never be able to get used to," Eric Clapton said of *Layla* in 1988. "It still knocks me out when I play it." One of the most recognisable rock songs, *Layla* begins with a seven-note riff of awesome expectancy, followed by an intense, intoxicating cry of unrequited love: *'What'll you do when things get lonely?'*

It was directed at Pattie Harrison, wife of George. Clapton was trying to lure her away from her husband, with whom he was good mates. That wasn't widely known when the song appeared in 1970 on *Layla And Other Assorted Love Songs*, but it was obvious to all concerned.

The opening riff was also there - taken from Albert King's *As The Years Go Passing By* - but the song was much slower than it finally appeared. "Eric took the song to Miami with him. We'd gone through it before," says Whitlock. "Eric brought that seven-note lick with him to the recording sessions. And then Duane stirred 'em up."

Duane Allman, guitarist with the Allman Brothers, was introduced to Clapton by producer Tom Dowd soon after sessions began on the album at Criteria Studios in Miami. According to Dowd, the sessions had been sluggish before he took Clapton to an Allman Brothers concert. Afterwards, Clapton invited the band back to the studio, where they jammed for the next 18 hours.

Within days, Duane Allman was playing at the album sessions, transforming the atmosphere as he and Clapton brought the best out of each other.

Whitlock's appreciation of Allman's playing with Derek And The Dominos is more measured. While he credits him with some inspirational performances - "The majesty of those opening chords on *Little Wing* is all Duane for sure" - he has a problem with some of his other contributions. "*Layla* would have been just as great without Duane on it," he says. "In many ways it would have been better. Both the slide parts he put on to the coda are out of tune. If Eric had been playing them it would have been different."

Derek And The Dominos attempted to record a second studio album, but the project was sunk by drugs and paranoia. *Layla* remains a stellar legacy. "It touched people where they needed to be touched," Bobby Whitlock says. "In their soul."

# 63 *Motörhead*
# Ace Of Spades

Although Lemmy always baulked at the notion of Motörhead being described as a heavy metal band, with *Ace Of Spades* they delivered one of the greatest heavy metal albums of all.

As Motörhead entered the new decade, they were operating at a frantic pace. Having released two albums in 1979, *Overkill* and *Bomber*, they were also working to a punishing touring schedule. Not for nothing would their live album be titled *No Sleep 'Til Hammersmith*. In such circumstances, lesser bands would have burned out. Not this band.

On August 4, 1980, Motörhead began recording their fourth album with new producer Vic Maile at his studio, Jackson's, in Rickmansworth. And it quickly became evident that Maile was the perfect man for the job. He had an intuitive feel for the band's music. And equally importantly, he didn't take any shit from them. As Lemmy stated: "Vic's strength was that he understood rock'n'roll. He was instinctive. And he had the same sense of humour as me. Basically, he was a c**t!" From Lemmy, this was high praise indeed.

The album was cut in just six weeks, and when the band heard the final mix, they were blown away. Maile had harnessed the full power of Motörhead in the studio.

The producer was, at times, a stern taskmaster. But by working the band that little bit harder, he got them sounding tighter, meaner and heavier than ever before, extracting performances of maximum intensity. Drummer Philthy Animal Taylor admitted that Maile had him playing "more solid." Lemmy said simply, "Vic got me singing instead of just shouting all the time." And as Fast Eddie proudly stated: "You can finally hear everything that's going on." Not that *Ace Of Spades* sounded polished: with Motörhead, that was never going to happen. It just sounded better - more in your face.

What Motörhead delivered on *Ace Of Spades* was 12 tracks of blistering heavy metal rock'n'roll. "This album is really fast," Eddie Clarke told *Sounds*. And he wasn't kidding. Motörhead had always played fast, but on *Ace Of Spades* they played, as Clarke said, really fast. "Maybe," the guitarist suggested, "we had some good speed. But whatever it is, I love it."

It was the fastest song on the album that would ultimately define the band's entire career: the title track. Two minutes and fifty seconds of hell-for-leather fury, *Ace Of Spades* is quite simply one of the greatest songs of all time. Issued as single on October 27, 1980 - 12 days before the album's release - it hit Number 15 on the UK chart and propelled the album into the Top Ten, where it peaked at No.4.

But there was more than one great song on this album. *Ace Of Spades* is full of essential Motörhead tracks: some faster than others, but all of them as heavy as a sack of gravel and as foul as a Hell's Angel's jeans. *(We Are) The Road Crew* is one of the greatest songs ever written about the touring life, right up there with AC/DC's *Ride On*. For Motörhead, being on the road wasn't just a part of the job: it was a way of life. '*I just love the life I lead/Another beer is what I need/Another gig, my ears bleed... Another bloody customs post/Another fucking foreign coast/Another set of scars to boast...*' The music matched the subject matter perfectly, its punishing rhythm replicating the merciless grind of a 20-gigs-in-21-days tour. And when the members of the crew first heard the song during a playback in the studio, one of them was moved to tears.

Three other songs represent Motörhead at their sleaziest. *The Chase Is Better Than The Catch* is the slowest and therefore longest track on the album, as it's basically the same idea only slower, and it has Lemmy confessing that he's a '*demon lech*' who likes '*a little innocent bitch*' and, naturally, '*a little whizz*'. *Jailbait* - the clue is in the title - is every mother's nightmare. And on the heavily metaphorical *Love Me Like A Reptile*, Lem finally meets his match in a cold-blooded, predatory female. He drools over this '*scaly baby*' with a '*soft white belly*' before promising to shock her '*like an electric eel*', which is not, strictly speaking, in keeping with the song's general theme - an eel is not a reptile but a fish - but, well, this is Lemmy, not David fucking Attenborough.

And to finish, there is arguably the meanest song this band ever recorded: *The Hammer*. A dose of archetypal Motörhead aggro, it has Lemmy reveling in the role of bogeyman, snarling all manner of threats ('*There ain't no way you'll see another day*') before delivering his final judgment: '*Believe me, The Hammer's coming... Down!*' For an album that fully encapsulated Motörhead's motto - Everything Louder Than Everything Else - *The Hammer* was a suitably deafening finale.

Even the cover image on *Ace Of Spades* was perfect: Motörhead, the classic rock'n'roll outlaws, posing as Western gunslingers with black Stetsons and bullet belts. Fast Eddie even sported a fetching poncho. But as Lemmy freely admitted, the desert setting was not authentic. "It was meant to look like the Wild West," he said, "but we did the cover shot at a quarry in South Mimms. The sky was natural. The only thing people don't know is that the spades on my trousers are only on one leg, so I could only have my picture taken from one side!"

year released
**1980**

producer
**Vic Maile**

THE

# 62 *Deep Purple* In Rock

Deep Purple's *In Rock*, released on the Harvest label in June 1970, was a revelation. Critics warmed to the confident songwriting, the expansive, Martin Birch engineering and the iconic sleeve art that depicted the five Purple members' faces carved into the surface of Mount Rushmore in place of the faces of US presidents. The delicious insolence of the image drew buyers in their thousands; the album stayed on the UK album chart for a thumping 68 weeks, peaking at No.4. After *In Rock* came the most successful period in Purple's history, with a run of what became classic albums (*Fireball*, *Machine Head*, *Made In Japan*, *Who Do We Think We Are!*, *Burn* and *Stormbringer*) released over the next four years.

Jon Lord, for years a quiet but significant force within Deep Purple, in an interview in 1971 looked back perceptively on *In Rock*, pondering: "The first three [studio] albums were pleasant, but directionless. Nobody knew quite what on earth the group was doing. Then we made a conscious effort to stop and think about writing material we all understood. And the result was *In Rock*, which was really our stage act. That was the turning point. And the point is, we believe in what we're doing together. We aren't too much interested in educating our audiences, we're more interested in entertaining. That's what it's all about."

He added: "We learned a terrific amount with *In Rock*. It took six months to make that album, and we think it paid off, really. I can honestly say that it's the first album we've been 100 per cent satisfied with. It gave us a hell of a lot of confidence. During that long time we learned a lot about ourselves and our music, and our sense of direction. We're very extrovert, really. We like to excite an audience, get involved with them."

Some reviewers had expected the new album to be classically influenced, probably because of Lord's interest in classical music, and also because of some song structures that had appeared on earlier albums, climaxing with *Concerto For Group & Orchestra*. However, Lord made it clear that this wasn't going to be the case, explaining: "I feel we're moving away from [classical music] now, because it was never intended to be part of the direction of the group; it was merely an experiment. We don't normally use any form of classical music now – except maybe in our solos."

Each member of the Deep Purple line-up that recorded *In Rock* had an indefinable but crucial contribution to make to the songs. As bassist Roger Glover remembered: "Ritchie [Blackmore] wasn't just the guitar player, he was a brilliant innovator. Things he wrote defy description. Ritchie was phenomenal in what he was doing in the late 60s and early 70s. He did things that you wouldn't even think of. He was a magnetic, dynamic writer. I don't think he could have done it in a vacuum by himself,

year released
**1977**
label
producer
**George Young**
**Harry Vanda**

In January 1977, AC/DC entered Alberts Studios in Sydney, and spent two weeks recording what came to be known as *Let There Be Rock*. The band were furious with their label in the US, who didn't like the band's previous *Dirty Deeds* album and were poised to drop them. "There was always a siege mentality about that band," remembers bassist Mark Evans. "But once we all found out that Atlantic had knocked us back the attitude was: 'Fuck them! We were seriously pissed off about it. We were going to go in and make that album and shove it up their arse." The result would be the first utterly explosive AC/DC album.

Malcolm and Angus weren't the only members of the Young family fired up by their ruck with Atlantic. The band's task of sticking it to their international label was aided in no small measure by the presence of their elder brother George, who was working at the time as an in-house producer for AC/DC's Australian label Albert Productions, alongside songwriting partner and fellow former Easybeat Harry Vanda. "If anything, George was even more determined to prove the Americans wrong

year released
**1970**

producer
**Deep Purple**

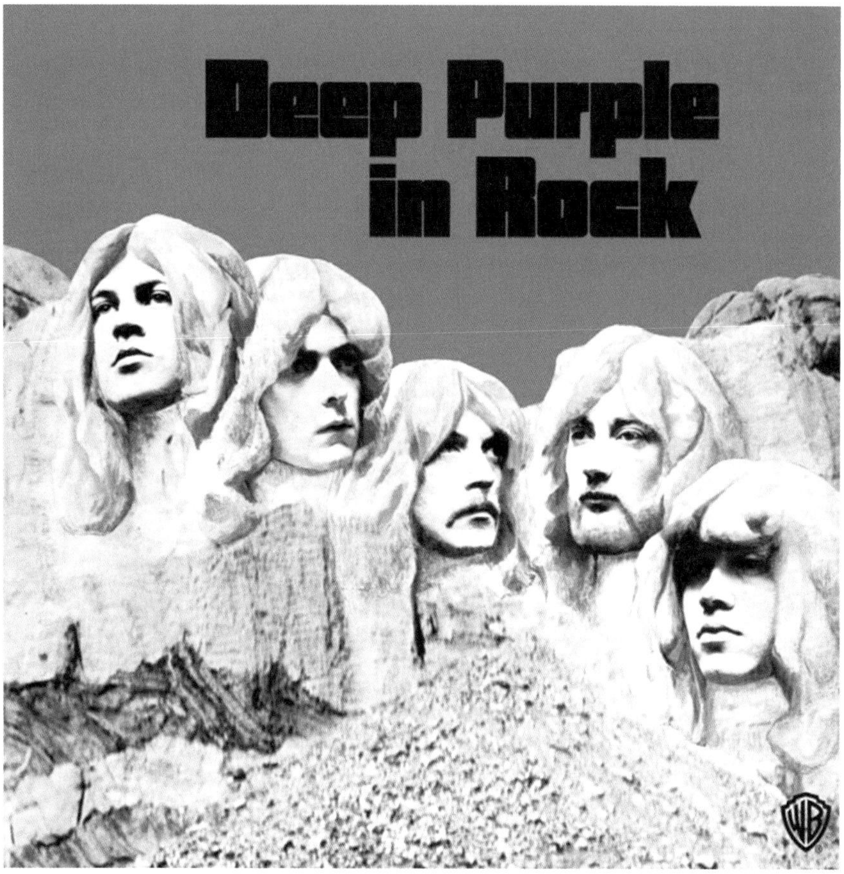


it did require the rest of us. But I'll certainly give him his due. He was the motivating character in the band."

Songs for possible inclusion on *In Rock* came thick and fast, and often without any obvious effort on the band's behalf. Asked how the band conceived the album's classic opening track, vocalist Ian Gillan shrugged: "I don't know how we came up with *Speed King*, any more than I know how Ian Paice started playing it, or how Ritchie Blackmore started playing it.

By the middle of the 70s a heavy rock template had been established, with extravagant, arrogant music being made by artists borrowing from the blueprint that had been drawn by *In Rock* as the decade began. "This album was unique, because it was the first studio one we [the Mk II line-up] did together," remembered Gillan, "but that joy we felt when we were making it was repeated quite a few times on later albums, too – but not all of them. We didn't realise what kind of a well we were tapping into."

The well that Deep Purple tapped into was bottomless. Heavy rock music was here to stay.

# 61 *AC/DC*
# Let There Be Rock

than Malcolm and Angus," says Evans. "And I think they got it right."

They certainly did. From the sound of a whisky-guzzling Bon counting in the intro to the swaggering opening track *Go Down*, a song about a real-life friend of his named Ruby, known for her fondness for *'lickin' on that lickin' stick'*, to the frantic finale *Whole Lotta Rosie*, about another lady friend acquainted with the singer's lickin' stick – this one *'weighing in at 19 stone'* – *Let There Be Rock* didn't let up for its eight-track, 40-minute duration. It sounded exactly like what it was. Written and recorded fast, before the vibe had time to fade, it was full of blood and spittle and anger and put-a-fuck-into-you fun, fuelled by cheap speed and cold beer, topped up with expensive whisky and at least a million cigarettes, some of them smelling distinctly 'funny'.

If the three albums that came before it – *High Voltage*, *T.N.T.* and *Dirty Deeds Done Dirt Cheap* – had an increasingly high quotient of brilliance, *Let There Be Rock* was the one where AC/DC truly found their place in the scheme of things, not least on the title track, a heartfelt ode to original, no-shit rock'n'roll as evinced by the fastest, most irresistibly hair-shaking piece of high-octane noise ever committed to what was still then just poor, weak vinyl. Elsewhere, *Hell Ain't A Bad Place To Be* stood as AC/DC's own *Brown Sugar*. "If you're a purist and like the guitars being completely in tune and things being completely studio-sterile, that song's gonna kill you," Mark Evans says of the latter, "cos the guitars are whomping all over the place out of tune. But it's just got that nasty, gritty feel about it that says AC/DC."

Indeed the whole album sounds like it's on the verge of spilling over into total feedback. It was recorded live in one room. Mistakes were tolerated if the vibe was strong enough, the energy audibly crackling over the speakers on tracks like *Overdose* or *Bad Boy Boogie*. The title song became the one AC/DC would end their set with for years to come.

Rhythm and backing tracks were all completed in the first week. Bon, who'd be given cassettes of the mixed-down, vocal-less tracks which he then "scribbled words to", did his vocals in the second week, during which Angus also laid down his guitar solos. Some of the new tracks, like *Bad Boy Boogie*, had previously existed in miniature form. "It was a title that was around and a riff that we'd messed around with at soundcheck," says Evans. "Others, like *Whole Lotta Rosie*, didn't look like they were gonna happen at first."

The idea of *Let There Be Rock* – indeed AC/DC's whole career – without *Whole Lotta Rosie* is unthinkable. Originally called *Dirty Eyes*, the band initially struggled to make it work. The song only clicked after a week of work. And yes, the titular character was based on a real person. "She was a Tasmanian girl," Evans chuckles. "A massive girl. Bigger than the lot of us put together.

# 60 *Def Leppard* Pyromania

When Def Leppard started to record this album in 1982, they claimed the ambition was to make something different from anything out there. Released a year later, *Pyromania* matched the boldness of that statement. Put in stark terms, it transformed hard rock. Twenty-five years later the album still sounds fresh and utterly vital.

In conjunction with producer 'Mutt' Lange, Leppard stripped away the barriers between hard rock and pop. They used samples when necessary, went for enhanced, massive choruses, and the record had a sound and style that was crisp and clear - perfect for American radio airplay. Above all they wrote a batch of songs of such a quality that every one is impressive. Some - *Photograph*, *Rock Of Ages*, *Rock Rock (Till You Drop)* - have become iconic; even the lesser-known *Comin' Under Fire* and *Stagefright* are a masterclass in writing melodic hard rock. The follow-up album, 1987's *Hysteria*, might have been a bigger seller, but *Pyromania* is definitive Def Leppard.

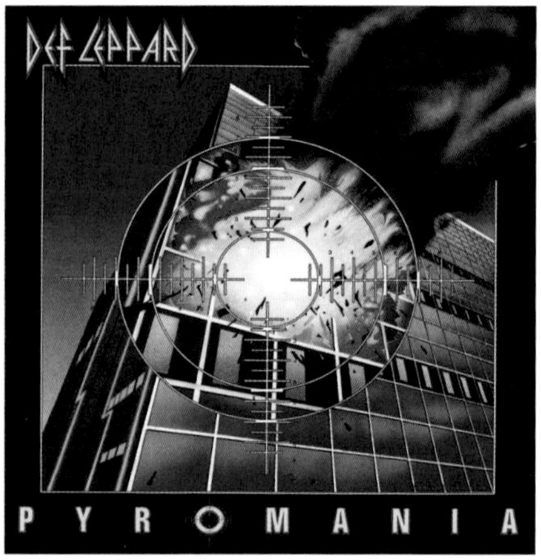


Leppard and Mutt Lange were a perfect fit. The band had thought so even before they'd heard *Highway To Hell* and *Back In Black*. They loved the late-70s new wave-era pop hits Mutt had produced: The Motors' *Dancing The Night Away*, City Boy's *5.7.0.5*, the Boomtown Rats' chart-topping post-punk anthem *Rat Trap*. With AC/DC's commercially huge *Back In Black*, Mutt proved that he was the best hard rock producer in the business, yet he was equally adept at the art of the pop single. Combining the two had always been Def Leppard's aim.

"*High 'N' Dry* was a big improvement on the first album," Joe Elliott says. "And with the third album, we wanted to make the same kind of leap. We didn't want to be making *High 'N' Dry II*."

Mutt Lange shared this vision. He told the band: "We can make a record that nobody's ever made before." Mutt listed the cutting-edge studio technology at their disposal - digital recording, new drum machines and synthesisers - and explained how these could be applied to the recording of hard rock."

Leppard wrote most of the songs for their third album in February 1982. Some of the songs were brand new, built from a stockpile of riffs the band had worked through after the *High 'N' Dry* tour. But they also remodelled a couple of older songs that hadn't made the cut for *High 'N' Dry*: *Medicine Man* was beefed up and renamed *Rock Rock (Till You Drop)*, and a previously unfinished track - described by Joe as "a dual guitar pop song" - was finally completed, and titled *Photograph*.

Aside from drummer Rick Allen, every band member contributed to the writing, as did Mutt Lange, who co-wrote all of the album's 10 tracks. Guitarist Pete Willis wrote the riff to *Rock Rock (Till You Drop)*. Their other guitarist, Steve Clark, a Jimmy Page fan, created the Zeppelin-styled epic *Billy's Got A Gun*. Rick Savage came up with the express-train rocker *Stagefright*.

Guitarist Pete Willis had become a liability. And after lengthy discussions, a decision was made. "We'd made the decision 99 times before," Elliott sighs, "and every time we'd been talked out of it, either by Pete or management."

The band had already identified a replacement for Willis: Londoner Phil Collen, guitarist with NWOBHM-era glam-rock band Girl and a good friend of Joe's. During the *High 'N' Dry* tour, Joe had called Phil at 2am following another drunken outburst from Willis. Willis was summoned to a band meeting and told in no uncertain terms that he was out.

On reflection, Elliott is keen to stress the importance of Pete Willis's contribution to *Pyromania*. The guitarist co-wrote four of the album's 10 tracks, including *Photograph*, the key hit single. And despite his run-ins with Mutt Lange, Willis also played the rhythm guitar parts on every track. Phil Collen joined the band for the final stages of recording, when they returned to London for overdubbing and mixing at Battery Studios.

The final mix of *Pyromania* was completed just before Christmas 1982. It had taken nine months to finish. However, at a cost of more than £1m it had to sell at least three million copies to get Def Leppard out of debt. Joe Elliott should have been a worried man. He wasn't.

"We knew we'd made a great record," he says. "And we knew it had the potential to be huge."

And so it was. During one amazing period in August, *Pyromania* was selling 100,000 copies a day in the US. The album climbed to No.2 on the Billboard chart - second only to Thriller. "We actually outsold *Thriller* for one week," Elliott says, "but that just happened to be the week that the *Flashdance* soundtrack went to No.1, with us at two and Jacko at three."

*Pyromania* was, as predicted, the birth of a legend.

year released
**1983**

producer
**'Mutt' Lange**

# 59 *King Crimson*
# In The Court Of The Crimson King

In mid-July 1969 a new British band called King Crimson, just signed to Island Records, began recording their debut album, just weeks after playing their first official gig and days after supporting the Rolling Stones in front of a crowd of half-a-million in Hyde Park. Two weeks later they had finished recording a remarkable, ground-breaking album that was sweepingly original, musicianly, creative, expansive; a true rock classic that many people consider to be the first true progressive rock album. When it was released, The Who's Pete Townshend called *King Crimson's In The Court Of The Crimson King: An Observation By King Crimson* (to give it its full title) "an uncanny masterpiece". And it was.

Crimson had rehearsed long and hard prior to entering the studio, and the songs' structures had also been worked up while gigging intensively in the few months the band had been together. The songs they had, that is. A problem they would have to address at some point was that they had barely more than half-an-hour's worth of music prepared. But the shortfall in material didn't seem to be cause for concern. "We were all twenty-four, twenty-five, twenty-six, and we'd all been around for quite a while," lyricist Pete Sinfield says, "so we had quite a lot of ideas and bits and pieces to fall back on when they were required.

With much bigger ideas than the budget and very limited time was able to accommodate, there was no room for a meticulous piecing together that the album might appear to be. "We went in and essentially recorded the tracks live, and embellished them from there, taking advantage of the multi-tracking – although we only had eight tracks," multi-instrumentalist McDonald recalls. The recording was completed between July 16 and August 15, with the band doing gigs between sessions. "We'd record and then go on the road for two or three days then go back to the studio. I'm surprised by the nonchalance that I see in the diary I kept."

That the album was completed in two weeks is amazing. That its best-known track, frenetic opener *21st Century Schizoid Man*, given its complexity and technical difficulty, was recorded in one take is nothing short of astonishing. "Contrary to what you might think, *Schizoid Man* was actually a breeze compared to other tracks," McDonald remembers. But then none of the tracks took long, and everything came together with a speed and smoothness that belies the end result.

Over the years, perhaps because guitarist Robert Fripp has been the only constant member of the band, it is often assumed that, right from the beginning, he was the beating heart of King Crimson and the man very much in the driving seat. Sinfield, however, points to another member of the band as the one pulling the strings during the recording of their debut.

"I think the driving force was Ian McDonald, really,"

year released
**1973**

producer
**The Who**

Arriving hard-at-heel after Pete Townshend's aborted *Lifehouse* project, was supposed to be his defining moment of the 70s, a rock opera to out-Tommy anything that had gone before. "If Tommy is rock opera, *Quadrophenia* is grand rock opera," says lifelong Townshend associate and Who biographer Richard Barnes. "If *Tommy* is tabloid, *Quadrophenia* is broadsheet. I think Pete moved The Who to another level with that record."

But by the end of February '74 The Who had stopped playing it entirely. "The whole thing was a disaster," griped Townshend. It would be 22 years before they attempted it again.

*Quadrophenia*, likened by Townshend in 1973 to "a sort of musical *Clockwork Orange*", was a deeply personal endeavour. Ostensibly about a young 60s mod at the crossroads of his adolescent life, it charts the spiritual yearning of main protagonist Jimmy Cooper through drugs, unrequited love, beachfront

year released
**1969**

producer
**King Crimson**

he says. "Ian was the one who wanted to do anything that we could possibly do within the scope and yet still have people listen to it. And I was the one floating around the outside knowing we should have an extraordinary cover and without the name on, and stuff like that."

Perhaps surprisingly, during the making of the album there was little if any feeling within the band that they were producing something special, and certainly no idea that they were making such a landmark record.

"I don't remember thinking anything like: 'Wow! That's great" or whatever," McDonald says. "Except maybe with *Schizoid Man*. I remember listening back to that and thinking: 'What the hell is this?!'

"When it was all finished there was a sort of glow of satisfaction – and relief," Sinfield remembers. "There was a feeling of, gosh, we've done something and it sounds really rather good. By any standards, there are parts of that album that shine out. And I think it has a timelessness to it as well – which I can tell you by the royalty statements even today.

# 58 *The Who*
# Quadrophenia

barneys, a string of useless jobs and unsympathetic parents. The mod scene sours quickly, his best mate runs off with his girl, he trashes his beloved scooter and makes a break for Brighton in a desperate attempt to reconnect with the thrill and camaraderie of the mods-versus-rockers skirmishes. But the summer of '65 is long gone. Consumed by despair, he rows out to sea to end it all, but has a sudden epiphany.

*Quadrophenia* the album is a record awash with metaphor – particularly the sea as both a destructive and redemptive force – and sprinkled with allusion to The Who's own past. It is, in fact, the idealism of 60s youth culture refracted through the lens of the cynical 70s, by big, rich rock stars who'd lived through it. It's as much about The Who as it is about Jimmy.

It's a complex, vaultingly ambitious work that is echoed in the music itself. Surging guitars and big vocals are tempered by brass arrangements, semi-orchestral strings and intricate layers of synths and piano. "At the time, Pete and I were writing to each other and I used to call him Tannhäuser because of *Quadrophenia*," says Barnes. "Which was apt because it does sound really Wagnerian with those horns. You can imagine these big, fat ladies in helmets, riding Vespas. It's a heavy, hard rock album but there are such delicate bits with violins and synthesisers. Pete has such a delicate touch. It's like porcelain and reinforced concrete side by side."

Received wisdom has it that the rest of The Who didn't quite get *Quadrophenia* to begin with, which Townshend concedes is "understandable" given that "it didn't really land completely as a collection of songs until about three weeks prior to starting to record".

But perhaps the one member who took to the project most readily was bassist John Entwistle, who was given free rein to add some ravishing horn parts to the mix, most notably the pumping brass salvos on 5:15, the semi-orchestral flourishes on the title track and the eruptive climax to *Love Reign O'er Me*.

*Quadrophenia* is the late bloomer in The Who's back catalogue. A record about the 1960s, recorded in the proggy fug of the 1970s. Even given its rather time-specific, niche-culture context, it still feels oddly significant today. These are songs that cut deep into the spiritual malaise; big, sweeping epics to get lost in or shake a fist to.

# 57 *Aerosmith*
# Rocks

Sometime mountaineer Dave Lee Roth claims that nothing gets a mule across a crevasse quicker than *Back In The Saddle*, the opening tracks on the fourth Aerosmith album *Rocks*.

*Rocks* swaggers and is funky as fuck (witness *Last Child* and *Get The Lead Out*). More than that, it's a big, brash album on which Aerosmith are at their most confident – not least because, prior to its release, the three 'Smith albums that proceeded it were still in the US chart.

*Rats In The Cellar* was inspired by the death of the group's drug dealer, and mid-70s rock doesn't come any more addictive than this. *Rocks* also made a young chap called Slash want to learn guitar.

"We recorded it in our rehearsal space, just outside Boston," says bassist Tom Hamilton. "We had the Record Plant recording truck pull into the garage, and we had a big room which we dressed with heavy curtains and divided up into a really neat recording room. There was a lot of laughter and a lot of camaraderie. Everyone was at their best on that album."

"Everyone talks about the drugs," steven Tyler says, "but if you want to talk about stuff that has any relevance here let's talk about something else. The drugs were part of our lifestyle then, but sleep deprivation was just as important here. We'd sit down with Jack [Douglas, producer], and get an arrangement in seven or eight hours and go and record it the next day.

"So, to me, that record is not about 'How much cocaine did you do?' It's got everything to do with me sitting in a dingy hotel in Hell's Kitchen writing the lyrics after a long day at the studio, back when 42nd Street was full of hookers and pimps and shady bars. *Rocks* sounds raunchy and dirty? Hell, our lives were raunchy and dirty. What else would you expect?"

*Rocks* is the album where it all came together, the time when the alchemy really worked. By now Aerosmith had hit their stride. The constant touring had transformed them into one of America's top-grossing live acts with an insanely devoted following known as The Blue Army.

Up until now it had all been foreplay, but now the band really had to deliver the climax – and *Rocks* was the ultimate musical money shot.

As Douglas pointed out, "This was the big album for Aerosmith. It had to make a big statement about how loud and hard they were, and how unapologetic they felt about being who they were: this brash, rude, sexual, hard-core band."

Every track is a masterpiece. Kicking off with the opening salvo of *Back In The Saddle* – the band's musical statement of purpose – it displays Aerosmith at their peak. It became a commercial blockbuster, going platinum on release. Seemingly Aerosmith couldn't get any higher. Although they had a bloody good go at it.

In reality the band were numbed by hard work,

**year released**
**1971**
**label**
**producer**
**Ian Anderson and Terry Ellis**

It begins with a tramp sitting on a park bench 'watching as the frilly panties run' and ends with a meditation on the nature of God. Tull's fourth album was nothing if not ambitious, yet thankfully low on pretension and high on sardonic rage.

The first half introduces *Aqualung* the tramp, 'eying little girls with bad intent' and *Cross-Eyed Mary,* the good-time girl who 'will do it for a song'. Both are archetypes that Anderson would return to again and again.

The second half deals directly with Ian Anderson's perceived disconnection between God and the church, an unlikely subject that he handles with his usual deft intelligence.

Jethro Tull have spent 40 years standing outside of generic conventions. Are they prog? Are they folk? Are they – as the Grammys once decided, at the expense of Metallica, no less – heavy metal? The answer, proved over decades and so many albums, is that they are a little bit of everything while, paradoxically, sounding like no one else. They are the most idiosyncratic and English

year released
**1976**

producer
**Aerosmith and Jack Douglas**

success seemed to be losing its appeal and the drugs began to take hold. Their collective intake was so high that management dissuaded them from touring outside the US in fear of a bust. The ominous cloud of addiction hung over the recording, bringing all its dark karma with it.

"We got good drugs because we could afford it, " guitarist Joe Perry admits. "All the big dealers started hanging around, so we only got the best stuff. We found a good, steady connection. At least until our guy in New York got murdered."

Again the lyrics proved to be elusive. At one time the album was going to be called *Aerosmith 5* in honour of all the unused instrumental tracks recorded while waiting for Tyler's contributions.

Miraculously, it all came together. With Tyler and Perry getting lost in their collective chemical excesses and rock star grandiosity, the rest of the band came to the fore. And of course there was the other 'honorary' band member, Jack Douglas – *Rocks* is a testament to Douglas's genius at pulling things together.

# 56 *Jethro Tull*
# Aqualung

of bands – one that is led, naturally, by a Scotsman. The identity of Tull is bound up in that of Ian Anderson, singer and player of acoustic guitar, mandolin, tin whistle, piano, violin and the most distinctive flute in rock. Anderson has driven the band into the deepest of folk roots, and messed around with electronica when it was giddy and new and barely out of the packet. He has written about prostitutes and tramps, ecclesiastical excess and pagan beasties. He's been as concerned by the decline in agriculture as he has in being an ageing rock'n'roller. He is a compelling oddity; a man who has adopted a series of semi-ironic, self- deprecating personas that have come to define the band he fronts.

*Aqualung* is best viewed as a halfway house between earlier blues leanings and the folk-informed full prog jacket that would ensue (*Thick As A Brick*). Though rich in conceptual continuity, as Frank Zappa might put it, 1971's *Aqualung* is not by any strict definition a concept album – a fact that Ian Anderson has peevishly pointed out over the years. Comprising a disparate collection of seedy, secular vignettes and rails against the hypocrisy of organised religion versus the concept of God, this dichotomy can also be viewed through the oppositional attributes of pastoral acoustic folk whimsy and riff-centric heft.

Much of its power and unlikely cohesion is a testament to the quality of the songwriting, which illustrates a band discovering its quintessential self. Bert Jansch and Roy Harper's narrative influences are notable throughout, though the remarkable *Mother Goose* – an Elizabethan madrigal replete with post-medieval recorders – harks back much further, revealing Anderson's antiquarian tendencies and plotting a long tail of historical social commentary.

It's Martin Barre's bombastic riffs on the title track and its offspring *Locomotive Breath* and *Cross-Eyed Mary* that really define the album, though, and they provided the radio-friendly platform that catapulted the band into mainstream American success – as unusual as that seems, viewed from a 45-year remove.

It remains an extraordinarily dynamic album, kick-started by the title track's thundering riff, followed by timeless classic rockers (*Cross-Eyed Mary*, *My God*) and interspersed with short acoustic ditties that could have come from the Roy Harper songbook (*Cheap Day Return*, *Wond'ring Aloud*). And *Locomotive Breath* remains the best live encore written by anyone, anywhere, ever.

Lyrically, side one paints some relatable portraits of society's oddballs and outcasts, while part of side two explores themes related to organised religion. This led the critics to pigeonhole *Aqualung* as a concept album. It wasn't really. But as a collection of literate work – as well as musical songs – it was seminal Jethro Tull – fist-waving, sensitive intelligence.

# 55 *Thin Lizzy* Jailbreak

Thin Lizzy [named, like all great rock'n'roll bands, after a big, shiny car] sparked to life in 1970 as a trio of Dublin freakniks who played a Mulligan's stew of traditional Irish folk mixed with bluesy rock'n'roll.

Led by the charismatic Phillip Lynott, a rare black Irishman with a wild, Hendrixy Afro and a mischievous glint in his eye, the young, scruffy group struggled to find their way until they discovered the simple pleasures of searing hard rock, soaring twin-guitar harmonies, mirrored basses and impish moustaches.

By the mid 1970s, the world had caught on, and the little band from Dublin became one of the best-known, and beloved, arena rock bands of all time. Thin Lizzy lived as hard as they played, and for every significant step forward in their career there was a crushing setback.

The band went through guitar players faster than most guitarists go through strings. The endless world tours took a physical and mental toll on the band. The members were plagued by poor health, erratic behaviour, violence and, in the case of their gregarious frontman, crushing chemical addiction. And yet they endured, enthralling audiences with their hard-driving tales of vagabonds, kings, fools and madmen.

If ever there was a rock band for the people, it was Thin Lizzy. Ah, but nothing lasts forever. Burdened by dwindling record sales and racked with addiction and dysfunction on all sides, Thin Lizzy finally called it quits in 1983.

On Christmas Day, 1985, Lynott collapsed at his home and was rushed to hospital. He passed away a few days later, on January 4, 1986. The official medical report cites heart failure and pneumonia, brought on by a drink and drug binge. Some, though, would contend that Lynott died from a broken heart, still mourning the break-up of his beloved Thin Lizzy.

*Jailbreak* is the album most people think of when the topic of Thin Lizzy arises, thanks to the worldwide smash hit *The Boys Are Back In Town*. Everything that's great about Thin Lizzy is in this song: the hard rocking swagger, the twin-guitar harmonies, Lynott's innate sense of melody, and a wonderfully evocative lyric about boys and girls, drinking and fighting. Incredibly, when the band recorded *The Boys Are Back In Town* in 1976, they didn't think it was anything special. But after US radio jumped on it, the song was a huge hit on both sides of the Atlantic. And over time it became something even bigger: one of the all-time classic rock anthems, and the song for which Phil Lynott and Thin Lizzy will always be remembered.

Uplifting, heroic, poetic and occasionally bare-knuckled, *Jailbreak* is the quintessential 70s riff rock album, full of timeless, rough 'n' ready rockers like *Warriors* and *Emerald*, as well as the infectious, surprisingly tender love song *Running Back*, and the

year released
**1980**
label
producer
**Tom Allom**

The year 1980 was the best year ever for heavy metal. So many classic albums released, including Black Sabbath's *Heaven And Hell*, Iron Maiden's self-titled debut, Saxon's *Wheels Of Steel* and Judas Priest's masterpiece *British Steel*.

From the first words that Rob Halford sang on *Rapid Fire* – *'Pounding the world like a battering ram'* – to the cacophonous finale of *Steeler*, this is as definitive a heavy metal album as Sabbath's *Paranoid*. Two brilliant singles hit the UK Top 20: party anthem *Living After Midnight* and the yobbish *Breaking The Law*. And in the dystopian vision of *Metal Gods* the band had their signature song.

A little context is needed. Yes, Black Sabbath came first. Iron Maiden and Metallica are bigger. But if there is one band, above all others, that defines the sound and aesthetic of heavy metal, it is Judas Priest.

"Metal is a very special kind of music," says Halford. And what this band has represented, for more than 40 years, is metal in its purest form: the screaming lead vocals, the duelling guitarists, the bludgeoning riffs, the

year released
**1976**

producer
**John Alcock**

timeless fan favourite *Cowboy Song*.

Little known fact: the cover artwork, intended to convey a vague sci-fi theme explored in the original sleeve notes by Phil, was designed by Jim Fitzpatrick, the same guy who designed that iconic poster of Che Guevara from the 60s.

After the success of *The Boys Are Back In Town* in the States, Phonogram decided to issue the single in Britain. Released on May 29, the single entered the UK Top 10 and peaked at No.8.

On the back of the single's success, the album too began to take off and, as a final thank you to the fans, Lynott left his hospital bed against doctors' advice to perform a one-off gig at the Hammersmith Odeon on July 11.

With *Jailbreak* finally hitting the upper echelons of the charts, Lizzy had made the jump into the next division. Success both at home and abroad brought greater incentives, although it also moved the band onto a new plain of indulgence. For now, they chose to ride the wave, and ultimately build on their success.

# 54 *Judas Priest* British Steel

leather and studs, the songs about death and destruction and motorcycles and, yes, heavy metal itself.

Inspired by heavy rock pioneers such as Sabbath, Led Zeppelin, Deep Purple and Cream, the nascent Priest recorded their debut, *Rocka Rolla*, in 1974. But it was two years later, with *Sad Wings Of Destiny*, that the band found their signature sound. In the 1980s Priest became one of the biggest metal bands in the world, with hit albums including *British Steel* and *Screaming For Vengeance*.

In the 90s there were darker days: first, when a lawsuit was filed against the band following the deaths of two young fans from Nevada in a suicide pact allegedly inspired by Priest's music; then when Halford quit to form a new band, Fight, and was replaced by Ohio-born singer Tim 'Ripper' Owens, poached from a Judas Priest tribute act.

But in 2003 Halford returned to his rightful place as Priest's master of ceremonies. And although Downing retired in 2011, the band have continued with Londoner Richie Faulkner as Tipton's foil on the defiantly old-school 2014 album *Redeemer Of Souls*.

In 2015 Halford told *Classic Rock*: "I've always been very happy that I'm a singer in a metal band. It's wonderful." And Priest are not just any heavy metal band, they're the most 'heavy metal' heavy metal band of them all.

Even 36 years after its release, the cover of *British Steel* still has the power to unnerve. Designed by Roslav Szaybo, it depicts a hand, cloaked in darkness, fingers splayed, clutching a giant razor blade so tightly that the glinting edges appear to cut into the flesh. Somehow, the absence of blood only serves to make the image more disturbing.

Judas Priest never intended the cover of their 1980 classic to be macabre. The sleeve was simply an extension of the album's title, conceived by bassist Ian Hill as both a nod to the striking steelworkers of the time and to what the band saw as their own quintessential Britishness.

The genesis of the cover began when vocalist Rob Halford noticed that Gillette razor blades bore the legend 'Sheffield Steel' and pitched the concept to his bandmates. While some had their reservations ("There was a bit of a debate, because a razor blade was an emblem of punk rock," notes Hill), the design was completed to unanimous approval. "As soon as we saw it," remembers former guitarist KK Downing, "we thought: 'This is as sharp-edged as we are.' It's so totally fitting."

Many Judas Priest fans would doubtless put *British Steel* at the top of their lists, and there's no questioning its brilliance, or its huge influence on the entire world of metal. You simply can't argue with classic tracks *Breaking The Law, Metal Gods* or *Rapid Fire* and *Living After Midnight* is one of the ultimate party metal anthems. The rest is nearly as good, and that's pretty fucking good by anyone's metal standards.

# 53 *The Beach Boys* Pet Sounds

Historically, *Pet Sounds* has never been taken quite as seriously as Bob Dylan's *Blonde On Blonde* or The Beatles *Revolver*. Perhaps this is down to the fact that The Beach Boys lacked the counter-cultural edge of Bob Dylan and The Beatles, or maybe it had something to do with its literal, artless front cover.

But that was then. In 2017, *Pet Sounds* is regarded not only as the equal of those records but, in some quarters, their superior. Certainly, together with the equally groundbreaking single *Good Vibrations*, which followed it five months later, it drew up an ambitious road map for rock's future.

It may have been a quantum leap for its composer, fragile 'man child' Brian Wilson, but *Pet Sounds* wasn't quite a bolt from the blue. Close scrutiny of the band's catalogue will reveal intimations of the album's lush, solipsist sorrow as far back as *The Lonely Sea*, from their 1963 second album *Surfin' USA*, or early ballads such as *The Warmth Of The Sun* and *In My Room*, while 1965's *Today!* featured a suite of songs on side two that evinced a harmonic sophistication and a desire to explore more mature themes than the usual surfing and hot rods.

*Pet Sounds*, though, was a sustained act of complex creation, one part work of orchestral ambition, one part proto-concept album. A nervous breakdown on a flight between LA and Houston in December 1964 had prompted Brian Wilson to refocus his energies from touring and promotion to the more enjoyable pursuits of songwriting and the boundless potential of the recording studio.

He had been further liberated by his introduction to marijuana and hallucinogenics the following year. Now, with The Beatles' *Rubber Soul* ringing in his ears and his competitive streak risen, he set out to make what he promised his wife Marilyn would be "the greatest rock album ever made". To turn the pocket symphonies in his head into gorgeous reality, he made two crucial moves. Firstly, he entrusted the task of translating his ideas about the loss of innocence and the imponderability of existence to advertising copywriter-turned-lyricist Tony Asher.

Secondly, he enlisted the help of ace session musicians The Wrecking Crew, including guitarist Glen Campbell and bassist Carol Kaye, veterans of Phil Spector's Wall Of Sound, with the precocious 23-year-old Wilson orchestrating the recording sessions himself.

The resultant songs – *Wouldn't It Be Nice, Don't Talk (Put Your Head On My Shoulder), I'm Waiting For The Day, God Only Knows, I Just Wasn't Made For These Times, Caroline, No* – were perfect miniatures of hymnal wonder, which expressed with devotional clarity the anxieties and longings of an adolescent poised on the cusp of agonising maturity.

If the role of the rest of The Beach Boys was diminished on a musical level, *Pet Sounds* was still

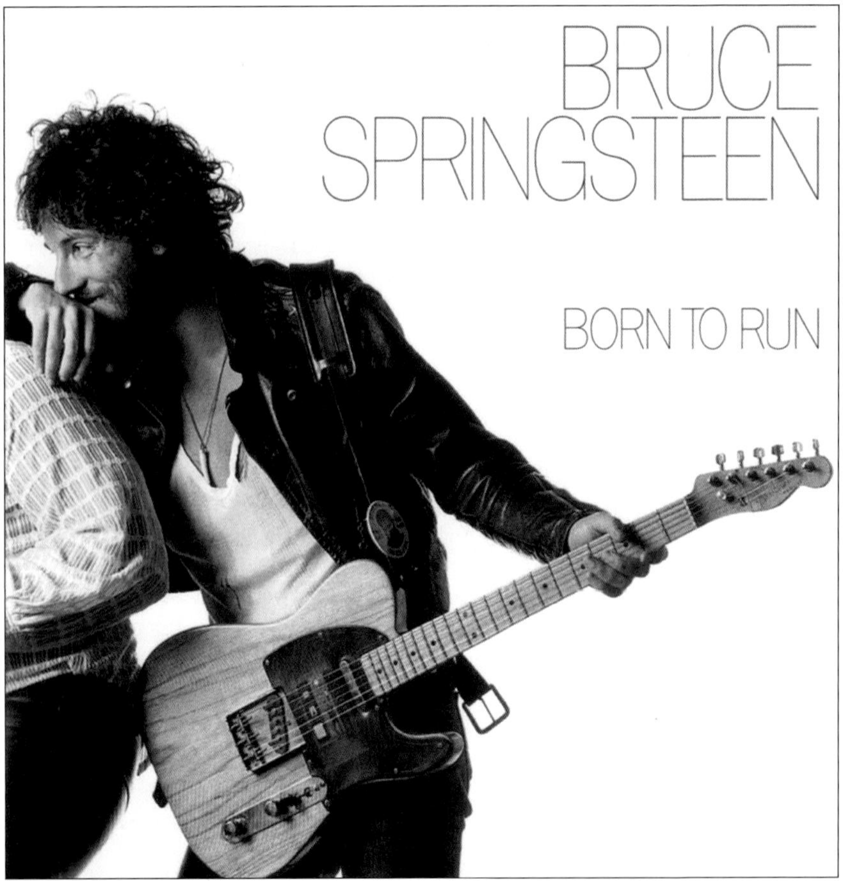


year released
**1975**

producer
**Bruce Springsteen, Mike Appel & Jon Landau**

This was the album that saved Springsteen's career after sales of his first two were disappointing, and also proved he could write anthemic rock that rivalled Phil Spector. While the title track and *Thunder Road* have always been live staples, it was the more romantic, orchestral songs like *Backstreets* and *She's The One* that are the album's overlooked gems. There are only eight tracks on *Born To Run*, but Springsteen slaved for almost two years making it. He rewrote each line of lyrics dozens of times, experimented with strings, and spent countless hours on minute details such as the running order. The result of his torture is Springsteen's masterpiece.

The finished album cover, with Springsteen on the front and Clarence Clemons on the back, had exactly the kind of classic rock iconography that Springsteen was attempting to capture in the music. Columbia were finally on board as well, and planned a pressing of 100,000 copies in the US – a large run considering Springsteen's previous record sales.

Radio embraced *Born To Run* and helped make it

year released
**1966**

producer
**Brian Wilson**

a triumph of vocal layering. It certainly wouldn't have been possible without the input of Wilson's brothers Dennis and Carl, cousin Mike Love, Al Jardine and new member Bruce Johnston.

In 2012, Mike Love suggested *Pet Sounds* was the work of a man "at the top of his game... as avant garde as pop has ever got", blowing his popular image as the villain of the Beach Boys story out of the water.

But Wilson wasn't done. *Pet Sounds* may have stalled at No.10 in the US after its release in May 1966, but any disappointment at its commercial performance was allayed by the arrival of a new single, *Good Vibrations*, in October.

With its modal shifts and multi-sectional mosaic of sound fragments painstakingly pieced together by Wilson over eight months in multiple recording studios, it set new standards with regard to what rock music could sound like and do, and blazed a trail for others to follow. It was the epic and euphoric antithesis to *Pet Sounds*'s glorious melancholia.

# 52 *Bruce Springsteen* Born To Run

Bruce's first Top 40 hit, but it was the live show where Springsteen won over most fans. When he played a five-night stand at the Bottom Line in New York in August, with one of the nights broadcast on radio, sales jumped again. By the time the band played their first ever UK date – November 18, 1975 at London's Hammersmith Odeon – Springsteen was an international star.

But with stardom came backlash, when a performer who'd previously been playing small college gigs was now gracing the national press. Most of the initial backlash was due to the *Time* and *Newsweek* covers. "I got calls from people who were upset about how much attention Bruce got," says Mike Appel. "Some were from publicists who said: 'When my artist saw this, they went ballistic, saying why can't you get me this kinda press?'"

In the years since 1975 the legend, and reputation, of *Born To Run* has only grown, and it often appears in readers' polls as one of the all-time Top 10 albums. Given its standing and status today, it is worth noting that in 1975, despite the press hype, it was nowhere near (No.3, in the US, No.24 in the UK) the runaway smash that Springsteen's *Born In The USA* was in 1984. Yet the album has continued to sell over the decades, and even Springsteen, forever the perfectionist, has found himself reassessing an album he didn't think was completely finished at release.

In discussing the album on *Wings For Wheels*, it sounded like it was still a part of his life that he couldn't completely let go of: "The primary questions I was writing about in the rest of my work life first took place in the forms of *Born To Run*. What do you do when your dreams come true? What do you do when they don't? Is love real? *Born To Run* was the album where I left behind my adolescent definitions of love and freedom. It was a dividing line." That was Springsteen the elder statesman of rock talking. But the young Bruce looked back on 1975, from the distance of 1976, with less ardour. "That was the most horrible period of my life," he said then about the record that would define the rest of his career.

The song *Born To Run* remains a staple on radio today, all these years after its birth. In a 1994 Greatest Songs Of All Time poll, conducted by *The Times* and the BBC, *Born To Run* was voted No.1 beating Dylan's *Like A Rolling Stone*. "I've been coming to Britain for quite a while, since the mid-70s," Springsteen said at the time. "The fans have been tremendously loyal. It's a kick."

In concert, it is often the moment when the house lights come on, and the whole audience stands up and pumps their fist in the air.

"It is a bit sacramental when we play it," Springsteen has said. "It falls like that in the course of the evening... I'm a lot like the rest of the audience. Once you write it, after that you just sort of listen to it."

# 51 *The Sex Pistols*
# Never Mind The Bollocks, Here's The Sex Pistols

Despite having released only one single by that point, by the spring of 1977 The Sex Pistols were the biggest news in British music. And yet the punk movement's most high-profile standard bearers still had to prove to a lot of rock fans that punk had some musical substance to back up the hype. The Clash, The Damned, The Jam and several others already had debut albums out, and The Pistols were being swamped by their own self-created chaos.

They'd recently sacked bass player Glen Matlock, and when they went into the studio in March 1977 with his replacement, Sid Vicious, they found that he couldn't play the required parts.

While the band signed and then unsigned to A&M records after being dropped like a hot potato by EMI, guitarist Steve Jones stepped into the breach to play the bass bits, and eventually, once the band finally inked a deal with Virgin, *Never Mind The Bollocks...* made it into shops at the end of October 1977. A less than promising background then, but as it turned out, it was worth the wait.

From the moment Steve Jones unleashes the titanic power chords of *Holidays In The Sun* to the final, nose-thumbing dénouement of Johnny Rotten's A&M-targeted, upward- tilted raspberry at the end of EMI, it remains triumphant, awe-inspiring and exemplary. In fact it makes me want to go out and waste my life all over again.

You know how it goes: the irresistible call to arms of *Anarchy In The UK*; the juicy, scare- the-dog swearathon of Bodies; the hippie euthanising charms of Seventeen; the Jubilee party-spoiling riff of *God Save The Queen*; and *Pretty Vacant*, the song it was even okay for grudging older brothers to like. It's been £3.99 in HMV since the last century, for God's sake. If you haven't already got it you'd better have a note from your mum.

The Sex Pistols' only proper studio album was just 39 minutes long, included four of their previous singles, and pre-dated the end of the band by a mere three months. Yet it remains one of the most influential and controversial records in history. With Johnny Rotten's abrasive vocals and provocative lyrics splayed across a wall of thrillingly direct guitars, *Bollocks* is a barrage of both gratuitous angst and elemental purity. While many punk 'classics' survive as nostalgia or well- meaning polemic, these compelling tirades against British society, hypocrisy and intellectual torpor still send rushes down your spine.

*Problems, Liar, Bodies* and *EMI* ('and you thought that we were faking') were miniature sonic snuff-movies, a dive into the previously unsayable. "My words are my bullets," said Rotten/John Lydon in 2008. "They meant a lot to my generation."

As 1978 dawned, he was growling: "Ever get the feeling you've been cheated?" and the Pistols were shot. But they'd hit the bullseye. Job done.

Sonically, the Sex Pistols' debut stripped rock'n'roll

year released
**1984**
label
producer
**Prince and the Revolution**

A maximalist magnum opus that's sold 25 million copies and counting, *Purple Rain* catapulted Prince into the immortal pop pantheon with its audacious blend of machine-tooled sex-funk, heavy metal guitars, porno-suggestive lyrics and MTV-friendly, high-gloss showmanship. The accompanying film may have been a polished turd of soapy melodrama but it transformed its diminutive star into a towering icon of the video age.

Remastered in 2015, the original album still sounds gloriously eclectic and mostly electrifying. From the skeletal robo-funk and Hendrix-oid guitar eruptions of *When Doves Cry* to the controversial, overblown perv-pop wank fantasy *Darling Nikki* and the epic blow-out finale of *Purple Rain* itself, this is Prince in his imperial pomp, cranking everything up to 11 with his tongue in both cheeks. Usually somebody else's.

*Purple Rain* was the album that made Prince a true superstar. Released in 1984, it was the soundtrack to the movie of the same name, a rock musical drama in

year released
1977

producer
**Chris Thomas and Bill Price**

back to its first principles. Visually, its sleeve did the same. "The only real thing about *Never Mind The Bollocks* was that it had to look ugly," recalled their late manager Malcolm McClaren. "We came up with the ugliest cover we could think of; that in a sense would attack the idea of super-graphics. I wanted to make ugliness beautiful."

"I don't know if Malcolm [McLaren, Pistols manager] ever read the lyrics of *Anarchy In The UK* or *God Save The Queen*," John Lydon told *Classic Rock*. "I don't know if any of them did. I just did what I did. I came in with my own imagery and wrote about aspects of life that completely altered the agenda, produced shock, awe and horror in the world. But it so needed it. From my point of view, these were the institutions, organisations, governments and religions that were ruining my life up to this point - ruining all of our lives. It wasn't just my own personal point of view, it was an oppression all of us were under. We needed to break free from the shackles that were demanding blind obedience to a monarchy. Why can't you question or challenge that? Why can't you raise an issue with it? Well, I did.

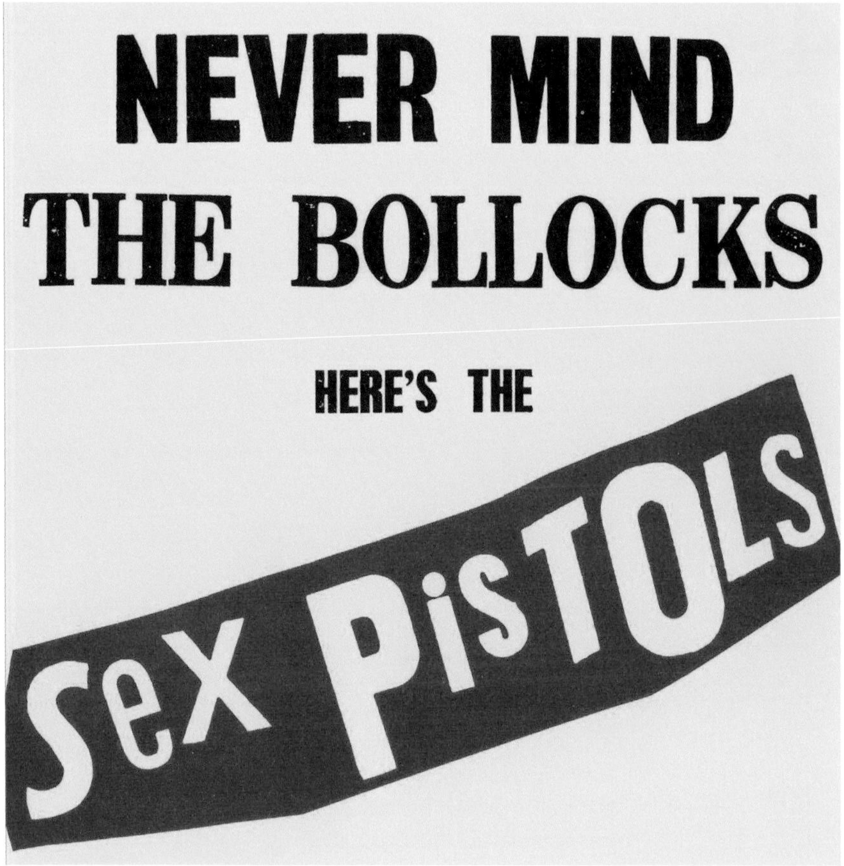


# 50 *Prince*
# Purple Rain

which Prince played the lead role as The Kid in a story loosely based on his own life. The movie was a box office hit, the album an era-defining classic. It was also the first Prince album on which he was backed by The Revolution - a group made in the image of Sly & The Family Stone, mixing male and female, black and white.

The album yielded two US number singles. The first, *When Doves Cry*, was a song that seemed to exist in its own world - a mesmeric funk track made unique by its absence of funk's lead instrument, bass. The second, *Let's Go Crazy*, was a quasi-religious rock'n'roll anthem on which Prince outgunned rock's reigning guitar heroes, Eddie Van Halen included. And the album's title track, which reached No.2, was his epic power ballad, an emotional tour de force climaxing in one of the greatest guitar solos ever recorded. The album hit No.1 in the US in August 1984, and stayed there until January 1985.

Such was the brilliance of Prince's guitar playing on *Purple Rain* that he starred on the cover of *Kerrang!* in 1984. The magazine's then-editor Geoff Barton, now of *Classic Rock*, explains: "We only had a live review. We couldn't get an interview because Prince very rarely gave interviews. But we put him on the cover because we believed in the power of his music and his phenomenal ability on the guitar. He was more in the mode of Hendrix than Michael Jackson. His playing on *Let's Go Crazy* is up there with the absolute best guitar gods. And for all the other influences in *Purple Rain*, it is very simply a fantastic guitar album."

In the end, perhaps the greatest gift of *Purple Rain* for Prince, beyond the stardom and the most enduring songs of his career, was simply that he found a way to belong to the music world at large. In the years after, he wrote and produced songs for The Bangles, Sheena Easton, Madonna, Chaka Khan and Stevie Nicks. Today that creative collaboration has continued with new artists such as Janelle Monae, Trombone Shorty and Zooey Deschanel.

In 1985, still in the heat of *Purple Rain*'s glow, Prince reflected on balancing roles as a band leader and bandmate. "I strive for perfection, and I'm a little bull-headed in my ways," he said. "Then sometimes everybody in the band comes over, and we have very long talks. They're few and far between, and I do a lot of the talking. Whenever we're done, one of them will come up to me and say, 'Take care of yourself. You know I really love you.'

"I think they love me so much, and I love them so much, that if they came over all the time I wouldn't be able to be to them what I am, and they wouldn't be able to do for me as what they do. I think we all need our individual spaces, and when we come together with what we've concocted in our heads, it's cool."

# 49 *Van Halen*
# 1984

If ever a rock band epitomised the American Dream, it's Van Halen. Formed in Pasadena, California in 1974 by four teenage kids from families that had migrated across the Atlantic in the pursuit of a better life, Van Halen were loud, brash, shamelessly ambitious, larger-than-life: classically all-American. And so was their pioneering spirit of rock.

Van Halen revolutionised hard rock music. When the band's debut album was released in 1978, punk had unsettled rock's old order; giants such as Zeppelin and Sabbath were on their last legs. But VH had seen the future. "This is the 1980s!" declared singer David Lee Roth, boldly if prematurely. "And this is the new sound – it's hyper, it's energy, it's urgent."

The key to that new sound was Eddie Van Halen, whose innovative two-handed 'tapping' technique made him the most influential guitarist since Jimi Hendrix. But VH wasn't a one-man show. Eddie's brother Alex went at his drum kit like a prizefighter. Bassist Michael Anthony underpinned Eddie's histrionics and provided killer backing vocals that had him rightly described as the band's "secret weapon". And then, of course, there was 'Diamond Dave', a wisecracking, splits-jumping, super-toned blond Adonis, son of second-generation Jewish immigrants, and hard rock's greatest showman. As Roth stated: "I once heard somebody say to the Van Halens: 'You guys play the music, the Jew sells it.' Well, you're fucking right!"

With Roth as cheerleader, Van Halen were America's favourite party band, their high-octane turbo-pop songs the soundtrack to the 'me' decade. But when Roth left the band in 1985 amid mutual hostility, much of the magic went with him, even if his replacement, Sammy Hagar, was ultimately a better singer.

Hagar lasted 10 years. His successor, former Extreme vocalist Gary Cherone, was out after one album. Hagar returned for a chaotic reunion tour in 2004, and two years later came the announcement that Roth was rejoining VH with, shockingly, Eddie's 15-year-old son Wolfgang replacing Michael Anthony. But a proposed US tour has been delayed indefinitely after Eddie entered rehab in March 2007.

Whatever happens next, Van Halen's place in the pantheon of classic rock acts is secure. With 56 million albums sold, they are 19th on the list of biggest-selling acts in the US. And at their best (with Roth) Van Halen ruled.

*1984*, the last of the definitive Roth-era albums ,was also the one that made Van Halen a household name on this side of the Atlantic when its lead single, *Jump*, hit No.7 on the UK chart. In playing this simple rock song on a keyboard, guitar hero Eddie beat all those airy- fairy synth-pop acts at their own game. *I'll Wait*, the album's other big pop crossover hit, was also powered by a keyboard riff, but the hard rock crunch of *Panama* and *Hot For Teacher* ensured that the band's hairy fan base wasn't alienated.

Opening with the unexpected sound of a warm electronic swell, *1984* seemed to herald the arrival of some new mutant, synth-driven Van Halen. But the truth was that the synths had taken outings on the previous two Van Halen albums, as well, and would likely have featured more had Eddie gotten his way earlier. The short instrumental title track and *Jump* follow in the footsteps of that weird time- fuck drone, *Sunday Afternoon In The Park*, from 1981's *Fair Warning*, one of two "synth" tunes on that album, and was followed by another two on the next year's *Diver Down*, featuring both Eddie (*Dancing In The Street*) and David Lee Roth (*Intruder*) on synthesiser.

The surprise on *1984* was that it seemed to underline the fact that the synths were here to stay, especially after the global success of Jump propelled the album to sales of eight million units in the first 10 months of release, thereby seeming to vindicate Eddie's ideas about what was good for the band.

More naturally Rothian in flavour, however, were the likes of *Hot For Teacher*, *Panama* and *Drop Dead Legs*. A little known fact about Van Halen is that they (along with Devo and Cheap Trick) had originally been under consideration for the starring roles in Allan Arkush's 1979 movie musical, *Rock'N'Roll High School* (which ended up starring the Ramones). But on the delinquent outing that is *Hot For Teacher*, they seem to make up for that missed opportunity. This is a tune on which the band truly swings – with Roth 'exuberating' to the max – over some bumpy territory that has previously been visited on tunes such as ZZ Top's *La Grange*, which itself had retraced a path that John Lee Hooker had cut some time earlier. Here, though, the tempo is ramped up to such a degree that it produces, as Eddie said, "a boogie beyond anything" he'd ever heard. It is excessive. But, in truth, any showing off found here merely compliments Roth's genius, dumb-ass, lyrical imagery, which trades brilliantly on the experience of childhood as a time of unfair and daily incarceration.

On *1984*, Van Halen could do no wrong... but by 1985 Roth was gone, and the band, in whatever guise, would never be as great again.

year released
**1984**

producer
**Ted Templeman**

# 48 *The Rolling Stones*
# Let It Bleed

The Beatles were more innovative, more popular, more of a cultural phenomenon. Led Zeppelin sold more records. But there has never been a better rock'n'roll band than the Stones.

Foremost, there are the classic songs: *(I Can't Get No) Satisfaction, Jumpin' Jack Flash, Honky Tonk Women, Brown Sugar, Sympathy For The Devil, Gimme Shelter, Tumbling Dice, Miss You, Start Me Up*. Then there are the classic albums: *Beggars Banquet, Sticky Fingers, Exile On Main St, Some Girls, Tattoo You*, and of course *Let It Bleed*. But the legend of The Rolling Stones was built on more than music.

There's the lifestyle: no rock star before or since has enjoyed such a legendary reputation for drug-fuelled rock'n'roll excess than Keith Richards; no other rock star has played the part of international playboy as expertly as Mick Jagger. And there's darkness: the death of original guitarist Brian Jones in his Sussex swimming pool in July 1969, which is still the subject of conjecture; the murder of 18-year-old fan Meredith Hunter, in December 1969, at the hands of Hell's Angels at the Stones' free concert at Altamont Speedway in California.

In recent years, it has become almost obligatory to knock the Stones. But at their peak – from the mid-60s to the late 70s – The Rolling Stones created some of the most important and influential rock music of all time.

Released the day before Meredith Hunter was murdered at Altamont, *Let It Bleed* came to symbolise the death of the 60s and the end of the age of love and peace. It was also the first Stones album to follow the death of Brian Jones, who was fired during its recording.

*Let It Bleed* wasn't all doom and gloom, but two menacing songs gave the album a dark aura: *Midnight Rambler and Gimme Shelter.* Despite all the hero worship of Robert Johnson, Muddy Waters, Howlin' Wolf and their back catalogues, the greatest blues song The Stones every recorded was one that Mick 'n' Keef wrote: *Midnight Rambler.*Based on the fiendish deeds of serial killer Albert DeSalvo, aka The Boston Strangler, *Midnight Rambler* was an extensive brooding psychodrama that had Jagger threatening to 'stick my knife right down your throat'.

*Gimme Shelter* was a vision of a world descending into violence. Richards came up with the smouldering intro while Mick Jagger was on the set of *Performance* with Keith's girlfriend Anita Pallenberg, shooting sex scenes that may well have turned into a real life affair. Keith sat at home stewing with jealousy, *Gimme Shelter* brewing. Producer Jack Nitzsche brought in soul singer Merry Clayton to add frenzied backing vocals: *'Rape! Murder! It's just a shot away,'* she sings. Clayton was pregnant at the time; the strain was such that when she went home after the session she miscarried.

Such are the interpretive powers of Mick, Keef and the boys, their version of Robert Johnson's dark

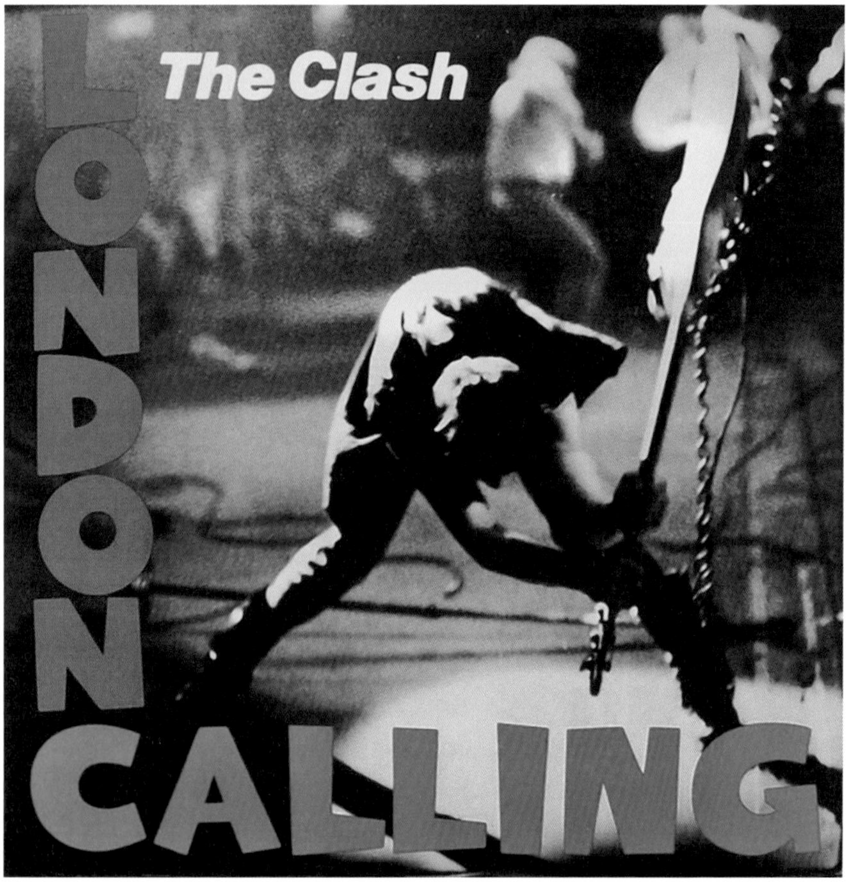


year released
**1979**
label
producer
**Guy Stevens and Mick Jones**

Most exciting rock'n'roll is made by people in their 20s for people in their teens. It's like a note slid under our bedroom doors by our big brothers and sisters, that says everything will be alright: we will get laid, we will fall in love, we will get high, our parents won't rule our lives forever. The Clash gave us all that – and then so much more. Because, while they were in love with 'the rock'n'roll woah' – and made music for guys with Ford Cortinas and dead-end jobs – *London Calling, Sandinista!* and *Combat Rock* are albums for grown-ups, albums you take with you after the anger subsides, when you start being less self-obsessed and begin to look out into the world.

Most rock'n'roll is solipsistic and inwards-looking – but from *London Calling* onwards, The Clash looked outwards. Their music wasn't about them, about how deep they were or how troubled, how wasted they were on drugs or the pressures of fame. It was about us, about you, about the big wide world that waited for you.

The street punk movement they'd inspired had

year released
**1969**

producer
**Jimmy Miller**

*Love In Vain* sounds like they wrote the thing themselves. Originally cut by the "King Of The Delta Blues Singers" in 1937, the song is about the pain of unrequited love, a feeling emphasised by Jagger's aching vocal delivery. *You've Got The Silver* is prime Keef, a swinging country blues number that saw his first lead vocal on a Stones record.

If *Let It Bleed* served notice that the summer of love was officially over, it did so in style. Epic closer *You Can't Always Get What You Want* might also be about the 60s dream - but it's not completely pessimistic. Musically uplifting, it's lyrically pragmatic. *'You can't always get what you want,'* sings Jagger, *'but if you try sometimes, you get what you need'*. Maybe peace, love and understanding were a long way off, it says, but we can get through it.

The London Bach Choir added an almost parodic quality to the song, their terribly English vocals at odds with the gutsy Americana of the rest of the record. True to form, they asked for their credit to be removed from the record after release, citing its "relentless drug ambience"

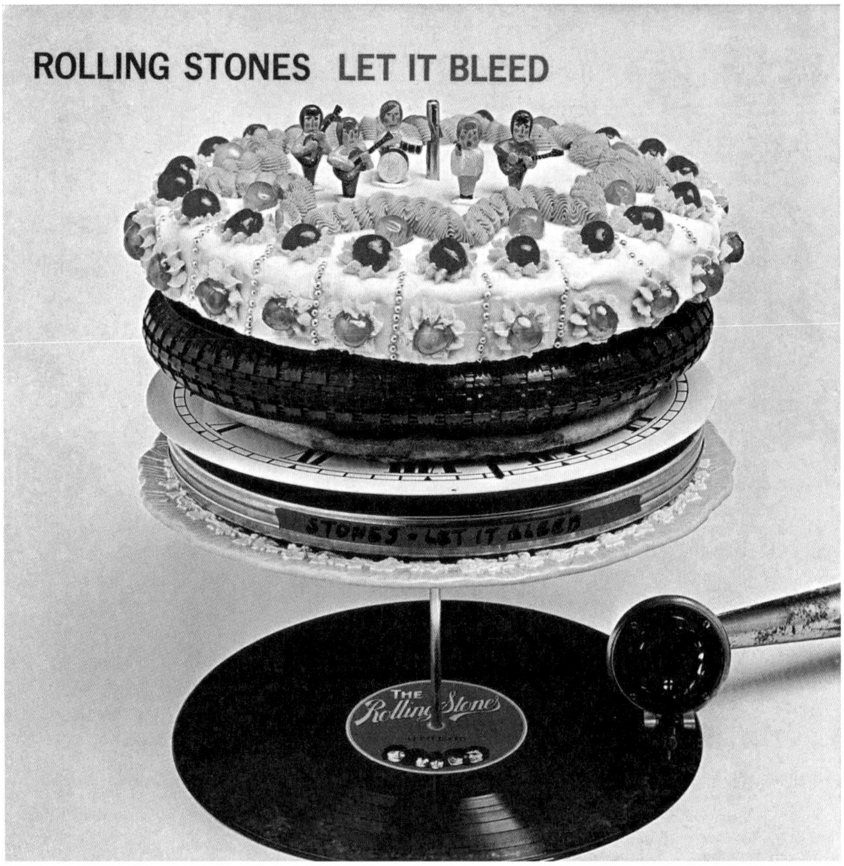


# 47 *The Clash* London Calling

morphed into the Oi! movement, but The Clash refused to be "little Englanders", musically and lyrically embracing a world beyond their roots, drawing on rock'n'roll, reggae, calypso, jazz, folk, blues, soul, and sometimes bolting them together (or taking them apart) with a natural genre-busting experimentalism that they rarely get any credit for.

As Chris Knowles points out in his brilliant collection of Clash opinions, *Clash City Showdown*, for a very long time *The Clash* was regarded as the band's finest album. American music critic Robert Christgau called their debut "the greatest rock and roll album ever manufactured anywhere" and ranked it as the greatest long-player of the 70s, while UK music weekly *Sounds* voted it the all-time greatest album in 1985.

*London Calling*'s stature really began to rise after *Rolling Stone* voted it the greatest album of the 80s in 1989 (the US version of the album was released in January 1980). A cynic might claim that us poor saps have followed *Rolling Stone* like sheep in our subsequent re-appraisal of the album. It might be fairer to see it as a more balanced reaction to the album after the frostier reception it had on release.

*London Calling* was neither a sell-out nor a conscious attempt to crack America. But it can also be seen as a mature musical and political response to a British pop culture that had been transformed by bands like the Specials and Dexy's Midnight Runners, and a bit of one-upmanship from a band at the height of their powers, encouraged to paint a richer picture by a man with a colourful background in rock'n'roll history.

Producer, Guy Stevens, had been a pivotal part of the 60s blues explosion, running Sue Records, hanging with Procol Harum and the like. Stevens was the svengali behind Mott The Hoople (guitarist Mick Jones' favourite band) and was on his uppers in 1979. Strummer and co dragged him out of the pub and into the studio. Inspired by their deranged father figure, The Clash kicked out the jams in a new, more musical way. By *London Calling*, drummer Topper Headon could play anything. Paul Simonon no longer needed the notes stuck on the fretboard of his bass. Strummer and Jones were at the peak of their songwriting powers. The sky was the limit.

*Train In Vain* grooves like classic soul. *Guns Of Brixton* conjures up genuine London reggae. *Rudie Can't Fail* was ska-punk in excelsis. The title track proclaimed a coming apocalypse -and welcomed it (*'London is drowning and I live by the river!'*). This was the party at the end of the world. *The Right Profile, Revolution Rock, I'm Not Down* - the songs on *London Calling* are a righteous, raucous rave-up.

Recording a blistering version of rockabilly cover *Brand New Cadillac*, Topper was dismayed at Stevens' ecstatic reaction at the end.

"We'll need to do it again," said the drummer. "We speeded up."

"All great rock'n'roll speeds up," said Stevens.

# 46 *The Allman Brothers Band* At Fillmore East

The Allman Brothers Band's 1971 double album *At Fillmore East* is often and quite rightly proclaimed as rock's greatest live release. It still sounds completely fresh, inspired and utterly original. It is the gold standard of blues-based rock'n'roll. After 45 years of such praise, it's easy to lose sight of what a radical album *At Fillmore East* really was.

It took a lot of guts for the band and their record label to put out a two-LP live album as their third release. After all, when it came out in October 1971, the band was something of a commercial flop. Though drawing raves for their marathon live shows that combined the Grateful Dead's go-anywhere jam ethos with a far superior musical precision, their first two releases had caused barely a ripple out in the marketplace.

The band's self-titled 1969 debut sold less than 35,000 copies and the following year's *Idlewild South* did only marginally better despite two singles, *Midnight Rider* and *Revival*. The band struggled to understand why. "When the first record came out at No.200 with an anchor and dropped off the face of the earth, my brother and I did not get discouraged," recalls Gregg Allman. "But I thought *Idlewild South* was a much better record and when that died on the vine, I thought, 'Damn, maybe we were wrong about this group.'"

But the lacklustre sales didn't match the increasingly large and rabid crowds The Allman Brothers were drawing on their relentlessly paced tours. Audiences loved the band's rare combination of blues, jazz, rock and country and their willingness to play until somebody pulled the plug. Finally, it dawned on the band and their management that a live album was the only way to capture the band's real essence.

What resulted was a recording of two shows at New York City's famed Fillmore East, which is a testament to a great band at the peak of their powers. Sadly, it would prove to be the final album ever completed by guitarist Duane Allman, who died in a motorcycle crash, aged just 24, shortly after its release. As such, it has proven to be something of an epitaph for both him and The Allman Brothers Band mark one.

"That album captured the band in all their glory," producer Tom Dowd said in a 1998 interview. Dowd, who died in 2002, was behind the boards for nearly a dozen Allman Brothers albums, including *At Fillmore East*. He worked with everyone from John Coltrane and Ray Charles to Cream and Lynyrd Skynyrd.

"The Allmans have always had a perpetual swing sensation that is unique in rock," he went on. "They swing like they're playing jazz when they play things that are tangential to the blues, and even when they play heavy rock. They're never vertical but always going forward, and it's always a groove."

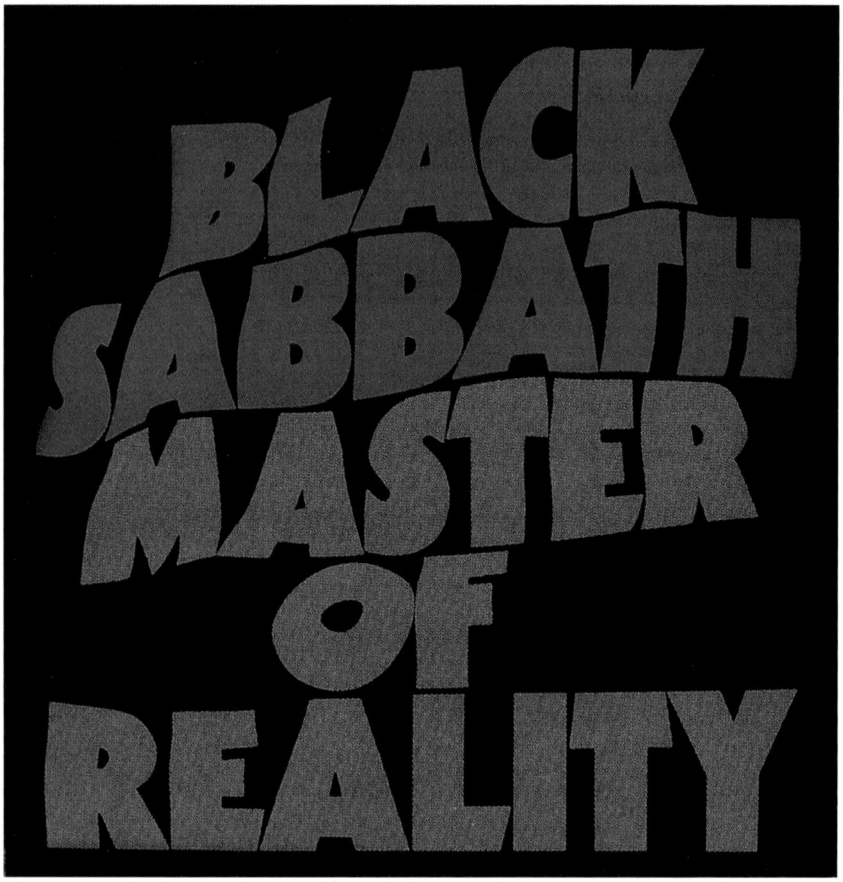


year released
**1971**
label
producer
**Rodger Bain**

The story of Black Sabbath is one of chaos, inspiration, luck and moments of outright genius – and never more so than during their stellar rise in the early 1970s. Between 1970 and 1975, the band released six groundbreaking albums – a run that still stands as one of rock's greatest hot streaks.

If 1970's *Paranoid* album raised Sabbath's profile on both sides of Atlantic, it was the follow-up, 1971's *Master Of Reality*, where everything truly came together. Producing the album themselves gave the band the opportunity to experiment – most notably, Iommi's decision to tune his guitar down by three semi-tones, to reduce string tension and make the instrument easier to play with his damaged fingers, inadvertently made Sabbath's sound even heavier, denser and doomier.

The result was one of the finest albums of their career – and one which would shape everything that came in its wake.

"The whole thing was an experiment," remembers guitarist Tony Iommi. "We tuned down to get more

year released
**1971**

producer
**Tom Dowd**

Certainly, the improvisation and length of the tunes on *At Fillmore East* were more similar to jazz than rock, with just seven songs spread over four vinyl sides, capturing the Allmans in all their bluesy, sonic fury. *You Don't Love Me* and *Whipping Post* both occupied full album sides, while *In Memory Of Elizabeth Reed* clocked in at 13 minutes. Still, from the clarion slide guitar of *Statesboro Blues* that opens the album to the booming timpani roll of *Whipping Post* that closes it, there is nary a wasted note in the 78 minutes of Fillmore music.

Propelled upward and onward by bassist Berry Oakley, whose free range style uniquely roamed the middle of the band's sound, and the rhythmic onslaught of double drummers Butch Trucks and Jaimoe, the group seemed ready to blast off in any direction at any time. Dickey Betts and Duane Allman spurred each other on to new heights of fretboard ferocity and creativity while also pioneering guitar harmonies. And Gregg Allman's authentic blues singing and surging organ vamps kept even the most ambitious jams firmly rooted to terra firma.

# 45 *Black Sabbath*
# Master Of Reality

power and a fatter sound. Of course, Ozzy started singing higher. He'd go, "Oh, I can reach that note now." However, when we got onstage, he couldn't do it."

"On the first album, we had two days to do everything, and not much more time for *Paranoid*," says drummer Bill Ward. "But now we could take our time, and try out different things. We all embraced the opportunity: Tony threw in classical guitar parts, Geezer's bass was virtually doubled in power, I went for bigger bass drums, also experimenting with overdubs. And Ozzy was so much better."

Lyrically, the album drew from war, religion and drugs. As far as the first subject went, *Children Of The Grave* was a potent and powerful anti-war statement. A startling successor to *War Pigs* on the *Paranoid* album...

"This is a workshop in heavy music. Even when we did it on the last reunion tour three years ago, it got the audience going like crazy. I know it's popular in the UK, but in America it really made a mark. When we first began to play it on tour in the States, it was just when the bodies were starting to come home from the Vietnam War, and the casualties. We had a lot of veteran soldiers turning up in wheelchairs at shows, and they'd come down to the front for this song – as they did for *War Pigs* – waving their flags, and singing along. It made for a very emotional and wild time."

Another significant moment on the album came with *After Forever*, which surprised many by talking openly about Christianity. Was this Sabbath distancing themselves from the Satanic and occult imagery of the past? Bill believes this song's implications to be profound in terms of the band's outlook on life.

"What we were doing on *After Forever* was asking relevant questions about the validity of Christianity, in particular Catholicism. We were voicing our own inner concerns about it all, asking everyone if they were prepared to accept what was being said, without questioning whether this was right or wrong."

*Master Of Reality* was released in July 1971, and immediately became a major success. In the US, not only did the record make it to number eight on the charts, selling half-a-million copies in advance, but in the UK it reached number five. By comparison, the *Paranoid* album reached number 12 in the States and number four over here. So the band had proven their somewhat surprise success in 1970 was no flashbomb-in-the pan.

Today, nearly 30 years on, the album not only stands in its own right as a great record, but one that has inspired succeeding generations of countless musicians.

"I know people feel that Sabbath invented heavy metal with our debut album – and that is true to some extent," Bill concludes, "but I believe that it's with *Master Of Reality* that we proved the potential and power of the music."

# 44 *Meat Loaf*
# Bat Out Of Hell

It's 1973. Jim Steinman has co-written an off-Broadway show called *More Than You Deserve*. Set during the Vietnam War, *More Than You Deserve* attracted a great deal of critical attention, not least for the performance of Marvin Lee Aday, a young singer performing under the name Meat Loaf.

"I used to be a lawyer back in the day," says David Sonenberg, a manager and lawyer who has worked with both Steinman and Meat Loaf since the mid-1970s, "and one of my earliest clients was Meat Loaf, Marvin Aday. He was in *More Than You Deserve* at the Public Theatre. At the time, [Broadway impresario] Joe Papp was interested in doing a show that Steinman had written, a futuristic *Peter Pan*, and Steinman had told him he didn't need to clear any rights with the James Barrie estate. So Papp asked me if I would go see the workshop."

Sonenberg duly went to see Steinman's new show, *Neverland*. "I was blown away," he remembers now. "It was sexy and crazy and a little violent. And there was a Peter, and a Wendy, and a Hook, and a Tink... I reported to Papp that we needed to clear rights."

*Neverland* was more than just a rock version of *Peter Pan*, it was also a reboot of *The Dream Engine*, his college musical from almost 10 years before. A major reboot.

Replacing the often stodgy choruses of *The Dream Engine* was a set of songs that seemed to come from a different galaxy. They had a little in common with the music Bruce Springsteen was now making – a rockier version of classic Phil Spector seen through a poetic 1970s lens – but where Springsteen was making his music leaner and more urban, Steinman's idea of a motorbike song made *Born To Run* look like an ode to a Raleigh Chopper. Steinman's vision was operatic. There was sex, and romance; drama and melodrama; love, death and the American guitar. And even in the golden age of album rock, these new songs were long. They were also great.

"Six of the seven songs which were ultimately in *Bat Out Of Hell* were in Neverland," Sonenberg remembers. "It opened up with Peter singing *All Revved Up*, and it was incredible."

*Neverland* never happened. And there were good reasons for that. "I sent the script to Great Ormond Street Hospital, who own the rights to *Peter Pan*," Sonenberg says. "And their solicitor said: 'I'm sorry, Mister Sonenberg, you lost me at the killer nuns.' There were killer nuns flying around, wearing habits and Victoria's Secret lingerie..."

*Neverland* was dead. But the songs Jim Steinman had written for it were still great. Now he and Meat Loaf embarked on a well-documented phase of their career together. They went from record company to record company, and instead of leaving a demo tape on someone's desk they performed the whole album, in the room, just piano and vocals.

As a plan it was insane, and it didn't work. It wasn't just being in a confined space with the two most terrifying men in rock, it was also *Bat Out Of Hell* itself. The mid-70s was, legend has it, a time of FM rock, when West Coast bands took it easy and even the greatest British bands – Pink Floyd, the other ones – were best appreciated on headphones with some spliff. Like the A&R men, very few listeners wanted a huge, screaming maniac leaping down their ears with songs about bats and motorbikes.

Famously, *Bat Out Of Hell* found its first music biz supporter in Todd Rundgren. Rundgren, whose own genre-blending music showed a similar defiant attitude to categories, also had a sense of humour. With Rundgren's support, and money from the tiny Bearsville label, the songs from *Bat* were finally recorded. But not without problems. There was, for example, the owner of Bearsville, rotund former Bob Dylan manager Albert Grossman. "Albert said: 'I'm not signing Meat Loaf,'" laughs Sonenberg. "I said: 'Why?' He said: 'Because he's too fat.' And Albert was twice the size of Meat Loaf!"

Despite this, Bat was made, and made well. In the wake of its ridiculous success, we take it for granted that *Bat Out Of Hell* is an extraordinary record. It sits in thousands of record collections next to *Rumours* and *The Dark Side Of The Moon* and, like those records, it sounds both immediately accessible and like nothing you've ever heard before. Most of this, of course, is down to the combination of Jim Steinman's music and Meat Loaf's incredible presence and singing powers, but Todd Rundgren's work can't be underestimated. From the famous revving-bike guitar on the title track – and fuck my old boots, is there a better opening song on any album than Bat Out Of Hell? – to the Spector drums on *You Took The Words Right Out Of My Mouth*, from the boogie melodrama of *Paradise By The Dashboard Light* to the gentleness of *For Crying Out Loud*, Todd Rundgren's work on *Bat* is as sympathetic as it gets. Not that anyone thought this at the time.

"We shopped it around for about a year," Sonenberg recalls. "It was finished, it was sounding amazing, and everybody hated it.They were literally establishing record companies for the sole purpose of passing on *Bat Out Of Hell*!"

year released
**1977**

producer
**Todd Rundgren**

FEDERAL

# 43 *The Jimi Hendrix Experience* Electric Ladyland

*Electric Ladyland* was not born easily. It took Hendrix an entire year to realise the towering and complex sonic edifice he was carrying around inside his head and heart. But then *Electric Ladyland* is a superhuman effort on many levels: a grand summary of Jimi's personal cosmology; an intricate construct made up of UFO lore, mythology, parallel universes, astral travel, alternative realities, reincarnation and the magical powers of a love supreme. The album is the quintessential Hendrix.

Back then, a year was considered an impossibly long time for a rock'n'roll artist to spend on an album. And in the process of making *Electric Ladyland* Hendrix's manager and confidante, Chas Chandler – the man who'd discovered Jimi and made him a star – would walk out on him. Jimi's band, the Experience, was starting to fall apart and would further unravel during the album's transcontinental sessions, which at times seem interminable. Throughout the recording, Hendrix was tangled up in legal difficulties stemming from years of contractual carelessness and blatant rip-offs. He was frequently obliged to halt work on the album in order to go out on the road and earn money for the next phase of the project and keep the whole boat afloat. By this point Hendrix, bassist Noel Redding and drummer Mitch Mitchell were already pretty beat up by a solid year of hard touring and the creation of two superb albums: *Are You Experienced* and *Axis: Bold As Love*. Their energy had been further drained by excesses of the highest order, intensified by copious ingestion of LSD and other popular intoxicants of the day.

*Electric Ladyland* would prove to be the final album that the Jimi Hendrix Experience recorded together. The group broke up shortly after it was finished. It would also be the last studio album that Hendrix saw through to completion during his life.

The album starts off with a brief, abstract tone poem, *And The Gods Made Love*. The result of lovemaking, in the ordinary course of nature, is procreation. And here it's happening on a grand, cosmic level. What we're hearing is no less than the creation of the universe. Tape manipulation techniques enable Hendrix and Kramer to evoke the momentous event in sound. A recording of tom-toms was slowed down to create an ominous sound like distant thunder. Jimi's voice is likewise slowed down to a god-like register not quite decipherable as human language.

*Have You Ever Been (To Electric Ladyland)* is an invitation phrased as a question, much like the line 'have you ever been experienced?' from Jimi's first album. In Electric Ladyland, 'angels spread their wings' to welcome us, as Hendrix appropriates one of his favourite tropes from BB King's blues classic *Sweet Little Angel*. It's kind of like Curtis Mayfield on acid with lots of sexy, supernatural angel babes. But no sooner do we settle down on a fluffy cloud than

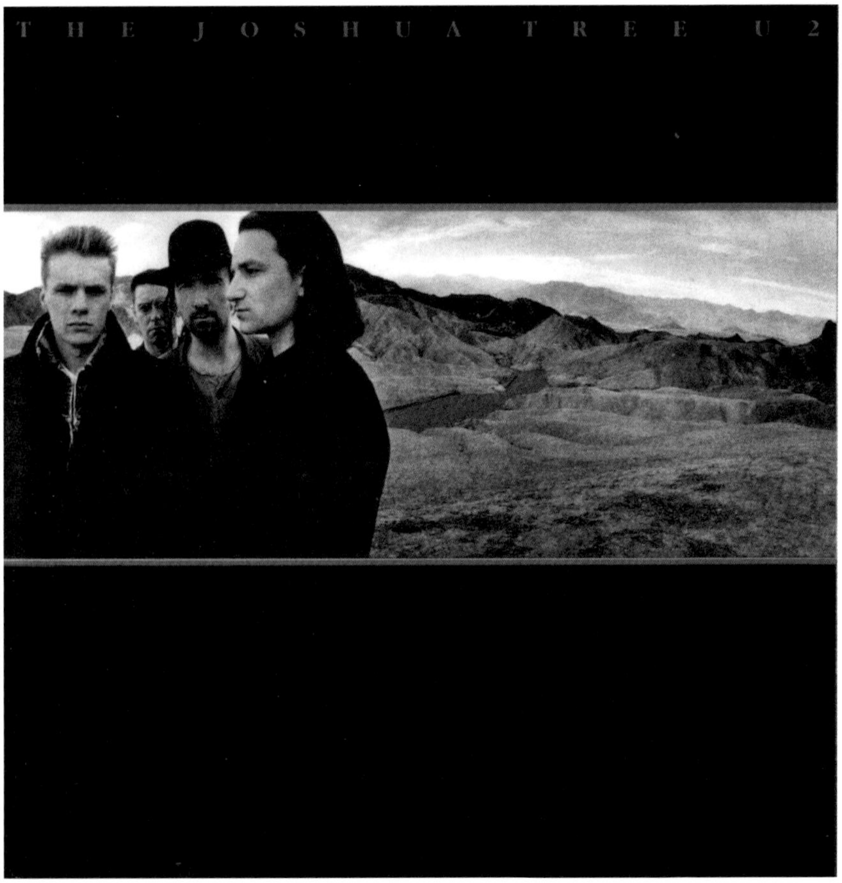


year released
**1987**
label
producer
**Daniel Lanois**
**Brian Eno**

In the moment of their grandstanding, late-afternoon Live Aid performance at Wembley Stadium on 13 July 1985, U2 got cast as the defining band of the eighties, made-for-stadium rockers with a conscience. However, to make that impression a reality they needed an appropriately epic, all-encompassing record.

On their previous and fourth album, 1984's *The Unforgettable Fire*, they had worked with debuting producers Brian Eno and Daniel Lanois to dial down their rabble-rousing default setting and fashion a more ranging, atmospheric sound. Like that record, *The Joshua Tree* was also made in Ireland with Eno and Lanois, but on this occasion they additionally channelled the grandeur of the American heartland that they had spent a chunk of the decade touring and the folk music born out of it. Its questing tone and boundless feel was set by frontman Bono's commitment to roving and a song that guitarist Edge wrote while the singer was off on one of his frequent travels.

Before and during the period U2 was holed up in their

year released
**1968**

producer
**Jimi Hendrix**

we get dropped abruptly back to earth –into the middle of *Crosstown Traffic*, no less.

The first vinyl side ends with another of Hendrix's best known tracks, *Voodoo Chile*. This freewheeling blues jam is one of several tracks that saw Hendrix bringing players from outside of the Experience into his creative circle. The track captures Hendrix at his most spontaneous and inspired, and forms a nice counterpart to the more carefully orchestrated guitar tracks on the album.

Hendrix's parting shot, however, is the real hair-raiser: *'And if I don't meet you no more in this world, then I'll meet you in the next one/Don't be late.'*

Interest in Hendrix is as strong now as it was 40 years ago, if not stronger. He is still that iconic rock guitarist whom even today's players try to emulate. *'Don't be late'* is a line that recurs in *Have You Ever Been (To Electric Ladyland)*, Moon, *Turn the Tides* and *Voodoo Chile (Slight Return)*. Jimi is goading us forward, egging us on. Guitarists today are still trying to catch up to where Hendrix was 40 years ago.

# 42 *U2*
# The Joshua Tree

Dublin studio, Bono and his wife, Ali, visited Africa and Central America. Proximity to grinding poverty and Reagan-era American interventionism prompted him to write the words to *I Still Haven't Found What I'm Looking For* and *Bullet The Blue Sky*. Back home in Dublin, meanwhile, Edge resolved to create the ultimate U2 live song and conjured *Where the Streets Have No Name*, his guitar chiming out across a wide-open landscape.

Alongside the haunted, but surging *With Or Without You*, and framed by photographer Anton Corbijn's context-establishing, Nevada Desert-set cover shot, these songs were the tent-poles of a record that was big and bracing enough to encapsulate the mood of that era and also the one of now, as U2 tour its thirtieth anniversary.

"We knew we had to make a big record," The Edge recalls. "We had equal parts fear and conviction going for us, and as maddening as that can be, that combination usually works."

Rarely do bands touted as the Next Big Thing go on to become the next big thing, but from the start U2 had all the ingredients: an distinctive sound, mostly due to The Edge's echo-laden guitar ostinatos, and an inexorable appetite for theatrics and experimentation. Jackrabbity upstarts when they released 1980's *Boy,* they issued a succession of wildly daring and successful albums. But by 1987, they were no longer callow young men, and the pedal-drenched guitar effects that defined their early albums were starting to sound like quaint clichés. With their maturity now equalling their ambition, they looked to America's roots music for inspiration. And the band's growing obsession with the US wasn't just hobby or diversion, it was a lifeline.

"We had hit a wall sound-wise," says the Edge, "so to suddenly discover all this great blues and gospel music, it seemed very magical, and we felt compelled to examine it."

On *The Joshua Tree*, U2 didn't just study American music, they channelled it, absorbing it into their collective DNA. The church gospel epiphanies of *I Still Haven't Found What I'm Looking For* and the Hendrixy blues of *Bullet The Blue Sky* came off as more than credible impressions; they were the genuine article. It helped, too, that Bono's lyrics had veered from desultory politics to matters of the heart, and in the gorgeous pulse of *With Or Without You* his soulful pleas are by turns aching and soothing, triumphant and tortured.

"It was an important record for us," says the Edge. "We had all grown up a bit, but we were still learning and questioning. It was a breakthrough, but we always try to use our breakthroughs to lead us somewhere else."

Twenty-four years after it was released and had sold 25m copies, Bono said: "At the time we felt guilty about our success, didn't quite feel as if we lived up to it. *The Joshua Tree* is a great piece of work. I know that now, but I didn't for ages."

# 41 *Aerosmith* Toys In The Attic

After Aerosmith's 1973 self-titled debut fell short of label expectations, selling only 30,000 copies, they lived in limbo, wondering if Columbia Records would drop them. But for Joe Perry, Steven Tyler, Joey Kramer, Tom Hamilton and Brad Whitford, failure was never an option. "The thought that we might not make it never occurred to us," Tyler wrote in his autobiography. "Everybody was totally committed."

They toured relentlessly, like "gypsies possessed", as Tyler put it. They got tighter. Their songs got better. Along the way they won fans while putting the fear into – and often upstaging – headliners such as Mott The Hoople, Kiss, Black Sabbath and Slade. "We were very competitive," bassist Tom Hamilton says today. "There's a lot of bands I like and respect now, but back then all I did was think of them as the people we wanted to blow off the stage." Before Aerosmith's second album, when producer Bob Ezrin famously pronounced them "not ready", the band doubled down with even more we'll-show-'em bravado. *Get Your Wings*, produced by Jack Douglas and powered by FM rock tracks *Same Old Song And Dance* and *Train Kept A-Rollin'*, scored well enough to get them back in favour with Columbia. Expectations were high for the third record.

Forty years on, that third, *Toys In The Attic*, stands out as a milestone, the album that lifted the group from scrappy openers to headlining superstars. With more than eight million copies sold, and classic rock hits *Walk This Way* and *Sweet Emotion* still sounding amazingly vital, Toys is the perfect distillation of Aerosmith's edgy guitar riffage, lewd humour and high-energy strut, and one of the first albums to proudly hoist the American flag in the rock pantheon alongside those by their Brit heroes The Who, the Stones and Led Zeppelin. "*Toys* has some of the most important songs we ever wrote," says Perry. "It set the precedent for how the band worked over the years to come, reshaped our sound and gave us a huge amount of confidence."

The confidence that had been building on the road carried over into the studio. "We were playing bigger venues before bigger crowds," says Perry. "Detroit, Cincinnati, Cleveland. We felt like if we could win the heart of America, the rest of the country would follow. And through constant touring we learned what kinds of songs and grooves went over best. As a songwriter you start thinking in terms of: 'If I was sitting in the audience, what would I want to hear?' That gave new focus to the songs that ended up on *Toys*."

For *Toys* read double-entendres. At times, Aerosmith's third album sounds like the Rolling Stones jamming with the New York Dolls as scripted by Benny Hill, with Tyler delivering *Uncle Salty* and the truly filthy *Big Ten Inch Record* with a knowing wink. Fun as those tracks are, though, the real gems on *Toys In The Attic* are the marimba-bolstered

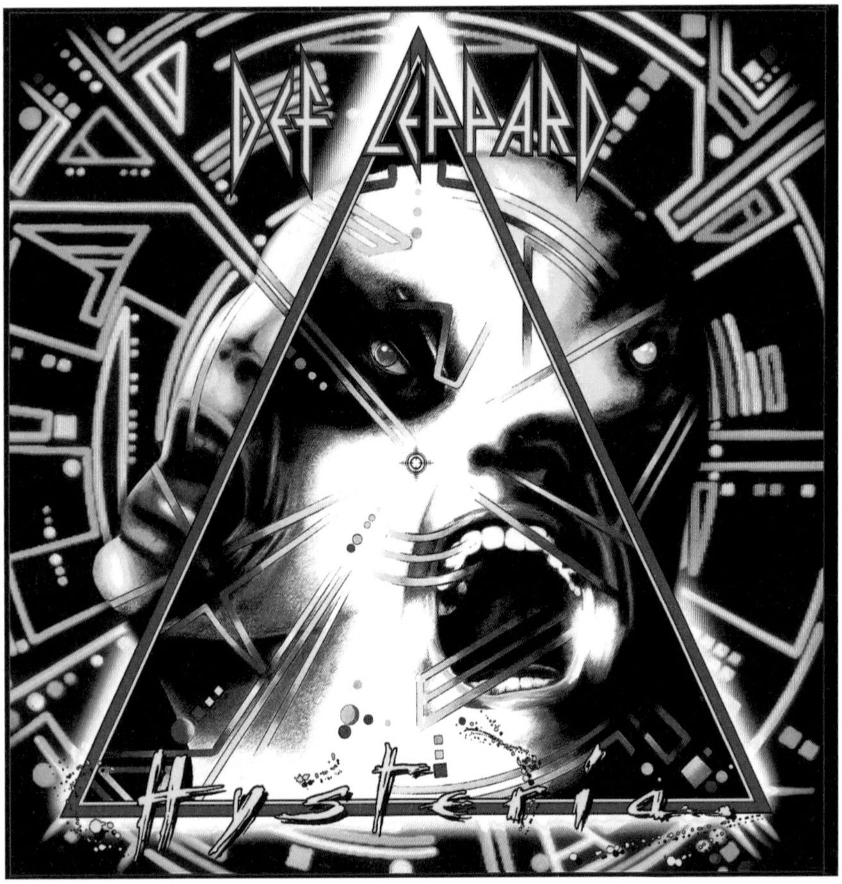


year released
1987
label
producer
Mutt Lange

Def Leppard were under no illusions about what they wanted to do: they wanted to become the biggest band in the world, and were prepared to do whatever it took to achieve their ambition.

Perhaps if they'd known exactly how much 'whatever it took' would turn out to be, they'd have knocked it on the head and got a job at B&Q. But it's a good thing they didn't, because the album that resulted from their very real battle against extinction turned out to be one of the classic British rock albums.

By February 1984 Def Leppard were already a big deal – well, in the USA anyway. The band that started out in a spoon factory in Sheffield had a respectable count of massive US gigs and six million sales of 1983's *Pyromania* to their name when they settled into a shared house in Dublin to start the grand cycle all over again.

To say they were worried would be an understatement. The pressures of success come from all directions – fans, management, your label, all need whatever you do next to be better than what you did last. But no one can tell

year released
**1975**

producer
**Jack Douglas**

*Sweet Emotion*, the pre-Run- DMC version of *Walk This Way* (Perry is reported to have written the music for the song in just five minutes), and the orchestrated ballad *You See Me Crying*.

*Toys In The Attic* was released on April 8, 1975. In the year of *Physical Graffiti*, Elton John's *Captain Fantastic* and Bowie's *Young Americans* it held its ground as a major contender. Three weeks after finishing up the album, the band were already into another run of touring - this time as headliners - that would take them through the end of the year. Fittingly, they ended in New York. Your correspondent, then at the tender age of 11, was at their triumphant Madison Square Garden show.

"*Toys In The Attic* was where I knew we'd made it," said Tyler. "[With that title] I was the kid who put my initials in the rock 'cos I wanted the aliens to know I was there. It's a statement of longevity; the record will be played long after you're dead. Our records would be up there in the attic, too, with the things that you loved and never wanted to forget."

# 40 *Def Leppard* Hysteria

you how to achieve that. Waking up after another drunken night in the city, drummer Rick Allen observed: "This is hysteria!" And, boom, they were off...

"We were scared," singer Joe Elliott recounts. "We had absolutely nothing in the way of ideas. We'd learned we couldn't write on the road; you were doing all these shows and interviews and appearances. If you managed to get an idea down, you were proud of the achievement rather than asking yourself whether it was a good idea. Besides, we'd enjoyed Pyromania so much, and we'd been living with that for nearly two years. We had nothing to go on."

If you're a band like Def Leppard, you already have a lot of the machinery in place. You know about constructing a song, you know about presenting drama and contrast, you know how to pitch the lyrics to give your audience the entertainment they're looking for. But, again, the caveat this time is that it's got to be double-perfect, bang on the button.

Fortunately, they had Robert John 'Mutt' Lange on board, the producer who had got so much out of them in their two previous studio epics, *High'n'Dry* and *Pyromania*. In classic 'sixth member' mode, Lange had already become part of the organisation and was happy to work on co-writing. "A lot of bands don't let the producer in," he commented. "Def Leppard let me right in."

*Animal* was the first single (*Women* in the US), and it gave the band their first UK hit - an extremely positive sign. Over the following months another five tracks were released as singles as the band headed out on tour, performing in the famous 'in the round' format (which required them to be taken from the dressing room to the stage, through the audience, in laundry carts).

Where fate had been throwing punches at Def Leppard it was now smiling on them. Sales of the album faltered, then stalled at around five million (which for just about any other band would have been a success). But then strip club dancers started using *Pour Some Sugar On Me* as their backing track, and word of mouth led to rotation play on radio stations across the United States. Suddenly the album was shifting tens of thousands a day. In the end it sold 16 million copies.

If any one track summarises the Def Leppard philosophy, it must be *Pour Some Sugar...* It's simple, it's anthemic, it acknowledges inspiration from a range of sources, and the lyrics are tongue-in-cheek, entertaining and upbeat. It's in the spirit of *I Love Rock'n'Roll* but is much more than that, with the careful blend of guitars, layered vocals, strong melody and shouty bits.

Elliott summed up both the secret to creating a classic album and the result of achieving one when he said: "We crossed over without selling out. We set out to be the biggest band in the world. And for a short while we were."

# 39 *The Doors*
# L.A. Woman

It's difficult to identify precisely what The Doors had that has seen their music and mystique seduce every new generation of music fans, but whatever it is, the blues-rooted *L.A. Woman* has it in spades. In turns driving, grooving, brooding, romantic and belligerent, it contains some of The Doors' best work: *The WASP (Texas Radio And The Big Beat), L.A. Woman, Riders On The Storm*...

November 1970. Sunset Sound, 6650 Sunset Boulevard. Jim Morrison, Robby Krieger, Ray Manzarek, John Densmore, engineer Bruce Botnick and producer Paul A. Rothchild are staggering through rehearsals for The Doors' sixth studio recording and the mood is deadly.

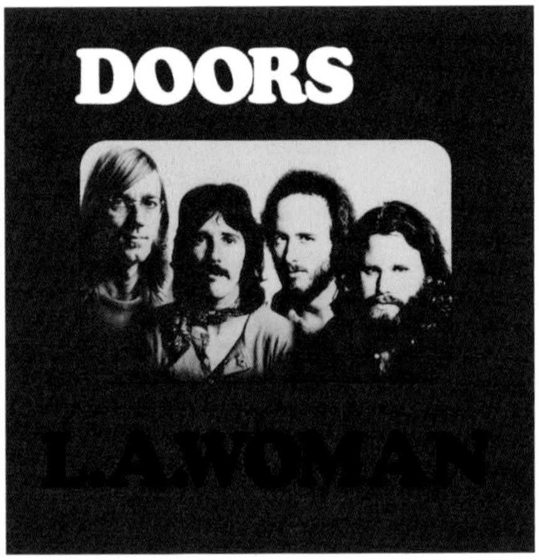


The band have busked through a meagre collection of material, including the germ of *L.A. Woman*, basic chords for *Riders On The Storm*, some blues jams and a couple of discards, namely the demo for *Hyacinth House*, and one track they've already finished. Tentatively called *Latin America*, it's been offered up for Michelangelo Antonioni's film *Zabriskie Point*. The director rejected the song after The Doors played it live for him.

"We played it so loud we blew his ears out," says Doors drummer John Densmore.

Equally unimpressed, Rothchild slumps over the console.

"You know what? I can't do this anymore. This isn't working. This music is like cocktail jazz. It's awful. You produce it. I can't".

Bombshell dropped, Rothchild sweeps up his belongings, gives everyone a brief hug, and exits to stunned silence.

Ray Manzarek recalled the day. "We were giving Paul a preview and he was bored. We played the songs very badly – with Jim – but there was no chi, no energy. We didn't want to be back in Sunset, and Paul couldn't bring us back to life. In that instant he was right. As soon as he left the room, that's when *L.A. Woman* started."

After Rothchild's departure The Doors went to a restaurant and considered their options. Sunset was out; likewise a return to Elektra's own studio. Krieger offered to produce but Morrison had a plan. "Why don't we just do it in our rehearsal room, in The Doors office? We like it there. Bruce – you produce it with the guys. You know how I work," he smiled. Once Elektra boss Jac Holzman agreed to the idea, Botnick transformed The Doors Workshop at 8512 Santa Monica Boulevard on the corner of La Cienega into a makeshift studio.

The squat two-storey building was near a variety of cheap motels, strip joints, liquor stores and burlesque bars – Morrison's kinda town. Botnick hauled the old eight-track board The Doors used on *Strange Days* across the street from Elektra and set up his brand new console on the first floor with an intercom microphone over his head to communicate with the band, out of sight downstairs.

Densmore didn't mind. "I used the same drum kit I had on the first record," he says. "I told Ray, I wanted to get the feeling Miles Davis had on *Live At Carnegie Hall*, where you could make a mistake, but you went for passion."

Jim Morrison was fairly straight during the early days of recording, at least by his extraordinary standards.

By the end of November, five of *L.A. Woman*'s 10 songs were near completion. The opening song *The Changeling* was plucked from one of Morrison's 1968 notebooks. A classic rocker à la *Roadhouse Blues, The Changeling* contained the mantra '*I had money, I had none*', summing up Morrison's attitude to life. An obvious single, said the band. Robby arrived with *Love Her Madly*, one of his 'girl's-driving-me-nuts' numbers. At Jac Holzman's insistence, it became the album's lead-off single, released a week before Morrison departed for Paris on March 1971. Krieger pleaded for *Riders On The Storm* but was overruled.

*Hyacinth House* was a Doors collaboration, whipped into shape by Manzarek, although Morrison and Krieger came up with the basic track while tripping at Robby's idyllic beachfront house in 1969. *Latin America* was renamed *L'America*. The original track was left intact, though Morrison overdubbed a guttural single word '*fuck*' and Botnick phased Densmore's drum break. Lyrically it was a slight piece concerning a short holiday Jim took in Mexico with his drinking crew. The song poem *The WASP (Texas Radio And The Big Beat)* with its marching band rhythm and phased drum break was another adaptation from 1968 and had often been played live before recording took place.

The Doors used a bass on every track, except *L'America*. Botnick hired the seasoned Jerry Scheff, who had just finished a stint with Elvis Presley in Las Vegas. Morrison, a Presley fanatic, was delighted. So was drummer Densmore.

"*L.A. Woman* was recorded in a state of high excitement," remembered Manzarek. "We dug our teeth into that song. It was all about passion and hauling ass. It felt like we were on Route 101, on the road from Bakersfield to San Francisco. You can hear our enthusiasm. Welcome to Los Angeles!"

The album that bore the song's name was released in April 1971, and it hit the Top 10 a few weeks later. It was a total triumph, but tragically, it would also prove to be Jim Morrison's last with the band.

year released
**1971**

producer
**Bruce Botnik**
**The Doors**

# 38 *Dio*
# Holy Diver

Best known as the Rainbow singer who left the band before they cracked the charts, and the man who replaced Ozzy in Sabbath, rock singer par excellence Ronnie James Dio kicked off his solo career in style with the third classic album he'd sung on. One of the brilliant heavy metal debuts, Holy Diver is a work of bravura and bombast.

This was a new beginning for Ronnie, but his past was in evidence both in his choice of two former bandmates (ex-Rainbow bassist Jimmy Bain and ex-Sabbath drummer Vinny Appice) and in the epic feel of the music. His masterstroke was the acquisition of 19-year-old guitarist Vivian Campbell, the man who "put the fast in Belfast", who gave the band a vital, contemporary edge.

Vivian Campbell was asleep when he got the call about joining Dio. It was the middle of the night, and his father had woken him to say there was a drunken Scotsman on the phone. It was Bain, calling from a hotel room, with Dio and Appice in the background, asking him if he wanted to audition for "this wee band" in London the next day.

For Campbell, Bain's offer was a no-brainer. His father sprang for the plane ticket and he flew to London the next day with just his guitar in hand.

With Campbell on board, things moved fast. Within weeks the four of them were in LA, working at Sound City Studios in Van Nuys, a courtyard with a rehearsal room on one side and a recording studio on the other. Although Dio already had two songs written – *Holy Diver* and *Don't Talk To Strangers* – the other tracks were all written at these sessions.

They'd rehearse in one room, then wheel the equipment across the parking lot to the studio to record. The material was a Frankenstein concoction of parts from older songs that Bain and Campbell brought to the table, the two tracks Dio and Appice had jammed on prior to going to London, and some artfully "thrown together" numbers recorded at the last minute.

The title track, credited solely to Ronnie, may have been a 'steal', albeit an subconscious one. While his lyrics – about riding tigers and being *'down too long in the midnight sea'*, which were either a reference to Lucifer's fall in the Book Of Revelations or entertaining mumbo jumbo, depending on your viewpoint – were entirely his own, its anthemic beat was reminiscent of Survivor's *Eye Of The Tiger*, a huge hit at the time Ronnie and Vinny were jamming in the singer's backyard. Even so, Bain insists that it was more of a collaboration that the credit suggests.

Certainly the album's other centrepiece, *Rainbow In The Dark*, was a collaborative effort. The riff taken from a Sweet Savage song called *Lady Marianne*.

"We played it for Ronnie and he immediately started singing the melody on top of it," says Campbell. "And then Jimmy went over to this little Yamaha and came up with the keyboard motif. We had the fucking song written in 10 minutes."

year released
**1972**

producer
**Jimmy Miller**

Given a critical kicking at the time, this double album has come to be widely regarded as one of the Stones' definitive records, even though (or perhaps because) it contains relatively few Stones favourites. At times dark, shadowy and bleak, at others it's relentlessly upbeat and rockin' – only repeated listening reveals all of its treasures.

The first reviews were cautious at best. "*Exile* isn't as immediately gripping as the Stones' last album, *Sticky Fingers*," said *Sounds* in May 1972. But, over time, this brilliant, far-reaching double album has been acclaimed as one of the greatest rock'n'roll records of them all.

*Exile On Main St.* is the loosest, funkiest and most soulful album the Stones ever made. And, reflecting Keith Richards's immersion into heroin addiction, the whole album has a gloriously decadent air, illustrated by the lazy roll of *Tumbling Dice*, which was a hit single.

"It was called *Exile* because we were basically booted out of England," Richards told *Classic Rock*. "It was either that or sweep the streets."

It might sound dramatic, but the Rolling Stones were in

year released
*1983*

producer
**Ronnie James Dio**

On the face of it, they worked well together. For the crunching *Straight Through The Heart*, Bain, Campbell and Appice knocked around one of the riffs the bassist had brought with him from Wild Horses, before Dio came in with the melody. The sound of the thundering *Invisible* was altogether more accidental. "We had one of the riffs," recalls Appice. "Then the next night we came in, we smoked a whole bunch of pot and our soundman put the tape in backwards. It started playing, and we all sat there laughing, going: 'You asshole!' But then we started saying: 'Wait a minute, that sounds good!' So we wound up learning the riff backwards. And that's the other part of *Invisible*. It's the riff forwards and the riffs backwards."

But it wasn't an entirely stress-free environment. "There was always a bit more tension in the room when Ronnie came to rehearsal," says Campbell of the friction between the band members.

Despite such issues, *Holy Diver* is a ready-made classic: a modern metal album that also harked back to Zeppelin, Lizzy and, of course, Rainbow.

# 37 *The Rolling Stones* Exile On Main St.

dire financial straits at the dawn of the 1970s. They owed a fortune to the Inland Revenue and, with top rate taxation under the Labour government running at 93 per cent, were unable to clear enough earnings to pay their back taxes. Keith took this high rate of tax personally. It seemed like yet another way for the establishment to persecute the Stones.

"So the feeling within the band was we've got to show them we're made of sterner stuff and prove you couldn't break the Stones just by kicking them out of England," recalls Keith. "We all looked at each other and said, 'Okay, we'll do it on the lam'."

So the band and their families reluctantly decamped for the South of France. "Well, if it's going to be France, it's got to be the Riviera, pal." Somerset Maugham liked to call it 'a sunny place for shady people' – it just seemed to fit. Keith moved into Villa Nellcôte, Villefranche-sur-mer.

During the war Nellcôte had served as the Gestapo headquarters (there were still swastikas embossed onto the air vents) and as no other suitable recording space could be found in the area, the band chose to record in its basement using the mobile recording studio that they'd previously rented out to the BBC to record sporting events.

"Finally this truck came in handy: a great control room on wheels, but there was a lot of slap-dash improvising because we'd never recorded outside of a studio before and this basement was... well, I can smell it now: every time I look at that cover, I can pick up a certain damp, oily, dusty flavour."

Nellcôte's basement was split into various compartments and the mobile truck was parked outside. Communication between the players, producer Jimmy Miller and engineer Andy Johns was therefore, at best, haphazard. But as the summer of '71 unfolded, the Rolling Stones' extended sessions, sometimes all-day, sometimes all-night, gradually bore fruit.

"A lot of the songs started off with an idea. Mick [Jagger]'s playing harp, you join in and before you knew it you had a track in the making and an idea working. It might not be the finished track; you're not trying to force it. As my father used to say: 'Keith, there's a difference between scratching your ass and tearing it to bits'."

Mick meanwhile was often absent from the sessions, attending to his pregnant wife Bianca who he'd married a month previously. Part of the magic of *Exile On Main St.* stemmed from the working relationship that had developed between Keith and fellow guitarist Mick Taylor.

"Brian [Jones] and I would swap roles. There was no defined line between lead and rhythm guitar, but with Mick's style I had to readjust the shape of the band and it was beautifully lyrical. He was a lovely lead player. I loved playing with Mick Taylor."

The guitarists' synergy paid off. *Exile...* is the Stones at their elegantly wasted peak.

# 36 *Nirvana*
# Nevermind

N*evermind* isn't just a huge-selling record; there have been far bigger. It's not even just an iconic set of songs. With the 12 songs on the album, Nirvana defined a generation, and in doing so came as close as anyone could possibly expect in the 90s to revolutionising the concept of rock'n'roll. Moreover, it seemingly came out of nowhere. What the Seattle trio (vocalist/guitarist Kurt Cobain, bassist Krist Novoselic and new drummer Dave Grohl in the place of Chad Channing) had done before - punk attitude combined with garage insouciance - had been impressive. But with *Nevermind* they really raised their game.

What has made *Nevermind* arguably the most important release of that decade is the songs. They were uncompromising. Kurt Cobain was writing about his moment, but also about all our moments. His 'secret' was in talking directly to himself. As with Axl Rose on Guns N' Roses' *Appetite For Destruction* four years earlier, Cobain didn't so much reach out to the disenfranchised masses as draw them into his world. Here were his agonies, his doubts, his frustrations, his rages - but opened up for everyone to see.

*Smells Like Teen Spiri*t is not just an anthem for Generation X, it's also an expression of self-disgust and uncertainty. This song defined a generation over twenty-five years ago and it's still damn near perfect. You can deny your love for *Nevermind*'s opener all you like, but when *Smells Like Teen Spirit* kicks in and you haven't heard it in a while... you will get shivers down your spine. Guaranteed.

Novoselic once said that *In Bloom* "originally sounded like Bad Brains, then Kurt turned it into a pop song." There's no reason why it couldn't sound like Bad Brains, but the fact Cobain refuted any notion of hardcore and embraced those wonderful vocal harmonies with Grohl is a titanic statement.

*Come As You* Are is Cobain's Beatles moment. It's that good. This song transcends Nirvana (and Killing Joke, whose song *Eighties* heavily inspired the main riff), clawing its way through the confines of rock music and essentially creating its own pocket of pop music. The chorus pedal achieves an aquatic guitar effect, doing nothing to stifle the track's appeal: a testament to Nirvana's warping of the weird to well-accessible at will. It's laid-back but Grohl's drumming suggests otherwise. It's everything you'd want from Nirvana post-*Bleach*. *Come As You Are* is *Nevermind*'s victory lap and arguably the ultimate Nirvana song.

*Nevermind* isn't all buzzsaw guitars welded to outstanding melodies, though. *Something In The Way* was originally recorded by Cobain on his battered acoustic guitar, with Grohl and Novoselic recording their parts later. The simple, heartfelt chorus is a shining example of Cobain's knowledge of the pop hook, while a haunting cello gives the track a mournful feel. The improvisational hidden track whacked onto the end, *Endless Nameless*, is a far cry from the rest of Nevermind, and opts for a noisy Melvins-esque attack on the senses. Which is fine by us.

year released
**1991**
label
producer
**Rick Parashar**

Although Pearl Jam eventually rejected the mainstream, the band's best album is also their most commercial: their magnificent debut, *Ten*. Instead of wallowing in misery following the demise of their band Mother Love Bone after the death of its singer, guitarist Stone Gossard and bassist Jeff Ament put together a much more back-to-basics band. In came Eddie Vedder on vocals, Mike McCready on guitar, Pearl Jam were born.

Disaffected youth was spoilt for choice in 1991. On Side A of the C90 tape in your oversized Walkman, the buzzsaw guitars and teen dispirit of Nirvana's *Nevermind*; on Side B, *Ten*, the debut album by Seattle rivals Pearl Jam, with plenty to soundtrack the imagined woes of the teenage existence. Geography and timing ensured that both albums were lumped together as blueprints of the nascent grunge movement, but really the only common currency was the chuckle-free world-views of Kurt Cobain and Eddie Vedder (as the Nirvana frontman sneered at the time, *Ten*'s squall of guitar solos, arena-ready hooks and overt classic influences were

year released
**1991**

producer
**Butch Vig**

*Polly*, the 'other' acoustic one, is downright chilling. As murky as *Something In The Way* may be, this Cobain track presents the story of the irredeemable Gerald Friend, a man who abducted, raped and tortured a 14-year-old girl. Despite its grim subject matter (which is handled excellently by Cobain, providing a perfect lack of empathy) it's a classic, and the best defence to anyone claiming Nirvana relied solely on the quiet/loud dynamic; there's a simple bassline and Chad Channing, in his sole drumming performance on the record, ever-so-rarely brushing his ride cymbal. And that's it. No frills. *Polly* is beautifully crushing.

Overall *Nevermind* is a remarkably dark record, the music stripped down, stark and gloomy – the antithesis of what one would expect from a mainstream mega-success story. Crucially, if you listen carefully you can hear the stirrings of all those demons that would cost Cobain his life three years later. More than anything else, *Nevermind* is Kurt's expression of will and unwillingness, his attempts to understand the world, while also coming to terms with the fact that he would never fully belong in it.

# 35 *Pearl Jam*
# Ten

hardly 'alt').

To listen to *Ten* in one sitting is an almost gluttonous pleasure, like eating too many chocolate liqueurs. It plays like a Greatest Hits and still sounds sufficiently huge. *Once* was always underrated, crashing in after the false start of the *Master/Slave* instrumental, but the opener is one of the album's strongest tracks, built on a seething vocal and a snake-charmer riff. Vedder in character as a vengeful maniac with pedal to the floor and '*sixteen-gauge buried under my clothes*'. A song to make your neck bristle and your fists bunch, it announced Pearl Jam as a band to treasure, right out of the blocks.

Pearl Jam themselves seem to have a problem with *Even Flow*, generally agreeing that they flogged the spark out the original demo with too many takes ("Not sure why we didn't use that one," said original drummer Dave Krusen, "but I know it felt better"). For everyone else, the version that made it onto *Ten* was a belter, driven by that muscular-yet-snake-hipped riff, and managing to sing about homelessness without getting up your nose.

And, yes, while *Alive*'s riff may now be held as practically the altrock Layla, it's still a stone-cold classic, from Gossard's stadium-ready intro lick to Mike McCready's spring-heeled solo (which he admits, incidentally, that he stole from Kiss's *She*).

When Texas teenager Jeremy Wade Delle shot himself in front of his classmates on January 8th, 1991, the seed was planted for what remains arguably Vedder's most powerful lyric. The blood-spattered MTV video was sensationalist, but the song is deathless, from Ament's opening chimed harmonics to the bereft outro. Strange to think that *Jeremy* almost didn't make the cut for *Ten,* the band struggling to balance the dynamics. "But this was an instance," remembered Ament, "when persistence paid off."

Those tracks are in good company, too: the honey-glazed verse of *Black* makes the bitter chorus land an even harder punch. Epic apparently badgered the band to release *Black* as the fourth single from *Ten*, but the line-up dug in their heels, helping the song to its enduring fan-favourite status. It's a bit of an odd one, *Black,* alternating between rock's most jaunty verse and most gut-wrenching chorus, but when Vedder delivers the devastating pay-off – '*I know you'll be a star in somebody else's sky, but why can't it be mine?*' – you'll feel a cold shiver of recognition. Stunning.

But the best moments are the ones you've forgotten about: the ghostly chimes of, say, *Garden*, or the resigned beauty of *Release*, while *Oceans* remains undimmed in its woozy brilliance. The latter is a work of strange, glowering beauty, and gave *Ten*'s first indication that Pearl Jam could shift gears. They all lend a flavour to this spellbinding album, and confirm that Pearl Jam were too colourful to be painted with the plaid brush.

# 34 *Ozzy Osbourne*
# Blizzard Of Ozz

Widely regarded as a busted flush after his sacking from Black Sabbath, Sharon brought Ozzy to his senses and somehow coaxed this excellent album out of him – with a little help from the late guitar genius Randy Rhoads, bassist Bob Daisley and drummer Lee Kerslake along the way. Tracks such as *Crazy Train*, *Suicide Solution* and the endearingly ridiculous *Mr Crowley* established Ozzy as an artist in his own right.

Rewind to 1979 and Ozzy Osbourne has fallen on hard times. Bullied out of Black Sabbath and holed up at Le Parc hotel in West Hollywood, he lurks amid the debris of excess: a hopeless, friendless, caged animal, seemingly resigned to his fate as rock's ultimate cautionary tale. "I really did think: 'This is the fucking end for me,'" he admitted to *Classic Rock*, three decades later. "I'd been booted out. I just got fucked up every day for three fucking months. Never went outside. Never even opened the drapes."

Into this scene of squalor and self-pity, enter Sharon Arden, with an industrial-strength dose of tough love. Though only in her late 20s, she was nonetheless a shit-kicking rock'n'roll authoritarian schooled at the knee of the formidable Don Arden (her dad), and the only person capable of mobilising the wallowing singer. "One morning, Sharon just came round and told me: 'Get your shit together. I'll manage you'. Ozzy recalls, with obvious admiration. "Once she was in the picture, things got rolling, y'know? Sharon absolutely deserves credit for getting that album out of me."

Auditions for musicians to work with Ozzy on his first album outside of Sabbath began with a notice on the board of Mates rehearsal space in LA. Months passed, until the arrival of Californian guitarist Randy Rhoads gave Ozzy his epiphany – "like God entering my life" was how he described it – and the pair left the US for initial writing sessions at Ozzy's family home in Stafford, West Midlands.

"Randy was one of these guys who, when we had a weekend off, he'd get in the truck with one of the roadies and just go off around England having guitar lessons," the singer recalls of their odd-couple dynamic. "He probably saw more of England than I ever have."

Rhoads and Ozzy were a natural fit. "In Sabbath, they'd just write something and say: 'Put a vocal on that'," Ozzy recalls. "I could get the range in the studio, but with a song like *Sabbath Bloody Sabbath*, I could never get it on stage. Randy was the first guy in my whole career to make it comfortable for me. When I had the melody in my head for *Goodbye To Romance* – the ballady, Beatley one – I sang it to him, and he says: 'Let's do it in this key.' He was very good at helping me out."

Despite Ozzy's residual 'satanic' caricature from the Sabbath years, there was light and shade in the *Blizzard Of Ozz* material recorded at Ridge Farm Studios in March and April 1980. "I like to go in the studio and make an album," he said. "For me, if it's just fucking headbanging from start to finish, that's not an album, it's just a fucking racket. I'm from the old school. In Black Sabbath we'd do jazz and all kinds of styles, it wasn't just fucking *Iron Man* every song. Anything that makes the album better. So when Randy says to me: 'Do you mind if I put this classical instrumental piece [*Dee*] on?', I said: 'What are you fucking asking me for? It's your album as well'. Just go for it, y'know?"

Lyrically, too, the subject matter was eclectic, with Ozzy taking in occult hero Aleister Crowley, pay-per-view hotel porn ("Randy used to call them 'bone movies'"), and the controversial *Suicide Solution*, later to spark a lawsuit from the parents of a Californian teenager who shot himself while listening to it. "But if you'd listened to the lyric, it's not about suicide as a 'solution'," Ozzy counters. "It's about liquid. It was about Bon Scott, to be honest with you – about drinking yourself to death."

Perhaps it was a little rich of Ozzy to judge anyone else's drinking habits. Although Sharon had made him functional, it's a mistake to cast *Blizzard...* as the 'sober album'. "Any band situation I've been in," Ozzy reflects, "the first album is always the most fun, because you've got everything to gain and nothing to lose. Recording *Blizzard Of Ozz*, there was a wonderful atmosphere: Sharon would come down, we'd all go down the pub, get pissed, come back, have some fun... loads of booze and drugs. It's when fucking business starts to get involved that it starts to get shitty. I don't understand the business side of it, still. My wife is the manager."

But even to an industry novice, it was clear that business was good. Released in September 1980, *Blizzard Of Ozz* swaggered into the UK album chart at No.7 and went platinum during a two-year run in the US chart. Just a year after facing the knacker's yard, Ozzy Osbourne was back at the head of the metal pack. *Blizzard Of Ozz* is a victory snatched from the jaws of defeat. And it sounds like it, with Ozzy performing with a backs-to-the- wall fire that he's never quite matched since.

year released
***1980***

producer
**Ozzy Osbourne**
**Randy Rhoads**
**Lee Kerslake**
**Bob Daisley**

# 33 *Rush*
# Moving Pictures

Released in 1981, *Moving Pictures* was a Top 5 hit in the UK and the US and has gone platinum four times over in their native Canada. But it's a line-in-the-sand Rush album. An oddball mix of heavy riffs, new wave shapes and 80s technology, it closed the door on the satin kimonos and sci-fi epics that defined Rush in 70s, and embraced a brave new world. In the 70s they had become the undisputed masters of progressive hard rock, famed for their epic conceptual pieces that played out over entire sides of vinyl. But with their first album of the 1980s - *Permanent Waves* - came a significant change.

"We began writing in a tighter, more economical form," says Lifeson. The result was that hit single, *The Spirit Of Radio*: a virtuoso-rock tour de force compacted into less than five minutes. And the song's lyrics fit neatly with this more direct approach. Bookish drummer Neil Peart, the author of all Rush lyrics since 1975, had previously found inspiration in ancient mythology and science fiction, but for *Permanent Waves* his writing was simpler, his subject matter more worldly.

Opener *Tom Sawyer* was the crystallisation of this new, modern Rush: a powerful, finely crafted hard rock song with a punchy yet deeply philosophical message. "*Tom Sawyer* is a real trademark song for us," says Rush guitarist Alex Lifeson. "Musically it's very powerful, and lyrically it has a spirit that resonates with a lot of people. It's kind of an anthem.

"On *Tom Sawyer*, the synthesiser is such a key part of that song," says Lifeson. "There was a good integration between the three of us and the keyboards. We still had that trio feel. Plus, we always felt that we had to replicate each song as faithfully as possible when we played it live, so *Tom Sawyer* was written in that way. There's no rhythm guitar under the guitar solo or anything like that."

It's a song that proved pivotal to the band's development. Geddy Lee has called it the "defining piece of music" from Rush in the early 80s. For much of that decade, keyboards took an increasingly important role in the band's sound. More than three decades on, the power of this song, and its message, has not diminished. "There's something in the lyric that people have always related to very strongly," Lifeson says proudly. "The spirit of independence and adventure. It's just one of those special songs.

"*Moving Pictures* was different for us in that it was more of a jam sort of thing," says Lifeson. "A lot of the material for that record was written off the floor. That was certainly the case with *Tom Sawyer*. We were rehearsing in a little farm outside of Toronto. We would typically just go in and jam and develop songs that way."

*Red Barchetta* highlights Neil Peart's abilities as a story teller, which, as the 80s dawned, were taking on a more nuanced style. Where it once took them the whole side of an album (see Rush's other entry at #19, *2112*) to tell the story of a future society where music is

year released
**1976**
label
producer
**Bill Szymczyk**

Hotel California was released on December 8, 1976, two weeks after the Sex Pistols' *Anarchy In The UK*. You couldn't get two records more diametrically opposed. Or could you? At the time, punk seemed designed to blow the likes of Eagles and their mellow country-rock vibes clean out the water. But closer inspection of their fifth studio album - the era's leading blockbuster MOR behemoth, along with Fleetwood Mac's *Rumours* - revealed a band disillusioned by political and social developments, moved to offer a critique of commercialism and excess.

You want punk? These five "middle-class kids from the Midwest" (Don Henley) came not to pursue the west coast myth but to bury it. It might have been the epitome of carefree freeway rock, but *Hotel California* was a dark affair, and certainly melancholy for a mega-seller (to date, 32 million sales and counting). If *Rumours* detailed the breakdown of relations within the Mac, *Hotel California* dissected the demise of the hippie dream, dismantling the notion of LA as some sun-kissed Utopia.

year released
**1981**

producer
**Rush & Terry Brown**

outlawed, they'd now got it down to 6:10 minutes. All you need to know about *Red Barchetta* is that it's set in a future where motor cars are banned, but where one young rebel borrows his uncle's *'old machine'* and gets chased by a bloke in a *'gleaming alloy air car... two lanes wide'*.

But while Rush were dipping toes in reggae and pop, they were still writing tracks like *YYZ*: a preposterous instrumental whose opening segment sounds like it was nicked off one of those punishing 70s King Crimson albums nobody actually listens to all the way through. Like *La Villa Strangiato*, *YYZ* was built to sate the appetite of bedroom air guitarists/bassists/drummers. And for all its tricksky fills, there's that moment of sublime, tuneful beauty at 2:53, when the synth kicks on.

*Limelight* is one of Rush's most memorable songs and most popular on the radio. As every Rush fan worth their salt knows, the song deals with Peart's increasing feelings of isolation as the band's stature grew, encompassed in such emphatic lines like *'one must put up barriers to keep oneself intact'* and *'I can't pretend a stranger is a long-awaited friend'*. The solo remains Alex Lifeson's favourite to perform live.

# 32 *Eagles* Hotel California

That it sold in such vast quantities says a lot about 1976 listeners' desire for a dose of realism from their rock'n'roll, even if the large majority would rather the delivery system be mellifluous acoustic-electric soft rock than raucous punk.

Not that *Hotel California* is just some breezy pop. Take the title track: country reggae, anyone? Has there ever been such an unlikely collision of opposites in a single song? Then again, have there ever been two lines – *'On a dark desert highway, cool wind in my hair'* – so evocative of a place and milieu? This is the dark side of the California dream writ large.

*Hotel California* was to mainstream US radio what *Bohemian Rhapsody* was to the UK variety – the ostensibly overlong number that broke the mould and forced programmers to indulge the artists' creative whims despite the restrictive (three-minute) format. Oh, and the guitar solo's not bad.

Often voted the best guitar solo of all time – duking it out with *Stairway To Heaven* for the top spot, usually – it's mostly Don Felder's work. Felder recorded a demo of the song a full year before the band recorded the album. When he turned up for recording sessions, he began playing a different solo, only for drummer Don Henley to call a halt to proceedings and insist he play exactly the same thing he had done on the demo. Felder: "Don Henley went, 'Stop, that's not right.' And I said, 'What do you mean it's not right? We're just gonna make these solos up.' He said, 'No no no, you have to play them exactly like what's on your demo.'" Felder had to find the demo and then "sit in the studio and re-learn what I'd already played a year before that."

The original running order of the album was designed to tell the story mapped out by the overarching LP concept: you're ushered into the *Hotel California* as the *New Kid In Town*, at which point you start enjoying *Life In The Fast Lane* and a bunch of *Wasted Time* before becoming a *Victim Of Love*, and so forth. *Life In The Fast Lane*'s boogie lite attacked bourgeois decadence with a smiling venom worthy of Johnny Rotten himself, although the fact that Eagles were mired in moral decay themselves somewhat undercut the potency of the message. Still, you'd forgive anything for *that* guitar riff.

Other highlights include sombre ballad *Pretty Maids All In A Row*, lighter-waving album closer *The Last Resort* and ballad *Wasted Time*.

Forget country: you could pen a credible thesis about Eagles being a great soul band, and *Wasted Time* – like *One Of These Nights* before it and *I Can't Tell You Why* after – is a superb R&B ballad just made for Don Henley's honeyed, husky tones. It's one of the many ironies about Eagles, the middle-class heroes of blue-collar good ol' boys, that these scions of summer good-times music were able to so adroitly capture the exquisitely sad onset of autumn. Producer Bill Szymczyk keeps things the right side of schmaltzy as Henley evokes end-of-an-era innocence like there's no tomorrow.

Which, according to this album, there won't be.

# 31 *Boston*
# Boston

Released in August 1976, the debut Boston album sent shockwaves through the music industry. It was a true Cinderella story – a band appearing out of nowhere, turning the world upside down and injecting fresh hope into a scene that was fast dying on its feet. To achieve this 'overnight' success, Boston leader Tom Scholz spent roughly six years ignoring his detractors, hidden in a basement tweaking songs, overdubbing and refining parts until the tapes literally began to disintegrate. Some laughed. Some were worried for his sanity. Most felt that he needed to get out a bit more rather than hang on to a crazy dream that was slowly slipping away. Then, one day, things changed. *Boston* made them the biggest new rock band of the 1970s, an American phenomenon, who dominated FM radio by crafting one of the biggest-selling debut albums of all time. Sales to date are in excess of 17 million and still going strong.

Born 1947 in Toledo, Ohio, Donald Thomas Scholz worked hard to get an education, one that would take him to the prestigious Massachusetts Institute Of Technology (MIT). After graduating, by day Scholz worked as a product design engineer for the Polaroid Corporation. By night, he played in a handful of local Boston bands, and dreamed about a career in music. And he made those dreams come true.

Sensing a schism between playing live and recording songs, Scholz decided the concentrate on the latter, building a 12-track home studio that provided him with a perfect place to create, critique and pull apart songs. It was a never-ending quest for perfection all right, one that produced little success as labels continued to pass in droves.

Working side-by-side with Tom in the studio was vocalist Bradley Delp, who was in many ways a secret weapon. By day he was a factory worker, making heating coils for coffee machines, but at night he was an amateur vocalist who had been in a number of bands before teaming up with Tom.

To begin with, the demos were again dismissed by virtually every label – and then they ended up on the desk of Epic staff producer Tom Werman. "After *More Than A Feeling*, which sounded quite like the final product, and halfway through the second song, I stopped the tape. I couldn't believe that this music was actually available to us," said Werman.

Epic signed them with one condition: the album would have to be re-recorded with a name producer. John Boylan, an experienced studio hound but mostly in the country rock genre, was assigned. Boylan met with Scholz, agreed that the demo tapes were sensational and that re-cutting the tracks was, in-effect, pointless. The two concocted a ruse to keep Epic off their backs, and Scholz went back to his home studio to finish the album.

Released in August 1976 (though the UK would have to wait until January 1977), *Boston* exploded out of the box, becoming the fastest-selling record of the decade, being further propelled by the single *More Than A Feeling*.

Scholz always knew that this was a special song and made it the opening track and flagship single. 40-odd years on, *More Than A Feeling* remains his and Boston's definitive statement. Everything about it is perfect: the melody, the arrangement, the multi-layered production, Brad Delp's wonderfully emotive lead vocal, a guitar sound like nothing ever heard before, and, of course, that revving riff famously echoed in Nirvana's *Smells Like Teen Spirit*. A top five hit in the US, *More Than A Feeling* launched Boston's career in spectacular fashion and gave rise to a whole new subgenre: Adult Orientated Rock. After this, the floodgates opened for Foreigner, Journey, Toto and so many others to follow. Unquestionably, *More Than A Feeling* is Tom Scholz's masterpiece. More than that, it might even be the greatest rock song ever created.

The second-best Boston song came right after the best one – as track two. Like so much of Boston's music, *Peace Of Mind* has an uplifting quality: in its freewheeling riff, its rich melody and dazzling vocal harmonies. And in the lyrics there is that sense of positivity that Scholz would carry through the band's entire career. Elsewhere on the record, *Smokin'* is a flat-out, high-octane blaster that stands toe-to-toe with Ted Nugent's *Just What The Doctor Ordered*, Montrose's *Space Station No.5* and Aerosmith's *Toys In The Attic* as one of the most ass-kicking songs of its era. *Foreplay/Long Time*, meanwhile, was the longest and most complex track on the album, split into two parts, with proggy instrumental *Foreplay* followed by the grandstanding rock anthem *Long Time*. One critic described as "a perfect marriage of Yes and Led Zeppelin".

Housed in an eye-catching sleeve, featuring giant guitar-shaped spaceships leaving behind a dying planet, the music captured the imagination of a public looking for a new, more cutting-edge sound. The guitars sounded like nothing that had been heard before, dense and full of rich sustain. Delp's vocals were a revelation, from heavenly whispers to piercing highs. The songs, honed to perfection by Scholz over the last seven years, were immaculately arranged and brilliantly executed. It was, in effect, a coup d'état of the most magnificent kind.

year released
**1976**

producer
**Tom Scholz & John Boylan**

# 30 *Metallica*
# Metallica (aka The Black Album)

With over 20 million copies sold worldwide, Metallica's eponymous fifth album, better known as 'the Black album' - in a fitting reference to the similarly packaged The Beatles' *The Beatles*, aka The White Album - is one of the biggest-selling metal albums ever. Famously, the San Francisco quartet had sold one million records with 1986's *Master Of Puppets* without releasing a single or ever making a promotional video, but five years on, their stated aim was to take over the mainstream, or as their drummer Lars Ulrich would memorably state, to "cram Metallica down everybody's fucking throat all over the fucking world."

Previous album *...And Justice For All* had been badly produced and under-whelming. If Metallica were to advance to the status of the gobsmackingly global - and Lars now had Guns N' Roses and Def Leppard in his cross-hairs - they needed to shape up. Now. "They were still only played on 10 radio stations in America," said co-manager Cliff Bernstein, to illustrate the point. For an ambitious man like Lars Ulrich, that would never do.

Over the 240 dates of their last tour, the band had compiled what they called 'The Riff Tape', a collection of riffs that James Hetfield, Kirk Hammett and (relative new boy) Jason Newsted had come up with. Its contents would form the basis of Metallica's next studio album. The first riff on The Riff Tape was one that Kirk Hammett had come up with. It would become the basis of what remains the band's most famous song, *Enter Sandman*.

Producer Bob Rock didn't fuck about. Rock had turned in big albums for The Cult (*Sonic Temple*) and Mötley Crüe (*Dr Feelgood*) and his speciality was rambunctious pop-rock which sounded fantastic pumping from a car radio. Rock put his new charges through nine months of demoing - basic training for metalheads. Lars took drum lessons, and Hammett got coaching from shred legend Joe Satriani. "In retrospect, the nine months we spent in this room were pure hell," said Lars later.

But it was worth it for the end result. "All 12 songs are ours," said the drummer. "They were written before we went into pre-production, but Bob was great at helping us build up the whole sound. Everybody put their ideas more on the table. Last time it was: 'This is my drum sound, and fuck you!'" Bob's forté was that he was able to drag good performances out of us, especially the vocals."

Hetfield rose to the occasion, especially with songs like *Wherever I May Roam*, about th e brotherhood of the band on the road, and *The God That Failed*, a particularly personal song about his childhood. The soundscapes that the band and Rock were creating, though lush and broad, had the new simplicity that they'd been aiming for.

That success brough its own problems. When he heard *Nothing Else Matters* for the first time, Kirk Hammett's initial reaction was 'James wrote a fucking love song to his girlfriend? That's just weird.' A sizeable proportion of Metallica fans felt the same way.

---

year released
**1971**
label
producer
**Jimmy Miller**

Housed in an iconic Andy Warhol-designed sleeve that, during the vinyl age, viciously assaulted all of your other records with its unashamedly impractical metal zipper, *Sticky Fingers* exemplifies all the Stones' best qualities over the course of ten essential selections.

By the time the album was first released, in 1971, the Stones had already released eight albums - steadily building the R&B, rock'n'soul foundations from which *Fingers* was able to thrive. It was also an important album for the band personally: marking the beginning of a new chapter, it was their debut studio set of the 1970s *and* their new Rolling Stones Records label - and for the first time there was no contribution from their now late founding member Brian Jones (while his replacement, guitarist Mick Taylor, featured on nearly all tracks).

From its sleeve to its closing track, *Sticky Fingers* demanded attention and didn't disappoint. It was and remains one of their absolute best, from the distorted opening guitar riff of hit single *Brown Sugar* to the Paul Buckmaster-arranged strings that close weary, yearning

year released
**1991**

producer
**Bob Rock**

Undeniably affecting, this open-hearted, tender ballad is arguably Metallica's most commercial song ever, meaning those who consider themselves 'hardcore' Metallica fans profess to hate it.

But it was *Enter Sandman* that battered down the doors to the mainstream for Metallica. An all-time metal classic, it was Lars Ulrich's skill in identifying and re-arranging Kirk Hammett's intro riff which transformed *Sandman*. But it's far from a 'pop' album. The sheer might of *Sad But True* is undeniable. Bob Rock describes the track's crushing riff as "this force that you just couldn't stop", and it's here more than perhaps any other track that Metallica stamped their authority as metal's new global kings.

*The Unforgiven* was another seismic leap forward. Laden with atmosphere and drama, it's a brooding meditation upon life, love and liberty worthy of long-time influence Ennio Morricone, a beautifully orchestrated, metallic symphony with not a single note wasted. A true masterpiece.

Their lives would never be the same again.

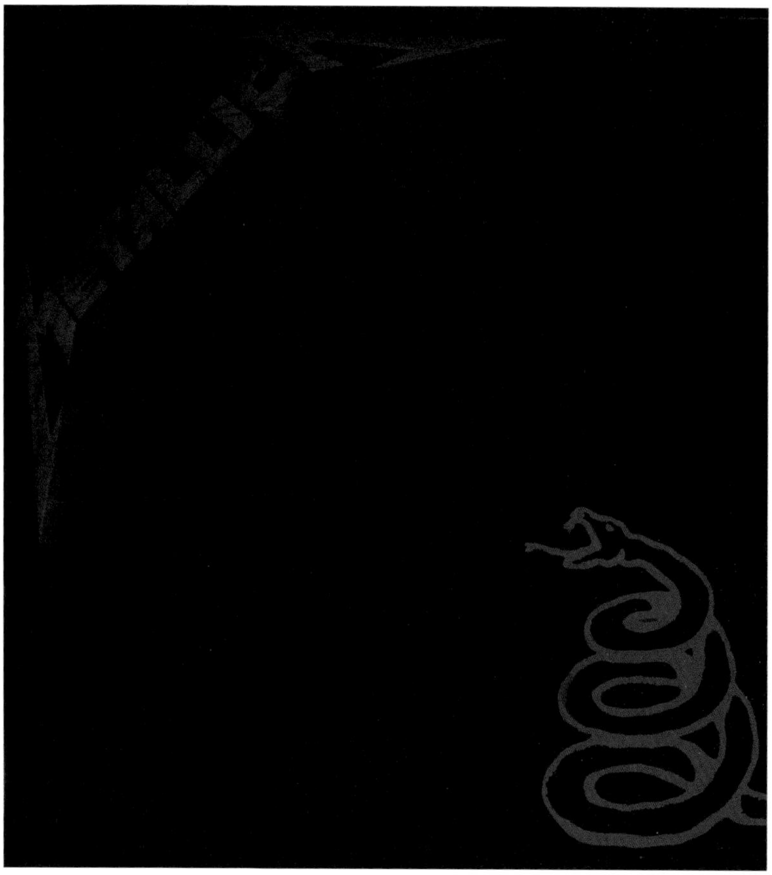

# 29 *The Rolling Stones* Sticky Fingers

ballad *Moonlight Mile*. Unsurprisingly, it topped both the UK and US charts.

The key sessions for the album occurred in December 1969 at Muscle Shoals Sound Studios in Alabama. It was here that the band cut evergreen party-starting staple *Brown Sugar,* with its controversial lyrics (has another song about slavery, racism, rape and oral sex ever gone straight to No.1 in the US and Canada?) and indestructible Keith Richards guitar groove. Muscle Shoals also gave rise to the Gram Parsons-inspired, country rock paradigm *Wild Horses* and a cover of Mississippi Fred McDowell's *You Gotta Move* (with Mick Taylor on slide guitar).

For all the controversy about whether or not Parsons contributed to the actual songwriting of *Wild Horses* (he recorded it before the Stones on The Flying Burrito Brothers' second album, *Burrito Deluxe*), hanging out with the country-soul man had certainly rubbed off. Sessions with Ry Cooder had also had a major influence. In his autobiography, *Life,* Keith Richards explains how Cooder had taught him the open G tuning that characterised much of his greatest work. (*The New Yorker* magazine recently quipped that Keith Richards and Ronnie Wood have been trying for thirty-five years "to do with four hands what Cooder can do with two".) The Stones' transformation from London mods to international roots musicians was complete.

Though the rest of the album was recorded at Olympic Studios in London and Jagger's country estate Stargroves, the album remains steeped in Americana. Other highlights include the brassy arrogance of *Bitch,* on which Bobby Keys' sax and Jim Price's trumpet duel with the guitars to great effect, the country rocker *Dead Flowers* and the Otis Redding-styled southern soul of *I Got The Blues,* on which Keys and Price emulate the Stax horns.

*Sister Morphine,* co-written with Marianne Faithful (who, although originally credited on the single version, was removed from album credits and had to fight a legal battle to get her credit reinstated) takes us on a slide into opiate oblivion. Started in early 1969, before Taylor joined the band, it features fabulous slide from Ry Cooder.

*Can't You Hear Me Knockin'*, with its irresistibly sliding, syncopated opening lick (velvety luxe and gravelly rock'n'roll at the same time) and organic blues jam is a beautiful thing. It's one-take extended coda, with its Santana-styled congas (courtesy of percussionist Rocky Dijon), propels Bobby Keys' sax improvisation and Taylor's inspired fluidity to dizzy heights.

By the time you get to the coked-out dreamscape of *Moonlight Mile* (when Jagger sings '*When the wind blows and the rain feels cold /With a head full of snow*' it's safe to assume he's not just singing about the miserable English weather), it's obvious they've come a long way from their early days of raw Chuck Berry covers. From *Beggars Banquet* in '68 to *Exile On Main St.* in '72, The Stones never put a foot wrong.

# 28 *The Who*
# Who's Next

A another classic band whose albums never score as highly in polls like this as you might think, The Who are possibly best loved for their extraordinary run of 60s singles than for their long-players. Which is odd, because a) they have made some classic albums and b) Pete Townshend is a man full of big ideas.

*Who's Next* was borne out of one very big idea, known as The Lifehouse Project, inspired by his grur Meher Baba. After labouring on it for years, Townshend presented what he had to his team. Producer Glyn Johns remembered: "We all had a meeting - the band, [manager] Bill Curbishley and I - and we got sent a script of the movie and I'd been sent acetates of Pete's extraordinary demos. At the meeting I said I didn't understand the script. I wasn't being rude, just pleading ignorance. Everyone else agreed, thankfully. But musically it was astonishing."

Townshend asset-stripped The Lifehouse Project's its constituent parts for *Who's Next*, and while it's tempting to harbour a romantic notion of what could have been, the relative simplicity of a traditional nine-track album setting seems to suit the proposed Lifehouse material perfectly well.

*Baba O'Riley* and *Won't Get Fooled Again* (the latter released in a chart-troubling single edit) stand strong on their own merits and, bookending the album, have come to define the band in their prime. *Baba O'Riley*'s trilling synth and organ-treated intro heralded another galvanising performance. Daltrey's cries of 'teenage wasteland' seem like a genuine call to arms.

As for the title, 'Baba' refers to Meher Baba, Townshend's spiritual leader, and 'O'Riley' tips the hat to electronic composer Terry Riley - another key influence on Townshend at the time.

*Won't Be Fooled Again* is talking about a revolution too - in fact, the line 'meet the new boss, same as the old boss' always seems relevant in today's politics. It's become a true-ism no-one even questions anymore (such a cliché, perhaps, that maybe it even explains the recent success of leaders who seem to totally debunk the past. At least, their supporters seem to say, they're not like the *last* boss...). The sentiment is matched by the music: Moon's crashing re-entry after the synth solo and Daltrey's microphone-spinning final primal scream are just two reasons why this is the ultimate Who anthem.

It was built that way. As rock music exploded, PAs got more powerful, and The Who moved from playing small clubs to enormous festivals and stadiums, Townshend set himself the task of creating music that could fill the spaces it would be played in. *Won't Be Fooled Again* was up to the job.

*Behind Blue Eyes* illustrates the light and shade of The Who - the delicate acoustic opening paving the way for the high-powered entry of Moon

year released
**1977**
producer
**Fleetwood Mac, Richard Dashut, Ken Caillat**

Few rock'n'roll stories are as downright weird as the strange tale of Fleetwood Mac: a 40-year saga involving drug-induced madness, bitter in-fighting, a 'fake' band that stole their name, a bizarre on-tour disappearance, two broken marriages, at least one coke-ruined nose, and the kind of bed-hopping normally seen in an old-fashioned West End farce.

Oh, and also involving some of the best rock music of the 60s, 70s, 80s and beyond.

On the simplest level, *Rumours* is a set of brilliant songs, beautifully played. That alone has made it the thirteenth-biggest-selling album of all time.

On a deeper level, these bitter-sweet, autobiographical songs spoke of the complex emotional turmoil at the heart of this uniquely dysfunctional band. John and Christine McVie's marriage was falling apart; Lindsey Buckingham had broken up with Stevie Nicks.

The album features so many hits singles it can feel like a greatest hits. Prime among them is *Go Your Own Way*, with a bitter and somewhat self-pitying lyric from Buckingham that has a very direct pop at Nicks. *'Packing up/Shacking*

year released
**1971**

producer
**Glyn Johns**

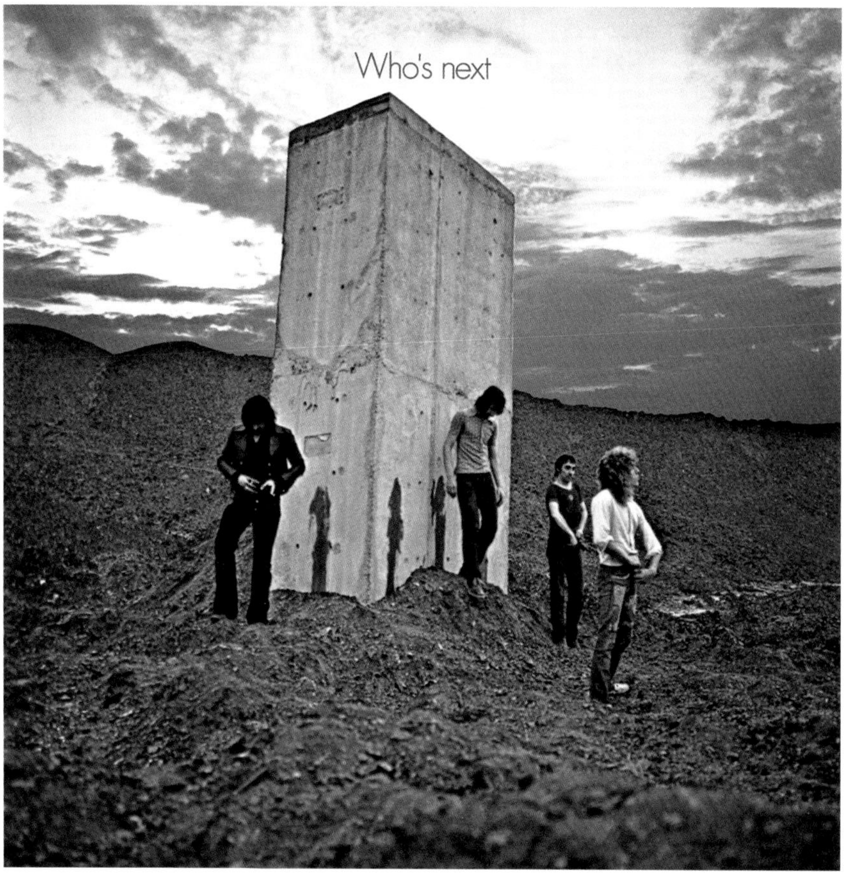


and Entwistle. As the harmonies mount, Daltrey takes total command of the vocal, leading them back to a tranquil close. A brilliant example of Who dynamics.

Roger Daltrey's vocal performance is astonishing. *Behind Blue Eyes* seems to serve as signature piece for both Daltrey and Townshend, while Entwistle's *My Wife* blazes with cannily deployed brass. A vast evolutionary leap forward that set the band's reputation in stone as one of rock's very best.

"You can't compare The Who to the Stones or Zeppelin," says Glyn Johns. "They're all completely different. The Who is a combination of three extraordinary musicians – the combination of Entwistle, Moon's flamboyance and Pete Townshend was like nothing I'd ever heard. It was never discussed, it was just the musical chemistry between them, and the energy level. It was peculiar to them, along with Roger Daltrey's voice which certainly contributed to the energy and power of the band. And the icing on the cake was Townshend's material which was completely extraordinary."

# 27 *Fleetwood Mac*
# Rumours

*up is all you want to do.'* Nicks flatly denies this was ever the case and resented the world being told so in a song, presumably even more so in a song that was so perfect for American radio. The drumbeat may have been nicked from the Stones' *Street Fighting Man*, but this tune is the very essence of Fleetwood Mac.

*Don't Stop* was written by Christine McVie as a positive, uplifting, 'moving on' song, the jaunty, barrelhouse feel of the piano riff helping to confirm the positive mood at the song's core. Fleetwood gives the number a certain driving intensity with that quasi-marching beat he does so well, and the shared vocals – one part Buckingham, one part McVie – adds another delightful musical colour.

The other band members weren't keen on Stevie Nicks' *Dreams* until Buckingham managed to take the song's basic chord structure and make three sections that all sounded different. The number moves along on an agreeably soothing bass line from John McVie and a simple Mick Fleetwood drum pattern as Nicks warns Buckingham against the dangers of thinking the grass will be greener without her. A delicate and haunting number beautifully delivered by Nicks.

*You Make Loving Fun* was written by Christine McVie about her affair with the band's lighting director (she told husband John McVie that is was about her dog, to avoid any unpleasantness...) and features a groovy little electric piano riff and a number of interesting guitar textures here.

One of the most famous and ambitious tracks wasn't a single, but could have been, despite being built out of a number of different pieces of music from all the band members. Given how *The Chain* moves from eerie vocal atmospherics to 70s rock workout in the space of four and a half minutes, the thing that is most impressive is that it does it so seamlessly and convincingly – while still sounding like it could be a massive hit single.

During the album's recording, John McVie was permanently sozzled and everyone was imbibing vast amounts of pharmaceutical cocaine dished out by the mirror-load.

"We were only like every other band of that era," Fleetwood told *Classic Rock*. "When I talk war stories with other bands, I think we weren't so bad. 'You did what?' We were lightweights compared to many. Look at the Stones or Johnny Cash, the stuff they took. We didn't do that, we were just boozers and mounds of cocaine. I thank God we didn't go to the opiate place. Cocaine eventually is bad, but we were still young kids. It didn't hamper us, it just meant we stayed up for three or four days and did some good music."

Nicks's *Gold Dust Woman* documented the madness of cocaine addiction (*'Rock on gold dust woman/Take your silver spoon/Dig your grave'*). She later confessed: "I curse the day I ever took cocaine." But it was at their most fucked-up, radiating paranoia and mutual enmity, that Fleetwood Mac created their iconic masterpiece.

# 26 *The Doors*
# The Doors

Earlier this year for *Classic Rock*, producer Youth wrote: "*The Doors* was one of the greatest debut albums by a rock group. What kind of band in 1966 would include a Kurt Weill/Bertolt Brecht song on their first album, or even start the first track with a bossa nova drum beat? The Doors were unique, then and now, mashing up Indian ragas with blues, jazz, rock, esoteric poetry and a phenomenal songwriting ability. Bottom line: they didn't have any bad songs."

*The Doors* heralded the arrival of a new voice in rock. Rock music itself was still in its infancy and tracks like the rousing, call-to-arms opener, *Break On Through (To The Other Side)* and the genuinely spaced-out *Crystal Ship*, with its (for the times) outlandish opening couplet – *'Before you slip into, un-con-scious-ness...'* – suggested a very different, far more advanced, into-the-night type of rock band than any seen before,

Jim Morrison was the ultimate LSD shaman rock star: dark, poetic and moody, unpredictable and fearless. The music was a uniquely 60s concoction of pop and a truly gothic form of rock, with layers of jazz stylings and neo-classical pretensions. Sometimes they veered a little close to the edge of MOR, yet listen to the seven-minute extended version of *Light My Fire* (apart from the album's two cornerstone tracks – the seven-minute-plus *Light My Fire* and the nearly 12-minute *The End* – most of the tracks were less than three minutes long) as it subtly and effortlessly morphs into a trance-inducing cosmic freak-out and you're listening to a band who know how to hook a pop audience –and then how to blow their minds.

Edited for radio, that glorious pop chorus, subverted by what now sounds like a quite innocent drug reference (but at the time was so controversial) became the defining hit song of the Summer of Love.

*The End* does a similar thing, with an epic catapult into The Heart Of Darkness, a seductive and hypnotic drone-like raga of organ and guitars, a psychedelic hymn and possibly their finest moment. The first of The Doors' epic songs, this was worked into an 11-minute frenzy during their residency at legendary Hollywood venue, the Whisky A Go Go, although some of the lyrics came from Morrison's time working on a student production of *Oedipus Rex* at Florida State University. "Every time I hear that song it means something else to me," Morrison said in 1969. "It could be goodbye to childhood." Was this the birth of rock opera?

In fact, the recording of *The End*, which would eventually roll out to almost 12 minutes in length – unheard of for a rock song at that time – precipitated one of the most oft-told stories from the making of the first Doors album. According to legend, the band was two-thirds of the way through playing the track, just after Jim had turned his on-stage announcement of wanting to fuck his mother into an incoherent yowl, and as he began to dervish around the studio he

year released
**1966**

producer
**George Martin**

In December 1965 and the first two months of '66, The Beatles' *Rubber Soul* album spent eight weeks at No.1 in the UK and six weeks at No.1 in the US, and was still in the US Top 20 when the group returned to Abbey Road studios in April '66 to begin recording material for their next new album. *Rubber Soul* had set a new benchmark, and was credited for having shifted the focus of rock music from singles to albums.

The first track the Beatles worked on was the epochal *Tomorrow Never Knows*, a psychedelic, pseudo-Indian cosmic soup dreamed up by Lennon four months earlier, inspired by the lines: "Whenever in doubt, turn off your mind, relax, float downstream," which he'd read in translator Walter Kaufmann's book *The Portable Nietzsche*. It was also the first track that 19-year-old Abbey Road engineer Geoff Emerick worked on, having that very morning been promoted from recording assistant. "I was extremely nervous," he recalled. "One request from John was that he wanted the vocal to sound like the Dalai Lama singing on a mountain top 25 miles away."

year released
**1967**

producer
**Paul Rothchild**

noticed – oh, the insult! – that engineer Bruce Botnick was watching a small black-and-white TV tuned to a baseball game. Jim, absolutely furious, smashed the TV to the floor while Botnick and producer Paul Rothchild sat stunned.

On *Break On Through*, an Elmore James riff slugs it out with Densmore's crisp bossa nova break-beat, while Manzarek plays his left-handed keyboard bass and Krieger pays tribute to Paul Butterfield's band's guitarist Michael Bloomfield. Morrison's vocal – which is a mixture of feral drawl and perfect diction – leads to the emphatic '*She gets high*' line, which had to be censored. Still awesome even 50 years on.

*Alabama Song*, the Brecht/Weill drinking song ('*Show me the way to the next whisky bar*'), was suggested by Manzarek, who had Austrian vocalist's Lotte Lenya's version on vinyl. Manzarek plays a fretless zither called a Marxophone. Authentically Weimar Republic, it was an influence on David Bowie, Alex Harvey, Nick Cave and more.

# 25 *The Beatles*
# Revolver

This, then, was in which the atmosphere *Revolver* – the album that transformed them from loveable mop-tops into psychedelic warriors – was created.

George Harrison brought *Love You To*. On *Rubber Soul*, Harrison had executed an effective sitar part on *Norwegian Wood*, but *Love You To* went much further. With minimal participation from the other Beatles, Harrison created the track with tabla player Anil Bhagwat and several Indian musicians from London's Asian Music Circle.

*Eleanor Rigby* served notice that Paul McCartney was a great storyteller and the arrangement seems to run counter to all the sonic experimentation littered throughout the album: McCartney, Lennon and Harrison are heard, backed by a pair of string quartets, arranged impeccably by Martin.

Side One closer *She Said, She Said* was inspired by an acid-fuelled party during which actor Peter Fonda commented, "I know what it's like to be dead".
A suitably lysergic meditation on the spiritual quest and driven by George Harrison's piercing guitar, and Ringo's circular drum figures, it was one of the worms in the Apple: a paranoid acknowledgement of the dark side of the 60s.

But if all of that serves to give *Revolver* serious chin-stroking credentials, it's worth pointing out that there's a lot of fun to be had. Harrison's *Taxman* was chosen to open the album, probably because of its dynamic opening bars and harsh, trebly chord slashes, but equally probably because of its sneering Scouse sense of humour. (Its most intriguing guitar-related fact is that the energetically crazed solo was played by McCartney. "I got the guitar and was playing around in the studio with the feedback and stuff, and I said to George: 'Maybe you could play it like this.' I can't quite remember how it happened that I played it, but it was probably one of those times when somebody says: 'Well why don't you do it, then?'")

There's the gloriously soporific *I'm Only Sleeping* (Lennon was once called "probably the laziest person in England" by a journalist), backwards guitar solo and all. And while Lennon never revealed what *And Your Bird Can Sing*'s cryptic lyric was about, you've got to favour the interpretation that it was an attack on Mick Jagger, whose 'bird' of the time, Marianne Faithful, could indeed sing. (Harrison and McCartney played the guitar duet on *And Your Bird Can Sing*: their first take was a distinctly Byrds-like folk-rock workout. A week later, they had another go, the guitar parts flowed better and the rock was decidedly more evident than the folk.)

There's *Doctor Robert*, a comical ode to a London doctor notorious for liberally dispensing drugs to his wealthy clientele; *Got To Get You Into My Life*, a song that seems like a traditional Stax soul-based McCartney love song, until you realise it's "actually an ode to pot, like someone else might write an ode to chocolate or a good claret"; and the classic pop of *Good Day Sunshine*.

There's also *Yellow Submarine*. But, you know, you can't have everything.

# 24 *Deep Purple* Machine Head

From the moment singer Ian Gillan and bass player Roger Glover had joined Deep Purple in June 1969 – replacing original singer Rod Evans and bassist Nick Simper – Deep Purple's career upswing had appeared unstoppable. The band's fourth studio album, *In Rock*, positioned them alongside Led Zeppelin and Black Sabbath as one of the Holy Trinity of bands who were forging the new, steel-plated sound that would define the early 70s. Nobody had thought to call it heavy metal yet. This was simply rock without frontiers; heavy, certainly, but metaphorically as much as figuratively, with lots of virtuoso light and shade in among the titanic riffs, operatic vocals and bludgeoning percussion.

"There was no genre," said Gillan. "There was no framework. You could just go where you want."

And Purple went exactly where they wanted, especially on stage. Their live performances sat part way between Zeppelin's ability to scale new heights of improvisation and The Who's no-holds- barred showmanship – gigs would often climax with Blackmore smashing his entire guitar and amp set-up.

Witnessing Blackmore's destructive displays, it was hard not to wonder if he was taking out his frustrations with his bandmates. Deep Purple had always been a combustible clash of personalities, and the arrival of Gillan brought another formidable ego into the mix. By the time of 1971's *Fireball* album, tensions between the livewire singer and the more conservative guitarist were becoming apparent.

Roger Glover tried to mediate but the growing clashes indicated that Deep Purple's next album was a car crash waiting to happen. It certainly got off to an inauspicious start when the original sessions for the album planned for November 1971 had be cancelled after Gillan came down with hepatitis halfway through a US tour.

Having decamped to Montreux to record, disaster struck again when the casino complex they were based in burnt down during a Frank Zappa show (an event that provided the inspiration for *Smoke On The Water*). *Machine Head* would eventually be recorded in the freezing, closed-for-the-season Grand Hotel on the outskirts of Montreux, using the Rolling Stones Mobile Studio.

And if they weren't being hostile to each other, they were provoking it in others. "We did *Smoke On The Water* there," said Blackmore, "and the riff I made up in the spur of the moment. I just threw it together with Ian Paice. Roger Glover joined in and we went outside to the mobile unit and were listening back to one of the takes and there was some hammering on the door. It was the local police, and they were trying to stop the whole thing because it was so loud. We knew that they were coming to close everything down. They were outside hammering and taking out their guns – it was getting pretty hostile."

Astonishingly, the adversity actually brought the band closer together. "It was all of us against the world," says Glover. "So there was a great feeling of camaraderie on that album."

*Smoke* set the template for heavy rock but it wasn't release as a single until the year after *Machine Head*'s release. The album went number within a week and changed public perception of the band. Suddenly, belatedly, people began to realise that Messrs Gillan, Blackmore, Lord, Glover and Paice weren't a Led Zeppelin or a Black Sabbath; neither were they the "pop" Purple of the late 60s. The band had hit on a unique, loose-limbed formula and were determinedly carving their own niche. Machine Head is a pivotal album because it set the template for Purple's entire future direction. And, of course, it's packed with timeless gems such as *Smoke...*, *Lazy, Highway Star and Space Truckin'*.

Reviewing a reissue for *Classic Rock*, Be Bop Deluxe legend Bill Nelson summed up the delights of *Machine Head* perfectly: "The album's first track, *Highway Star*, has Lord's chunky riffing on what sounds like an over-amplified Clavinet. It sets the sonic scene for the vast majority of the album: tough, insistent, focused and inventive Blackmore's opening guitar chords suggest something that Pete Townshend might have windmilled into the world with the early Who. The track swiftly settles into a punky machine-gun chug, hurtling along at a speed that underpins the song's theme. These days, we'd mix the drums louder, but Ian Paice drives the band hard, despite his kit being at the rear of the mix. Up front, Ian Gillan's vocal nails the archetypal tight-trousered rock god wail, even though the lyrics fall only just the right side of *Spinal Tap*-ism. When the organ solo kicks in, we're almost into Gothic prog territory, some technically tricky runs revealing the high level of musicianship at work. Blackmore's solo sounds as if it could have influenced the twin guitar harmonies of bands such as Lynyrd Skynyrd or The Allman Brothers. It also includes a line that sounds like a direct steal from Fleetwood Mac's 1969 single *Oh, Well*."

Aggressive, driving, tight-trousered, technically-tricky gothic prog? That was *Machine Head*.

year released
**1972**

producer
**Deep Purple**

# 23 *David Bowie*
# Aladdin Sane

'Ziggy Stardust in America' is the usual line trotted out for *Aladdin Sane*, the follow-up to Bowie's breakthrough album. But with good reason: Bowie's last album with the Spiders From Mars, *Aladdin Sane* was written on the road, inspired by the USA and steeped in sex, drugs and ruthless ambition.

Bowie wrote the songs for *Aladdin Sane* on tour buses, limousines, trains and hotel rooms all across the USA. Though not as conceptually overt as *Ziggy, Aladdin Sane* was his most ambitious lyrical work to date: a cooler, more loveless affair than its summery, blustery predecessor.

The new Ziggy – the character of Aladdin Sane – was a stranger in a strange, dystopian land populated by sexually predatory celebrities, terrorists and snipers, coke dealers, ferocious groupies, Andy Warhol starlets, smacked-out rock-star casualties – and he was loving every cocaine-tooting minute. The Top Rank Suite, Stoke-on-Trent (which saw the last British date before his departure) this was not.

After their debut gig, wowing the Music Hall, Cleveland, Bowie and guitarist Mick Ronson concocted *The Jean Genie*, nicking The Yardbirds' version of Muddy Waters' *I'm A Man* and turning it into an erotic coke-and-fuck fest in keeping with the jubilant mood of the tour. Roadie Will Palin recalled the song's birth as an on-the-road chant, jammed up by Ronno and Bowie's pal George Underwood, Ronno's riff accompanied by shouts of "Bus, bus, bus, bus, bus, bus, we're bussin'."

In LA Bowie started writing *Cracked Actor* after taking a stroll down Hollywood Boulevard. Borrowing a cue from the Velvet Underground's *Loaded* epic *New Age*, written about Shelley Winters, Bowie's song depicted a 50-year-old has-been homosexual entering into an S&M tryst with a 'trick' he's picked up on Sunset and Vine. The most debauched lyric he'd written, *Cracked Actor* is often interpreted as an old lech taking advantage of a young lad: it's actually the other way around.

In California, Bowie hooked up with Iggy Pop and started writing another song in his honour, *Panic In Detroit*. A train ride from Seattle to Phoenix gave rise to *Drive-In Saturday*, a futuristic post-apocalyptic sci-fi twist on American 50s rock'n'roll that namechecks Carl Jung, NY Doll Sylvain Sylvain (Bowie misspelled his name and used it as a brand name for a pre-Viagra pick-me-up: *'He's crashing out with Sylvian/ The Bureau Supply for ageing men'*), the model Twiggy (*'Twig the Wonder Kid'*), and Mick Jagger. It was prescient in predicting a time when video porn would be mainstream.

The biggest change in the line-up was new keyboard player Mike Garson, whose influence is all over the album. The second biggest change, said producer Ken Scott, was that, "Bowie's confidence level had exploded. All our ears and ideas had changed, and we were looking for different things. The drum sound was much more live than it had

year released
**1967**
label
producer
**Chas Chandler**

An album? *An album?!* It's easy now to think of *Are You Experienced* as just, you know, just another rock album, albeit a landmark album. Everyone knows it's important, sure. What's hard to fathom now, 50 years later is that, when Jimi Hendrix landed on British soil and formed the Jimi Hendrix Experience in 1966 he may as well have been beamed down directly from Mars.

Brian May, for one, didn't actually even *believe in him*. "I'd heard the solo on *Stone Free* and refused to believe that someone could actually play this," said May. "It had to be some kind of studio trickery, the way he talks to the guitar and the guitar talks back to him. I was already playing in a band called Smile and I thought I was a reasonably good guitarist, so I knew it wasn't possible..."

Eric Clapton took Pete Townshend to see him. "The thing that really stunned Eric and me was the way he took what we did and made it better," remembered Townshend. "I thought I'd never, ever be as great as he is, but there's certainly no reason now why I shouldn't try. In fact, I remember saying to Eric, 'I'm going to play

year released
*1973*

producer
**Ken Scott & David Bowie**

been before. With David's arrangements, he threw a lot more in than he did in *Ziggy*. Then there was the addition of Mike Garson. There'd been acoustic piano before, which Ronno or Bowie had done, but they're not the greatest keyboard players in the world, so Mike made a big difference. On *Ziggy*... it was all very sparse – there had been two bits of synth – that was it. On *Aladdin Sane* there were a lot more keyboards, Mellotrons, a Moog synthesiser, as well as acoustic piano."

*Watch That Man* was a perfect opener. It told the story of a wild party and all-night debauches with the Dolls in New York, high on cocaine and lust. The perfect closer to this American sojourn was *Lady Grinning Soul*, theme song for an imaginary James Bond movie, supposedly written in honour of Claudia Lennear – also the subject of the Stones' *Brown Sugar*. The Stones themselves were out-rocked on *Let's Spend The Night Together*, while *Time* drew from the same well as *Rock'N'Roll Suicide*.

To split this band after *this* album? Bowie *had* to be a lad insane.

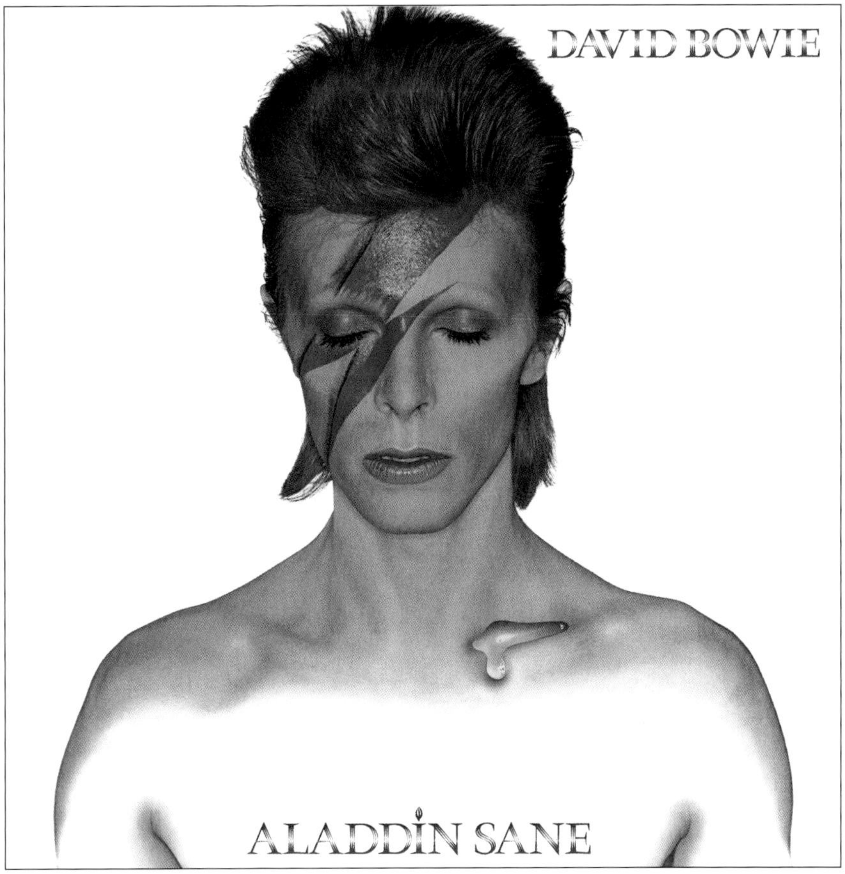


# 22 *The Jimi Hendrix Experience*
# Are You Experienced

him off the stage one day.' But what Eric did was even more peculiar. He said, 'Well, I'm going to pretend that *I am* Jimi Hendrix!'"

Hendrix hadn't fallen from the sky, of course, he had been coaxed over from his life as a struggling New York backing musician by former Animals bassist Chas Chandler. But his guitar-playing skills were truly other-worldly and debut album *Are You Experienced* gave the world the chance to hear what he could.

What Hendrix managed to do with his guitar, the sounds he occasionally teased, often thrashed out of that lump of wood with strings attached, put him in a league of his own. From screeching feedback to delicious dollops of wah-wah, his tone was an absolute bolt from the blue. Then there were his solos. A guitar solo was no longer a means of getting from the bridge to the final chorus, instead, Hendrix's solos were moments full of colour. When he was in the mood it sounded like his fingers were about to burst into flames.

But *Are You Experienced* isn't just some guitar-wankathon – it's packed full of killer songs. Not just great songs, but daringly innovative material. There's the guitar attack of *Foxy Lady, Fire* with its bonkers, off-the-wall funk feel, and, on the original US release, stripped-back ballads such as *The Wind Cries Mary*. This record showed Hendrix as a thoughtful, soulful songwriter as well as a smokin' riff master.

Of course, it wasn't a one-man show; Noel Redding's bass lines were the catalyst for a huge bulk of the Experience's tunes, and the album benefits greatly from the amazing jazz feel of drummer Mitch Mitchell, an imperious player who took centre stage on *Fire*. Then there was the three-four rhythm which carried *Manic Depression*. Granted, Neil Peart and Mike Portnoy gobble up such meters for breakfast, but odd time wasn't exactly commonplace in mid-60s rock.

*Are You Experienced* changed our musical landscape in so many ways it made your head spin. It gave a glimpse of just what could be achieved with a guitar. The reverberations from Jimi's experiments across its tracks can certainly still be felt today. It also brought a treasure trove of genres together, from rock and soul to psychedelic funk and even folk. It was graceful, with flickering moments of beauty like *May This Be Love*, and it was trippy and experimental (*Third Stone From The Sun*, the title track). It blew the minds of Beck, Page, Clapton, Townshend and beyond and, in doing so, ensured that the 60s ended in a squall of feedback and the ring of high-hats.

It put Jimi on the map as the greatest guitarist of his time and one of the most iconic rock stars the world had ever seen.

So, no, this isn't just *an album*. To paraphrase Henry Miller, it's a kick in the pants to God, Man, Destiny, Time, Love, Beauty... what you will. The true birth place of rock music as we know it.

# 21 *Rainbow*
# Rainbow Rising

Even by the standards of the 70s, the story of Rainbow's classic second album - and its messy aftermath - is a tangle of creative genius, colourful characters and personal tensions. *Rising* captured the band at their peak. Driven by guitarist Ritchie Blackmore's single-minded vision, it pioneered an epic sound whose influence can still be heard today. In the space of 18 months, Blackmore had assembled one of the greatest rock bands ever - and then dismantled it.

The guitarist had left Deep Purple following 1974's *Stormbringer* album, tired of the band's relentless recording and touring schedules, growing funk-rock influences and, ultimately, their refusal to record a cover of *Black Sheep Of The Family* by cult trio Quatermass. Blackmore realised he was losing his grip on the band he formed, and quit to put together Rainbow with members of US rockers Elf, a former Deep Purple support band fronted by singer Ronnie James Dio.

Having recorded Rainbow's self-titled 1975 debut album with the members of Elf, Blackmore had no intention of retaining a group he felt had the charisma of a bar band. Dio was in, but the rest were replaced. Scottish bass player Jimmy Bain joined from Harlot. Drummer Cozy Powell - already a legend, who had been playing drums since the age of 12, had a stint with Jeff Beck (one of Blackmore's favourite guitarists), and two hit singles as a solo artist. Keyboard player Tony Carey completed the line-up. The band decamped to Munich with Deep Purple producer Martin Birch.

The resultant album, *Rising*, is the sound of a band on fire. Recorded in the days before digital edits, the album has the intensity of a band getting it right in just a couple of takes, driven by Blackmore's intense desire to prove a point to his former Purple bandmates. And then there's the voice. "Ronnie was not only a talented singer, he was an amazing songwriter," said Tony Carey. "Even on the throwaway songs, which would be *Run With The Wolf* and *Do You Close Your Eyes*, he was ferocious. All five-foot-two of him."

The album kicks off with the keyboard crescendo of *Tarot Woman*. "I especially like the Minimoog solo Tony does on *Tarot Woman*," said Blackmore. "It was the first solo he did for the song. He said he could do much better, and went back and played for about an hour, but it never compared to the first solo."

The album's centrepiece is *Stargazer*, a nine-minute epic that combines Blackmore's love of classical music with Dio's vivid, fantastical lyrics. The track is built around a cello-inspired main riff, but the highlight is Blackmore's uninhibited lead playing and searing slide work (a recent addition to his repertoire). The sweeping, Eastern scales add to the grandiosity.

"It's amazing how many guitarists use the same

year released
*1970*
label
producer
**Rodger Bain**

It's fitting that Black Sabbath's second album, *Paranoid*, topped the UK album charts in the first year of a new decade. In capturing the zeitgeist, the eight tracks created by the Birmingham four-piece put a definitive musical full stop to 1960s hippy ideals propagated by Haight-Ashbury, free love and flower power.

The long shadow of the seemingly endless Vietnam War had sapped the naïve optimism young people had felt during much of the previous decade. The mood was changing, getting darker. And who better to provide a musical representation of this altogether doomier worldview than four working class, socially deprived young men from the bleak and industrial city of Birmingham? As vocalist Ozzy Osbourne put it in his typically laconic manner, "'Be sure to wear a flower in your hair'? What's all this flower shit? I've got no shoes on my feet."

*Paranoid* was produced by Rodger Bain and recorded in London at two studios, Regent Sound and Island. Many have claimed that it's the most powerful example

year released
**1976**

producer
**Martin Birch**

old lines," said Blackmore. "They never dare touch Arabic or Turkish scales." For added grandeur, Blackmore brought in the Munich Symphony Orchestra, led by conductor Rainer Pietsch. But not everything went to plan.

"The orchestra was too flowery, and there was too much detracting from the simple melody," Blackmore says in retrospect. "We kept taking out parts, and I felt sorry for Rainer because he was so proud of this grandiose piece he had written. We got down to the bare bones, and mixed in some Mellotron to even out the orchestra not sounding cohesive or in tune."

*Rising* was released on May 17, 1976. Although it has a running time of just 33 minutes and 28 seconds, Blackmore obviously felt it was complete, as he held back songs (notably *Kill The King* and *Long Live Rock'N'Roll*). *Rising* has become a hard rock totem and was a major influence on the new wave of metal approaching. Blackmore, though,wasn't that impressed: "Although I thought the overall sound of the record was very punchy, it lacked warmth and bass. It was very 'toppy'."

# 20 *Black Sabbath* Paranoid

of heavy metal music in its purest form. US outfits like Iron Butterfly and Blue Cheer released loud, raw, guitar-heavy albums before *Paranoid* came out, and Sabbath's English contemporaries Led Zeppelin had put out their hugely significant debut album a full 20 months earlier. But it's *Paranoid*'s relentless stripping of the traditional blues guitar phrasings favoured by earlier rock bands, together with Sabbath's seemingly tyrannical expunging of sex from the lyrical palate, that makes the album a game changer and a defining moment in heavy metal.

This is an album that's unashamedly built on a bedrock of riffs, riffs and more riffs. Bill Ward's drumming is appropriately brutal, but there's an absolute singularity of purpose in the way the songs subordinate themselves to guitarist Tony Iommi's playing that makes numbers like *Iron Man* and *Electric Funeral* come across as utterly relentless and unstoppable. But riffs aren't the only weapons in the Sabbath armoury on this album. Bassist Geezer Butler's lyrics are perhaps surprisingly intelligent – if thoroughly pessimistic – for a group that wasn't afraid of bludgeon.

*War Pigs* is an articulate exposé of warmongers, despite the lazy rhyming of '*Generals gathered in their masses/Just like witches at black masses*'. *Hand of Doom*, meanwhile, offers an unflinching look at hard drug use amongst former soldiers as a means of coping with what was later recognised as Post Traumatic Stress Syndrome.

And then there's Ozzy. It's perhaps only now, a staggering 47 years after he delivered these performances, that we can see just how different a vocalist he was. Not for him the preening usually associated with band frontmen. Ozzy never sounds like he's there to fluff up his own ego like, say, early Robert Plant. No, his defiantly sexless vocals are just another tool, willingly and effectively subjugated to this collective musical juggernaut.

Given the band's addiction to musical brutality the album's one moment of introspection, a jazz-inflected, almost whimsical piece titled *Planet Caravan*, should feel mis-placed and plain wrong. Yet somehow it works, perhaps as an extreme counterpoint to *Paranoid*'s overall dedication to power.

It's no coincidence, meanwhile, that the track from which the album takes its name remains Sabbath's musical calling card. *Paranoid* was the last track to be written – a three minute filler – and plainly has its roots in Led Zeppelin's *Dazed And Confused*, as well as *Communication Breakdown*, the opening song on their debut album, just recently released.

But the end result was something new, thrilling and commercial (going to No.4 in the Uk singles chart). Its unvarnished lyrics ('*Happiness I cannot feel and love to me is so unreal*'), jagged riff structure and avoidance of unnecessary frills have proved to be the bedrock of this unique band's quintessential heavy metal sound for the best part of half a century.

# 19 *Rush*
# 2112

The future is a tricky beast to predict. When George Orwell's *1984* was first published in the late 1940s, the year in which the novel is set must have seemed light years away. And while many of Orwell's predictions came uncannily true (Newspeak, omnipresent government surveillance, etc), he failed to anticipate the popularity of Bananarama. Similarly, while Stanley Kubrick's *2001* remains a stunning piece of cinema, the actual year itself offered precious little in the way of groundbreaking outer space exploration – the US was too busy invading Afghanistan.

Rush were lucky in setting *2112* so far into the future that only the Methuselahs among us will discover whether or not the Priests of the Temples of Syrinx ever assume control. (Not as lucky as Zager and Evans, mind you, but lucky all the same...)

To truly appreciate the brilliance of Rush's *2112* – concept and title track combined – one must reflect on the zeitgeist of the 1970s, and specifically the year 1976. Rush had released three albums up to this point – a self-titled first album, *Fly By Night* and *Caress Of Steel* – but by and large, the band were still, to echo a track title from their aforementioned debut, finding their way.

Their bosses were not impressed. "After *Caress Of Steel* flopped, the record company, Mercury, had made it very clear to us that we were disappointing them," remembered singer and bassist Geddy Lee. "We figured we'd be dropped if the next record didn't do well. Deep down, I think we were all convinced that our careers were over and we would have to get 'real' jobs. So *2112* saved our career. There's no question about that."

The theme of *2112* began to reflect that antagonism. "My memory is that Neil [Peart, drummer and lyricist]... wrote the story for *2112*, based on *Anthem* by Ayn Rand – an anti-totalitarian science fiction story. Neil and I had also read another of Ayn Rand's books, *The Fountainhead*, and that was an inspiration to us. *The Fountainhead* is a story about an architect who was determined not to compromise his aesthetic, his vision, and he would do just about anything, even radical things, to stand up for his art and his right to be an individual. That spoke volumes to us while we were making *2112*. We felt we were being pressured to compromise our art. People don't like it when you term hard rock or prog rock as art, but to us, as creators of that music, it is our art."

'Art' was a dirty word at the time. 1976 was categorically not the best year in which to release a record such as *2112*. Babylon was all set to burn, Rush's hard-rock sci-fi shtick was widely regarded as out of place and out of time, and their promo photos – three gawky, long-haired Canadians wearing satin kimonos – didn't help their cause one iota.

As spring '76 turned into summer '76, Britain began to wilt and wither under a relentless heatwave, daytime temperatures regularly exceeding 90 degrees Fahrenheit in old money. The fields and meadows became more parched than Paul Gascoigne after a month in rehab.

Despite this hostile environment, Rush stuck their heads above the sun-scorched parapet. News of *2112*'s excellence spread by word of mouth more than anything else, and when the band toured the UK for the first time in '77 – at the height of punk, no less – an army of pale-faced rock fans emerged from the shadows to greet them like conquering heroes.

Listening to *2112* today, one is struck by both its brilliance and its brevity. The main concept suite, which occupied side one of the original vinyl record, lasts a shade over 20 minutes. The five songs on the flip-side (as was) are all around the three or four minute mark. But sometimes less is more, and the title track – which of course details the failed struggle of a lone man to bring the joys of music back to a dystopian world – remains an awesome piece of work.

It's comfortingly familiar too. Even if you haven't heard *2112* for years, you'll recognise immediately every last Alex Lifeson power chord, every last shrill Geddy Lee warble, every last Neil Peart pitter-patter drum pattern. There's an endearing naivety to the piece too – this was no work of premeditation, just an honest outpouring of fantastical thoughts.

The best part of the *2112* story has always been when the central character discovers an abandoned guitar (*'What can this strange device be?'*) and learns slowly how to master its six sonorous strings. Lifeson's initial gentle tentativeness is genuinely evocative, and when he finally gains the confidence to let rip it's no exaggeration to describe the moment as life-affirming.

On release, the *NME* called the band fascists, because of the Ayn Rand connection and Rand's right-wing beliefs. Geddy Lee, whose parents were Holocaust survivors was extremely angry and upset: "Ayn Rand was the inspiration for *2112*, but we had no connection to her right-wing politics. *2112* was an anti-totalitarian, anti-fascist story." The critics could snipe all they liked. Within a year, *2112* had gone gold. It's now triple platinum in the US and double platinum in Canada.

year released
**1976**

producer
**Rush & Terry Brown**

RUSH

# 18 *Pink Floyd*
# The Wall

Bricks. Hundreds of them. Spanning the stage. Scraping the rafters. It's February 7, 1980, and the Los Angeles Memorial Sports Arena has never seen anything quite like the debut performance of Pink Floyd's *The Wall*. During the first part of the show, a blockade has been built between us and them. Now, 45 minutes later, a one-brick hole remains, where Roger Waters stands, picked out by spotlights, singing the eerie, valedictory *Goodbye Cruel World*. As he delivers the kiss-off, 'Goodbye', a final brick flips into position and he is entombed. Blackout. House lights up. End of Act One.

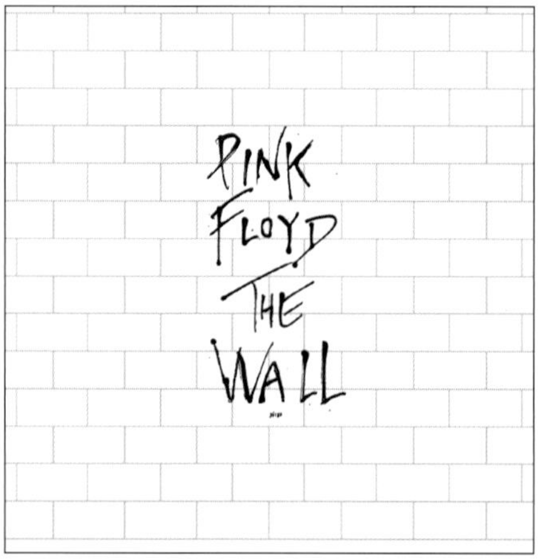


It's fair to say The Wall tour of 1980/81 was the antithesis of the no-frills rock'n'roll schlep. As challenging and bitingly satirical as its 1979 parent album, the 31-date odyssey (and Alan Parker's subsequent 1982 film) had been floated, in embryonic form, right from the start. "When Roger conceived *The Wall*," Floyd artist Gerald Scarfe said, "he told me he wanted to make it into an album, then into a show, and finally into a film. We got on well. We had the same ironic-stroke-sardonic view of the world."

That world view was apparent on the album, Floyd's eleventh, for which Waters presented his bandmates with a narrative tracing a picaresque anti-hero, Pink, through a wretched childhood, brutal education, failed marriage and hollow stardom, all under the cloud of his father's death at war.

Pink, of course, was a proxy for Waters himself, whose own father had perished at Anzio in 1944. "In its essence *The Wall* was an autobiographical work," he told the BBC. "I grew up carrying a burden of a huge sense of guilt. I probably felt responsible for my father's death. I had recurrent dreams I'd murdered somebody and I was going to get found out."

As for *The Wall*'s iconography, the flashpoint came in Montreal, when Waters spat at an unruly fan during Floyd's 1977 In The Flesh tour. "I felt this extreme feeling of alienation from these hundreds of thousands of people, all swilling beer and hooting and shouting," he explained. "I suddenly had a visual image of an arena with a wall built across it and a band performing behind this wall.

"I remember thinking: 'This is a great idea.' So I started to talk to the other guys in the band, and of course everybody thought I was completely insane."

Somehow he convinced them, although sessions were fraut and Pink Floyd as a band were effectively over by its release. Maybe the animosity fed the recording, or maybe Waters just felt that way already. Either way, *The Wall* is a dense double-album diatribe on isolation, indoctrination, society and the bastards who try to control us.

From the bombastic, opening *In The Flesh* to the surprisingly anti-climactic *Outside The Wall* the plot is peppered with metaphors, flashbacks, nightmares and dreams. What saves it is the compelling musical drama that keeps you hanging in there while it all unravels.

There's an abundance of musical highlights, great lyrics, clever dynamics and some great storytelling (that really only made sense when you saw the movie). The sigh at the begining of *Mother*, before the lyrics take you into Pink's interior monologue (*'Mother do you think they'll drop the bomb/Mother, do you think they'll like this song?'*). *Nobody's Home*'s endlessly quotable lyrics may be the greatest insight into rock star alienation ever written (sitting in front of the TV in an American hotel room with *'the obligatory Hendrix perm and the inevitable pinhole burns'* and *'13 channels of shit on the TV to choose from'*). And there's show-stopping lines, like *Vera Lynn*'s opening, *'Does anybody here remember Vera Lynn?/ Remember how she said that we will meet again, some sunny day?'*

*Another Brick In The Wall Part 2* condenses Roger Waters' pessimism into one schoolboy-pleasing anthem, driven by producer Bob Ezrin's direction to Gilmour to "Go to a couple of clubs and listen to what's happening with disco music". They added the four-to-the-floor beat and it became their biggest hit, introducing them to a new generation. Ezrin was possibly the ideal producer. Not only did he have form in making particularly bleak concept albums – think Lou Reed's *Berlin* – but Waters felt that he needed a creative foil. In fact, Ezrin was responsible for moulding the then sorry story into a workable shape. "In an all-night session I rewrote the record," he said. "I used all of Roger's elements, but I rearranged their order and put them in a different form. I wrote *The Wall* out in 40 pages, like a book, telling how the songs segued. It wasn't so much rewriting as redirecting."

"I needed a collaborator who I could talk to about it," Waters said. "Because there's nobody in the band that you can talk to about any of this stuff. Dave's just not interested..."

Maybe. But on *The Wall*'s most enduring and best-loved moment, *Comfortably Numb*, its power and simplicity, is heightened with, not one, but two of the finest guitar solos ever recorded.

year released
***1979***

producer
**Bob Ezrin**

# 17 *Metallica*
# Master Of Puppets

The heaviest album in the top 20 is the record that transformed the band from being cult thrash heroes into a major heavy metal force – easily the most important band of their generation in the genre.

The third Metallica album, not only is *Master Of Puppets* rightly regarded as an all-time metal classic, but some still believe this to be the finest album the band have ever created. It was the first album Metallica put out in America on a major label, Elektra (they were still signed to Music For Nations in the UK and Europe),and was to be the last to feature Cliff Burton, the bassist tragically dying during the band's subsequent tour.

It's hard to overestimate how important this album was not just for Metallica, but for metal in general. Says Alter Bride's Mark Tremonti: "When I heard the opening bars of *Battery* it completely blew my mind. The whole album made me a believer. I like that it was heavy and brutal at some points, but that it was so beautiful at others. And I loved the way they had their finger-picked, clean, classical-influenced versions and then beat you over the head with the electric guitar in the chorus. It was like a heavy metal concerto; almost as if Bach had come down and assisted a metal band in writing an incredible album." (In fact, the bass part played by Burton during the intro to *Damage Inc.* was inspired by the classical piece *Come, Sweet Death* by Bach.)

Nestling here next to albums by venerated masters like Bowie, The Beatles and Zeppelin, it's clear that the impact of *Battery*, of the majestic, four movement *Master Of Puppets*, of the slow-burning *Welcome Home (Sanitarium)*, the beautifully atmospheric, classically composed *Orion* and the punishing *Damage, Inc.* has not diminished one iota with the passing of time. On an album conceived around themes of manipulation and control, Metallica's mastery of the form is absolute and unerring, the performances a peerless harnessing of power, dynamics and mood.

The first Metallica album entirely written by the four musicians who would record it, the songs on *Master Of Puppets* were assembled in the garage of 3132 Carlson Boulevard in the spring and summer of 1985 and presented to producer Flemming Rasmussen perfectly arranged in demo form before the quartet decamped to Sweet Silence studios in Copenhagen in late August to record it. Upon its release, UK music magazine *Sounds* hailed the set as nothing less than "a landmark in the history of recorded music."

Structurally, *Master Of Puppets* aped the format of its predecessor, *Ride The Lightning*,but here Metallica's ideas were more developed, their confidence in their own abilities more pronounced. In a sense, *Ride The Lightning* was the bolder album, a fearless stylistic leap forward from *Kill 'Em*

year released
**1972**
label
producer
**David Bowie & Ken Scott**

'To Be Played At Maximum Volume', advised the back of the sleeve, and that is indeed the best way to enjoy Bowie's creative pinnacle. *Ziggy Stardust* marks the moment when Bowie got it absolutely right.

Like all good concept albums it felt like a journey, from the apocalyptic *Five Years* to the pain-racked *Rock 'N' Roll Suicide*. Unlike most concept albums, the abundance of pop hooks meant it sounded just as good heard in snatches on the radio. While Bowie would never be better, you can argue that the album belongs equally to guitarist Mick Ronson.

Morrissey once said of his hero Oscar Wilde that "He wasn't complicated yet he still left you lying on the bed panting because it was so real and truthful" and *Ziggy Stardust* had a similar impact on a generation. Opening track *Five Years* introduced a scenario where *'earth is really dying'* and as news of its fate echoes through the market square, Bowie, our narrator suddenly breaks from dispassionate description to tear down the fourth wall and draw the listener into the very heart of the narrative. The

year released
1986

producer
Flemming Rasmussen

*All*, but where that album played host to Metallica's first dishonest song - the transparently commercial *Escape*, a song the band came to loathe so much that they declined to play it live for almost three decades - *Master Of Puppets* is both uncompromising and uncompromised throughout, the work of men now utterly convinced of their own destiny.

So it's challenging but utterly convincing. A bold record that still moves people today. "*Master Of Puppets* is definitely a more uncommercial album than *Ride The Lightning*," insists producer Flemming Rasmussen. "Definitely. *Master Of Puppets* is Metallica celebrating that they've got a major label deal and that they no longer give a shit. It was them saying, 'We're just going to do the stuff we like and if the record company doesn't like it, then fuck them.' I think that was the attitude. And it worked too. There's not one bad song on the album, not a single one. It is just fabulous from start to finish. They had that youthful attitude of 'we're better than everybody else in the whole world' and they were just out to kick some ass."

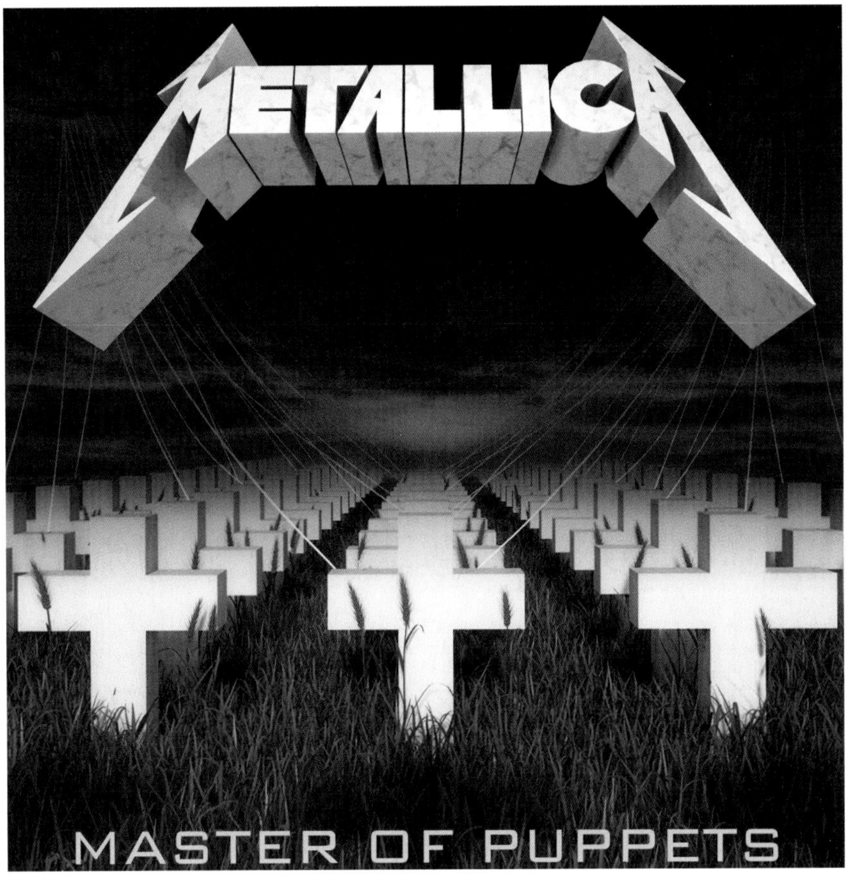


# 16 *David Bowie* Ziggy Stardust

## (aka *The Rise And Fall Of Ziggy Stardust & The Spiders From Mars*)

words '*I think I saw you in an ice cream parlour*' initiated a direct link between Bowie and a teenaged constituency that would last a lifetime. As hairs involuntarily rose on the back of countless necks, Bowie's enduring star was born.

*Starman* was the hit single –the track behind the *Top of The Pops* appearance that blew minds and had dads tutting. But those perfect tumbling drums and snake-hipped groove makes it irresistible. *Suffragette City* is little bit Jerry Lee, a little bit Stones, and climaxes in a deliciously salacious '*Wham bam thank you ma'am*'-punctuated false ending, It is glam rock in excelsis.

*Hang On To Yourself* was propelled by a driving Eddie Cochran-informed, Ramones-presaging Trevor Bolder bass line and lyrics about a girl, a groupie, who '*wants my honey not my money*' '*a funky-thigh collector*' who '*can't dance, we don't talk much/ We just ball and play/But then we move like tigers on Vaseline*'. This was rock'n'roll recast in a new, exciting language.

*Moonage Daydream* was seductively encoded with sci-fi word-play and gay slang, this gender-blurred androgynous '*mama-papa*' moved on from sexually confused '*rock 'n' rolling bitch*' to happily filling a pew at '*the church of man-love*'. As things rapidly escalate from inspired to ecstatic, Ronson unleashes an überglamtastic, truly space-age concluding guitar solo to-die-for.

Ronson, said photographer and insider Mick Rock, "was Ziggy's anchor. His guitar gave the music its rock'n'roll edge. In performance he played the perfect robust foil to David's ambiguous persona. He also did all the live and studio arrangements. It's impossible to imagine Ziggy's magical rise without him."

The album's closer, *Rock 'N' Roll Suicide*, is one of the most perfect closing songs ever constructed. It begins by putting a self-analytical cigarette into its listener's mouth ('*Time takes a cigarette, puts it in your mouth*'), it's understated, acoustic...it's wearing a denim shirt. But it's noticed you, and how wretched you feel, stuck between childhood and adulthood: confused, unacknowledged, alone. Then, as if reading your mind, at 1:39, Bowie delivers the line: '*Oh no, love, you're not alone*' and in an instant your 60s Kansas monochrome life turns 70s Oz Technicolour.

Fireworks illuminate your soul, your heart swells in your chest and those, hitherto dormant, neck hairs are back up again. At 2:27, Ziggy Stardust tells you '*You're wonderful*' and from that moment on, you belong to David Bowie. It's as simple as that. As Mick Ronson's glorious, final, string-driven crescendo rings out, you simply cannot wait for it to end.

Not because it's not the most marvellous moment in any pop music you've ever heard, but because the sooner it ends, the sooner you get to play it again.

# 15 *Queen*
# A Night At The Opera

The arguments still rage. "Queen were a *singles* band!" someone will say. "Like The Kinks, The Who and ELO! It doesn't make them a bad band – not at all! But *Greatest Hits I & II* – those are their best albums..."

Don't listen to them. Queen were perfectionists. Sure, they mastered the single. Famously, they're the only band where every member wrote a number 1 single. Bassist John Deacon wrote *Another One Bites The Dust*, drummer Roger Taylor penned *Radio Ga Ga*, guitarist Brian May sculpted *We Will Rock You* out of the finest rock clay, and frontman Freddie Mercury wrote *A Day At The Races*' most famous song –arguably the most famous song in the whole of rock – *Bohemian Rhapsody*.

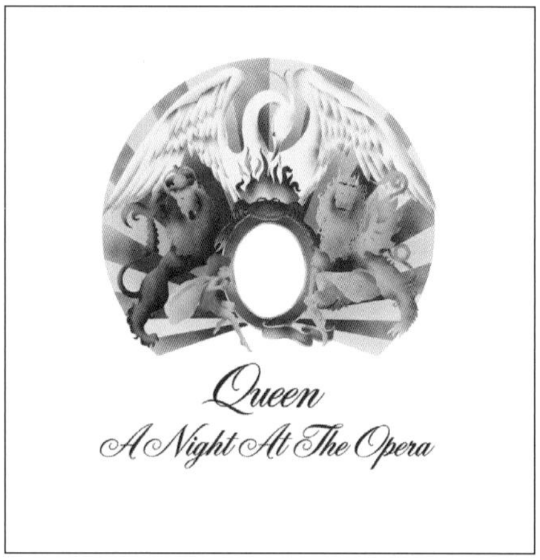


Over-familiarity, *Wayne's World* and over-exposure might have taken the shine off *Bohemian Rhapsody*. Yet more than 40 years after its release, its daring fusion of heavy metal, show-tune balladry and light opera remains the high watermark on *A Night At The Opera*, and a tribute to 70s Queen's collective imagination and sheer bravado. It broke the mould in 1975, and no-one has even dared to try and compete with it since.

"Working with Queen, you can't put it in normal terms," the album's producer Roy Thomas Baker once explained. "Queen can't work like any normal group. They utilise each other's talents to the fullest. The middle operatic section in *Bohemian Rhapsody,* for example, took about six to seven days to record in total. It was multi-tracked and there were so many harmonies that it takes quite a while to sort it out. It's the same case with Brian May's harmony guitar work.

"A lot of the band's ideas are revolutionary," he said. "You've got a band that has a relatively heavy rhythm section, is versatile musically and sings exceedingly well. The Queen situation is unique."

*A Night At The Opera* wasn't really where they found their feet – the previous year's *Sheer Heart Attack* was where their songwriting really came into its own – but it was the album where the public finally caught up, thanks to the greatest calling card of all time, in *Bo Rhap*. Warned by everyone, including friend and DJ Kenny Everett that, at six minutes, it was too long for the radio, Everett then played it 14 times on his radio show that weekend. An American DJ followed suit and suddenly the record company felt compelled to release a song they thought was commercial suicide.

It was the Christmas No.1 in 1975, stayed at the top of the charts for nine weeks and became the UK's third best-selling single of all time, after *Candle In The Wind '97* and *Do They Know It's Christmas?* which, let's face it, don't really count.

One song does not an *Opera* make, however, and there's more to the album than *Bohemian Rhapsody*. There's John Deacon's *You're My Best Friend*, a lush pop song that sounds like T.Rex remodelled by the Beach Boys, it was Deacon's first hit single, reaching the UK's top 10. Not that his bandmates liked it: Taylor thought the lyrics (dedicated to Deacon's wife Veronica) too soft and Mercury refused to play electric piano, making Deacon play it instead. But what did they know?

Freddie himself brought *Love Of My Life*, a romantic ballad (reputedly written for Mercury's soon-to-be- ex-girlfriend Mary Austin) that became an audience singalong at shows in the late 70s. Roger Taylor had a love song too –except his was about his car. *I'm In Love With My Car* was the B-side to *Bohemian Rhapsody* and vintage Taylor. With his blond girl's hair and fine line in self-aggrandising, laddish rock songs (see also: *Tenement Funster*), *I'm In Love With My Car* captures the essence of Queen's barefaced cheek and grandeur. Plus, any song that rhymes 'forget her' with 'carburettor' can't be all bad, can it?

So there's love songs, there's charm and wit – but there's vitriol too. Freddie Mercury could be a vicious sod, and *Death On Two Legs*, the opening track on *A Night At The Opera*, apart from being close to its best, is certainly its most vicious. Lyrics such as '*You suck my blood like a leech*' were aimed at Queen's ex-co-manager Norman Sheffield, and were so vituperative the now late Sheffield threatened Queen with a lawsuit. From its Hammer Horror movie intro through May's scything guitar solo and Mercury's impassioned '*You're tearing me a-p-a-r-t*', this is Queen at their rococo rock finest.

And we've almost gone all this way without mentioning Brian May. His '*39* – a song he once described as "sci-fi skiffle" – has a sing-song campfire melody and simple charm make it May's best song on the album. Not that he was slacking. Most guitarists would have been happy to put their feet up after coming up with the various riffs, solos and licks on *Rhapsody*. Instead May is on fine form, establishing the gorgeous melodic style that would become his signature. Team work makes the dream work.

"We're just very different," Mercury told *Melody Maker*'s Harry Doherty at the time. "We do things in a style that is very different to anybody else. There are literally scores of songs that have been rejected for this album. If people don't like the songs we're doing at the moment, we couldn't give a fuck.

year released
***1975***

producer
**Roy Thomas Baker**

# 14 *Led Zeppelin* Physical Graffiti

As Led Zeppelin wrapped up their 1973 US tour, cracks had begun rippling through the band's foundation. This was not entirely surprising. Zeppelin had released their first five albums – all platinum sellers – and toured the States nine spine-crumbling times between 1969 and 1973. They were the biggest band on the planet, but it had come at a cost. Moreover, the proggy gyrations and obtuse lyricism of their fifth album, *Houses Of The Holy*, had confounded many fans and fuelled the scorn of petty critics all too ready to write off the band's posturing as pseudo-cerebral cock rock.

After a brief hiatus, Zeppelin regrouped in the spring of 1974 and convened at a remote estate in Headley Grange, where they dove headlong into a verdant songwriting frenzy that would yield their enduring masterpiece – the utterly enthralling *Physical Graffiti*. Clocking in at nearly an hour, the new material was so provocative, diverse and at times bludgeoningly heavy that rather than prune off a single track to fit onto one 40-minute album, they reworked unused tunes from their previous three records and released *Physical Graffiti* as a double album. Cocky? Absolutely, and yet as Jimmy Page – who also produced the record – would correctly point out years later, they were the only band who could successfully pull off something so grandiose.

From the sizzling funk of opener *Custard Pie* to the dizzying tempo changes of *In My Time Of Dying*, it was clear that along with their battering mastery of electric blues, Zeppelin had broadened their outlook considerably. Forays into elegant acoustics (*Bron-Yr-Aur*), California country rock (*Down By The Seaside*) and roof-busting Dixieland blues (*Boogie With Stu*) fixed Zepp's ambitions beyond amped-up Elmore James worship. The apex was *Kashmir*, that mesmerising Middle-Eastern paean to heaviness, powered by Bonzo's hypnotic *Levee*-esque stomp and a sweeping orchestral backsplash.

Guest reviewing the recent reissue for *Classic Rock*, producer Youth perhaps summed it up best: "Side two ends with another cornerstone and possibly their finest moment, the mighty *Kashmir*. Another epic running to over 8 minutes and testament to Bonham's unequalled status as best drummer of all time. Engineered by Ron Nevison (who also engineered another best ever double album contender, The Who's *Quadrophenia*), Bonzo's drums are phased, there's a strange time signature which belies the simplicity of the beat and the sheer voodoo of it twixes your head. Bonham is like Hannibal, riding through the Alps on huge elephants... an ecstatic trance inspired by the deserts of India and North Africa..."

Robert Plant himself has commented: "I wish we were remembered for *Kashmir* more than *Stairway To Heaven*. It's so right; there's nothing overblown, no vocal hysterics. Perfect Zeppelin."

He may have seen his wish come true. *Kashmir*'s

year released
**1968**

producer
**George Martin**

The album you voted the greatest double album ever made doesn't even have a name. A simple white sleeve with the words 'The Beatles' embossed on the cover, the allbum that came to known all over the world as 'The White Album', seems to be a conscious reaction to *Sgt. Pepper*'s technicolour universe, a record without a concept, an LP that was too numb to feel, or to commit to anything with feeling (famously, on rocker *Revolution*, Lennon claims that when we *'talk about destruction, don't you know that you count me out... In'*).

By 1968, the band were sick of the sight of each other. But just as telepathic harmony between the four Beatles had led to perfect pop, so growing disharmony bred the raw, discordant fury of rock. The most significant of a series of events that activated The Beatles' metamorphosis from exemplary pop group to prototype rock band was the death of Brian Epstein. The band learned of their manager's barbiturate overdose on August 27, 1967 while studying transcendental meditation with Indian guru Maharishi Mahesh Yogi in Wales. Within the week, they announced

year released
**1975**

producer
**Jimmy Page**

stock has risen over the years and at the reunion gig in 2007, it got the biggest roar of the night.

*Physical Grafitti* also endures and grows in popularity, partly because of it's sheer consistency. It's not four sides of filler propped up by a couple of classics. Belters like *The Wanton Song* and *The Rover* removed any doubt that the band might have lost their way after *Houses Of The Holy*, while meat'n'potatoes rockers like, uh, *Houses Of The Holy* and *Sick Again* tapped into the abandon of Zeppelin's earliest influences.

*Ten Years Gone* is spellbinding, *Night Flight* is staggering, while for connoisseurs, *In The Light* could easily be the album's masterpiece. With John Paul Jones' genius to the fore, it's an unparalleled masterpiece of atmosphere, while the druggy insolence of Page's effortless playing sounds like he just staggered out of a session for Iggy Pop's *The Idiot*. (*In The Light*'s closing moments also see some stunning Bowie/Visconti-like harmonic overdubs.)

Rock music's greatest double album ever made? Or is that...

# 13 *The Beatles*
# The Beatles (aka The White Album)

their decision to manage themselves.

Without Epstein's cautious hand on the tiller, The Beatles were let off the leash creatively. Lennon was hit the hardest by his death, and as he enthusiastically self-medicated with lashings of LSD, the balance of power steadily shifted towards McCartney.

On a trip to India in February 1968, with the Maharishi, they set about writing new material. And with the only Western instrument to hand being an acoustic guitar, the White Album's sound was born of necessity. Donovan taught John to fingerpick and, utilising the technique, Lennon wrote *Dear Prudence* (an exhortation to young actress Mia Farrow to join in) and *Julia* (ostensibly about his late mother, though also about Yoko, the 'Oceanchild' in the lyric; Yoko literally means 'child of the sea' in Japanese). In all, Lennon, McCartney and Harrison wrote 17 of the songs that would appear on the White Album while in India. And, for the very first time, even Ringo wrote one.

But John was still locked inside his own private hell. Trapped in a loveless marriage, obsessed with thoughts of Yoko and unable to sleep (an insomnia diarised in the White Album's *I'm So Tired*), he wrote *Yer Blues*. Reminiscent of Fleetwood Mac and the other blues boomers, the song was indicative of the fact that Lennon was far from happy. "When I wrote '*I'm so lonely, I want to die*'," he admitted, "I'm not kidding. That's how I felt, up there, trying to reach God and feeling suicidal."

Having travelled to India in search of direction, Lennon found only disillusionment. He left Rishikesh in a huff, accusing the Maharishi (falsely, as it turned out) of making a pass at Mia Farrow, an incident chronicled in the accusatory *Sexy Sadie*. Back in London, he left his wife and moved in with Yoko. The two started taking heroin. And as Yoko sat in sessions at Abbey Road, the LSD-driven Technicolor pop lightness of *Sgt. Pepper* gave way to darker rock shades as the opiates held sway. Guitars distorted as moods blackened, and Yoko's very presence initiated an edginess that mirrored the social chaos occurring outside of The Beatles bubble: a happy accident that only served to enhance the band's rock'n'roll relevance.

*Revolution* took Chuck Berry riffing to violent extremes. McCartney, competing with the sound and fury of The Who, tore through *Helter Skelter*. *Yer Blues* is the sound of pure disaffection (that John later dismissed as a parody of the British blues boom). Harrison's *While My Guitar Gently Weeps* goes a more graceful root, bringing Eric Clapton in for the solos.

Age, and technology, has been kind to the White Album. Listened to on vinyl, it's a frustrating experience, with moments of genius punctured by corny pop, annoying song sketches and the experimental *Revolution 9*. In 2017, however, where anyone can make a playlist of its best bits, it really *does* sound like the greatest double album ever made.

# 12 *Iron Maiden*
# The Number Of The Beast

Widely regarded as one of the greatest heavy metal albums of all time, *The Number Of The Beast* turned Iron Maiden into superstars. Their first album with Bruce Dickinson, it brought them top 10 hits in the UK and established them as major players on the world stage. It also contains some of the finest songs ever written in the name of heavy metal.

The first chance anyone had to hear the new Iron Maiden was in February 1982, with the release of first single *Run To The Hills*. A Top 10 hit in the UK, *Run To The Hills* is one of the most celebrated metal anthems of all time. It introduced everyone to the 'Air Raid Siren' - that's Bruce Dickinson, obviously - and completely nailed Maiden's swashbuckling, gung-ho approach and insane levels of energy in just under four minutes of triumphant, euphoric heavy metal abandon. It's still ridiculously exciting 35 years later, despite regularly falling from favour in the band's live sets. *Run To The Hills* is, inevitably, the people's choice.

The b-side of *Run To The Hills* was Total Eclipse. Its appearance as a b-side meant that it didn't get included on the album, something the band would later regret.

"I knew that I had joined a great band," said Dickinson. "I also knew I could make it even better. I had a vision for *The Number Of The Beast*: my voice glued on to Maiden equals something much bigger. We did it fast - four or five weeks. We'd be in the studio till five or six in the morning. The one mistake we made was putting *Gangland* on the album instead of *Total Eclipse*. We picked *Gangland* because it was the first thing we ever recorded together properly. But the rest of the album was fantastic. *Hallowed Be Thy Name* was a precursor to *Rime Of The Ancient Mariner* [from 1984's *Powerslave* album]. That song, and the whole album, took Maiden to a different level."

*Hallowed Be Thy Name* was recently voted Maiden's best song by readers of *Metal Hammer* magazine and it brought the pre-encore curtain down on virtually every one of the band's gigs for at least two decades after *TNOTB* was released. One of their greatest ever epics, and quite possibly quintessential Maiden song, *Hallowed...* gives you everything that's great about this band in seven overwhelmingly dramatic and exhilarating minutes. Machine Head, Cradle Of Filth, Dream Theater and Iced Earth have all recorded cover versions, which serves to prove what a vast influence this song - and the album that it appears on - has had on generations of metal musicians.

The artwork and the title track, meanwhile, connected with schoolboys everywhere. In 1982, British music was in a weird place. Punk had fizzled out. The Jam and The Clash were about to split up. Phil Collins was at No.1 with a cover of a Supremes song. Duran Duran and Culture Club ruled the mainstream. *TNOTB* connected with a new

year released
**1978**
label
producer
**Ted Templeman**

In 1978, bands like Sabbath, Zeppelin and Deep Purple were either defunct or entering the last phases of their career, and classic hard rock was largely a thing of the past. And then along came Van Halen. Singer Dave Lee Roth had learned a thing or two from Jim Dandy, the frontman for Black Oak Arkansas, and in some ways, Van Halen were a throwback to a bygone era. But despite what appeared to be bad timing, they offered a classic rock'n'roll experience and a new post-Hendrix guitar innovator.

Signed by Ted Templeman to Warners, home to two of guitar hero Eddie Van Halen's favourite bands (Deep Purple and Black Sabbath), Templeman agreed to produce their debut album (he had previously worked with Montrose and Little Feat, among others).

Templeman and engineer Donn Landee's contribution to Van Halen can't be overstated. The pair had been working together for years and had developed an intuitive sense about how to magnify the essence of what a band was. For Van Halen, that meant playing together in a room - and overdubs be damned.

year released
*1982*

producer
**Martin Birch**

generation of kids who wanted an exciting and dangerous new band that offered escape. Derek Riggs' album sleeve was as smart and funny as it was scary. "Eddie represented the idea that the youth of today were being wasted by society," Riggs told *Classic Rock*. "He started out like that, anyway, and I made him more scary."

Maiden wanted Vincent Price to intone the familiar *Book Of Revelations* intro for the title track, but after the horror movie legend reportedly demanded £25,000 they gave the job to little-known voice actor Barry Clayton (who promptly dubbed himself 'Vincent Cut-Price'), whose pitch-perfect reading brought just the right amount of drama. Fuddy-duddies everywhere fanned themselves with a scented handkerchief and worried that the world was going to hell. It was – and going to hell had never sounded so good.

"Before *The Number Of The Beast* we were part of the New Wave Of British Heavy Metal," said manager Rod Smallwood. The band had quickly out-grown the scene. "After *The Number Of The Beast*, Maiden was a worldwide major act."

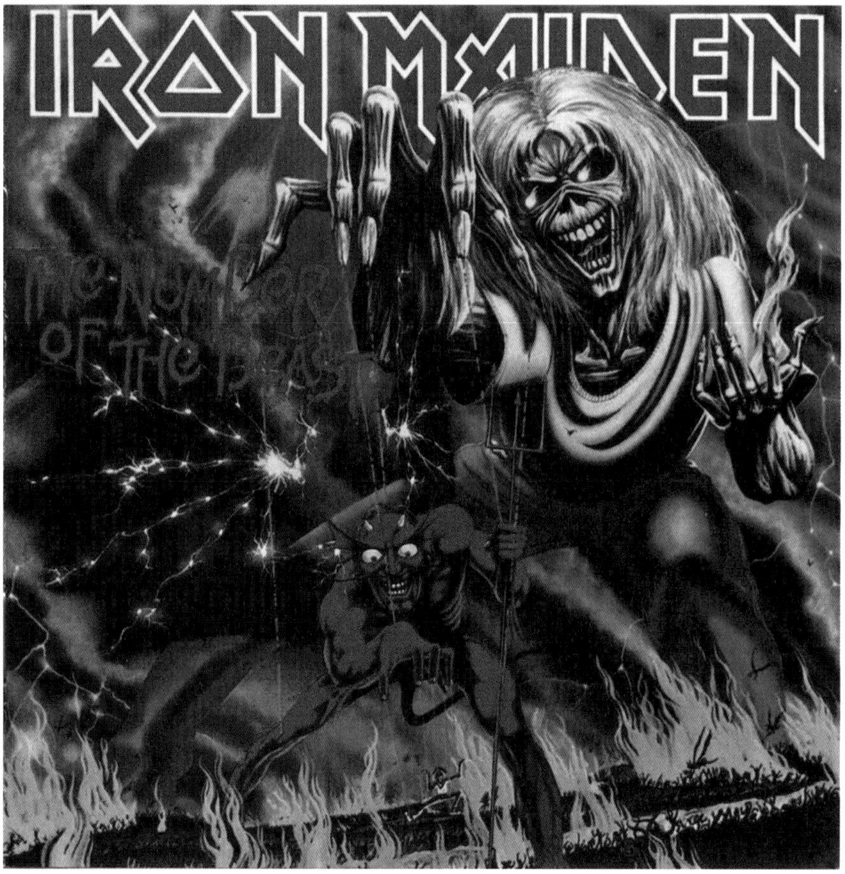


# 11 *Van Halen*
# Van Halen

Templeman realised that in order to capture the bombast and beauty of the band's live performance, he would need to keep things simple and organic. With that in mind, he cut virtually every track live, without overdubs (the exceptions were *Runnin' With The Devil* and *Jamie's Cryin'*). The sound had people sitting up and taking notice. "It was a turning point for me when I heard that record," admits producer Mike Fraser, a veteran who has worked with everyone from Aerosmith to AC/DC. "It was hard rock done in a pop manner maybe for the first time with heavy guitars and slap reverb on them. It was a real head-turner. All the songs were there and with the production they managed to create a new sound. It was flawless."

Nowhere was this new sound better illustrated than on the band's take of The Kinks' classic *You Really Got Me*. A song they'd been covering for years in the clubs, it took on new dimensions in the studio. The guitar tones were both monstrous and majestic at the same time. Rolling out his vintage Marshalls and plugging in his hot-rodded Stratocaster, Edward provided an early glimpse of what he would call his "brown sound".

Roth might not have had the most technically perfect voice in the world, but ultimately, what lifted the album was Edward Van Halen himself – the guitarist redefined the very vocabulary of what a rock guitarist could do. If there was one track that instantly placed the guitarist in the pantheon of greats it was *Eruption*, his spontaneous, two-handed tapping instrumental masterpiece. It showcased a technique that would initially mystify and ultimately mesmerise every guitar player who heard it.

*Ain't Talkin' 'Bout Love* ushered in the next decade of rock. Everything that came after, the endless torrent of 80s flash metal, the glam and glitter and ant-snorting and overdosing and assless leather chaps and misspelled words and guitar solos that sound like exploding bombs and throngs of long-haired punks puking beer in parking lots, it all sprang from this effortlessly charismatic ode to David Lee Roth's penis. No one can touch this song for sheer ferocity, not even prime-time GN'R. It is the sound of the greatest rock'n'roll band in the world operating at full capacity. A complete stunner then, now, and forever.

*Jamie's Cryin'*, *Ice Cream Man* – *Van Halen*'s highlights retooled rock music for the 80s. Close to 40 years on, the band's debut album has lost none of its shine, nor any of its importance. Before it, hard rock was in serious danger of becoming staid and lifeless. Afterwards, every self-respecting rock band cited it as a touchstone. It's not just one of the great debut albums, it's one of the great albums full-stop. You can hear its incomparable sound and bravura attitude echoing through the 1980s and beyond, its success revitalising not just the Sunset Strip, but similar scenes all over the world.

# 10 *Led Zeppelin* Led Zeppelin

Recorded over nine days, a total of just 30 hours in the studio, Led Zeppelin's debut album was fully recorded and mixed at a total cost, including artwork, of £1,782. While the punk velocity of *Communication Breakdown* blazes and *Good Times Bad Times* grooves, there's a dark, brooding ferocity brought to Willie Dixon blues staples *You Shook Me* and *I Can't Quit You Babe* that transcends mere technique. *Dazed And Confused* provides Page with his broadest canvas for live extemporization, while *How Many More Times* defines the Zeppelin template of über rock pomp and power.

Opening with the rhythmic battering-ram that is *Good Times Bad Times*, the immediate impression you got from hearing *Led Zeppelin* for the first time was one of pure shocking power, its opening salvo summing up everything the name Led Zeppelin would quickly come to represent. A pop song credited to Page, Jones and Bonham built on a zinging, catchy chorus, explosive drums and – at exactly the right moment – a flurry of spitting guitar notes, it pointed the way forward for rock music in the 70s, towards heavy-duty riffage and mallet-swinging drums.

Its counterpart, meanwhile, on side two, another Page-Jones-Bonham composition titled *Communication Breakdown*, with its spiky, downstroke guitar riff and grafting of the ostinato from Eddie Cochran's *Nervous Breakdown*, was proto-punk; the sort of speeded up, one-chord gunshot the Ramones would turn into a career a decade later. (Black Sabbath, meanwhile, would bolt *Breakdown*'s powerchord chugging to the *Dazed And Confused*'s piercing riff to make *Paranoid*.) While *Your Time Is Gonna Come*, the third of the three originals on the album, is something else again: a wonderfully understated pop song built, in the fashion of the time, around a Bach fugue, played by Jones, then swept into a completely different musical zone by Page's pedal steel guitar – an instrument he had literally picked up in the studio that day and begun to play.

The rest of the album, however, though equally impressive in the scope of its sonic architecture, was quite shamelessly unoriginal in its material, as exemplified by its final track, *How Many More Times* – also credited to Page, Jones and Bonham but a composition clearly based on several older tunes, primarily *How Many More Years* by Howlin' Wolf, a number which Plant and Bonham had performed in Band of Joy, inserting snatches of Albert King's *The Hunter*. The 'new' Zeppelin version opened with a bass riff snatched from the Yardbirds' earlier reworking of *Smokestack Lightning*, plus more than a passing nod to a mid-60s version of the same tune by Gary Farr and the T-Bones also re-titled *How Many More Times*. There was even a lick or two appropriated from Jimmy Rodgers' *Kisses Sweeter Than Wine* as well as – bizarrely – a slowed-to-a-crawl take on Beck's solo from the Yardbirds' 1965 pre-Page hit *Shapes Of Things*.

All of which they might have gotten away with if so much else on the album didn't also take its cue from the work of others, largely without acknowledgement. *Babe I'm Gonna Leave You*, was Page's reworking of a traditional ballad first heard outside contemporary folk circles on a Joan Baez album (and later credited to American folk singer Anne Bredon) while *Black Mountain Side* was Page's instrumental version of fellow Davy Graham disciple Bert Jansch's 1966 recording of another traditional Gaelic folk tune titled *Black Water Side*.

Even the *covers* on the Zeppelin album drew accusations of plagiarism. *You Shook Me* was considered a rip-off of the version recently released on the Beck Group's *Truth*. Jimmy has always claimed it was simply "a coincidence" but Zep manager Peter Grant – then also working for Beck – had given Page an advance copy of Beck's album weeks before its release, and John Paul Jones had actually played Hammond organ on the *Truth* version. In fairness, listening to both tracks decades later, what is most striking is the lack of similarity between the two tracks. The Beck version is short and gimmicky, while the Zeppelin version is almost three times as long, portentous, with swampy bottleneck guitar more redolent of the original's swooning rhythms, while Page's guitar solo is fluid, haunting and mysterious, not bitty or showy like Beck's.

The most blatant steal on the first Zeppelin album, though, occurred on the track ironically destined to become one of the most closely associated with Jimmy Page: *Dazed And Confused*. Credited solely to Page, the original version of the song had been written by a 28 year old singer songwriter named Jake Holmes. Although acoustic, it included all the signature sounds from the Zeppelin version including the walking bass line, the eerie atmosphere and the paranoid lyrics. Again, Zeppelin took it to a different place entirely. Holmes' version is modest and unimpressive. Page's skill as guitarist and arranger, however, transformed it into a psychedelic epic.

Strictly speaking, not the most original debut album, then. But as first steps go, Led Zeppelin was pretty sure footed. The gauntlet had been thrown. Jimmy Page was making his mark.

year released
**1969**

producer
**Jimmy Page**

ZEPHYR

# 9 *AC/DC*
# Highway To Hell

*Highway To Hell* was AC/DC's big breakthrough, their first million-seller. And, sadly, the last record that Bon Scott ever made. It was a triumph rescued from the jaws of disaster, an album with so much commercial expectation riding upon it that Atlantic Records originally attempted to bully the band into covering The Spencer Davis Group's 1966 hit *Gimme Some Lovin'* in a desperate bid for chart action. Mindful that the pressure was on, Malcolm Young (and the group's new hot-shot manager Peter Mensch) fired original producer Eddie Kramer, hired in Robert 'Mutt' Lange, and forced his band to knuckle down for three month's solid graft in the studio. The result was the most polished, professional and powerful album of the quintet's career – and subsequently their first million-selling disc in America.

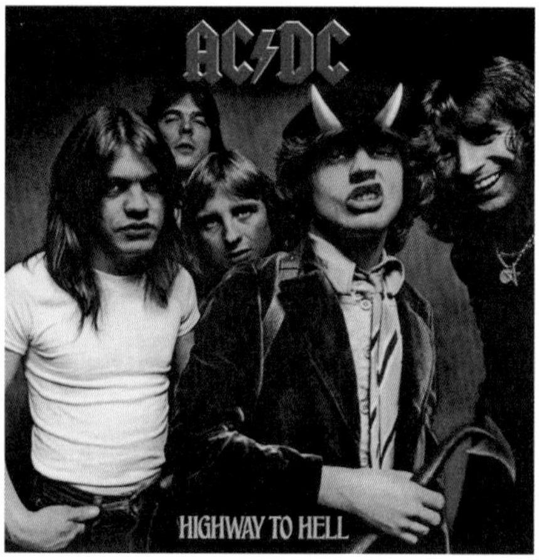


Mutt Lange's genius was to translate all the blood, sweat and tears squeezed out of his charges in London's Roundhouse Studio into an album that sounds effortless, care-free and spontaneous. AC/DC never lacked balls, energy or thuggish aggression, but on *Highway To Hell* their swinging punches were delivered with precision and poise, impacting with heart-stopping force. The devil, as ever with Lange, is in the details. The lairy gang vocals on the chorus of *Walk All Over You* (close your eyes and tell me you can't instantly see Malcolm Young shuffling forward towards his mic stand as you read those words). Those economical, brutally effective guitar stabs on the verses of *Touch Too Much*. The breath-robbing full-tilt climax of *If You Want Blood*. The unstoppable, rolling momentum of *Girls Got Rhythm*.

The first track they worked on was *Highway To Hell* itself. The instantly arresting guitar-drum intro had been demoed with just Angus grinding away on guitar while Malcolm bashed at the drums. All was nearly lost when an engineer took the only cassette of it home, where his young son playfully unravelled it. Fortunately, Bon, who was always rewinding his own worn-out cassettes, put it back together the following day and the tune that was about to transform all their lives was restored.

The fact that the intro sounded like Free's *All Right Now* was not lost on Lange, who hired Free's old engineer Tony Platt to help him mix the final edits. "He was looking for someone that would give it that kind of dry, punchy rock thing," said Platt. "That feeling of time and space."

It was a sound that characterised the whole album. Tracks like *Touch Too Much* – retrieved from a flailing, earlier incarnation and remade into a top-notch toe-tapper – and the pulsing *Get It Hot* were, on the surface, cornerstone heavy rockers, yet, as Platt points out, they had proper groove. Even the scorching *If You Want Blood (You've Got It)* was impossible to listen to without moving yourself out of your seat.

George Young had always encouraged his charges to simply give it their best shot and damn such niceties as tuning and time-keeping, but Lange insisted on everything being in perfect balance, melodically, rhythmically and harmonically. They were tighter and leaner and he even coaxed from them tracks that took their foot off the pedal long enough to almost be called ballads. In the case of *Love Hungry Man*, the beat was essentially no different to *Highway To Hell*, but the idea was much less in-your-face. With the final track, *Night Prowler*, Lange even took them back to the kind of electric blue melancholy they had only dared to chance once before – on Bon's totemic *Ride On* from *Dirty Deeds Done Dirt Cheap*. Bon's lyrics recounted the tale of a beast that waits for you to *'turn out the light'* before it *'makes a mess of you'*. If the music hadn't been so convincing, the song might have fallen into Alice Cooper-type schlock-horror. It wasn't theatrical – it just sounded mean and dirty.

Lyrically, other tracks, like the bouncing *Girl's Got Rhythm* and *Beating Around The Bush* – the latter remodelled from the discarded *Dirty Deeds* track *Backseat Confidential*, with a new, flintier riff barely one remove from that of Fleetwood Mac's *Oh Well* – came straight out of the same bottom drawer as the rest of Bon's dirty-minded fantasies. But musically, this was a whole other universe. *Walk All Over You* and *Shot Down In Flames* were pop-rock taken to its zenith.

Bon, throughout, is at his most commanding, compelling and irresistible, cock o' the walk in a rough 'n' tumble, spit 'n' sawdust world where "nobody's playing Manilow", rolling with the punches (both *Beating Around The Bush* and *Shot Down In Flames* lay out scenarios in which the horn-dog singer's ego takes a bruising) and always on the sniff for the next adventure, as detailed so memorably on the album's title track. *Classic Rock* once described *Highway To Hell* as "not just AC/DC's greatest song, [but] the ultimate rock anthem, period" and the song is Bon as he'll always be remembered – cocksure, rambunctious and ready to take on the world with a gap-toothed grin, come whatever may. It's the sound of freedom, the sound of the world's greatest rock 'n' roll band at their most feral and fearless. *Highway To Hell* is Bon Scott and his band at their most gloriously, thrillingly alive.

Shazbot. Nanu nanu.

year released
***1979***

producer
**Mutt Lange**

CANARSIE
SOCCER

# 8 *The Beatles*
# Abbey Road

The legacy of The Beatles transcends generations and strides unfettered across cultural divides. The mere mention of the name, and the individual members, dead or alive, opens doors and builds bridges around the world (as Paul McCartney is fond of saying, "nobody is Beatle-proof"). Strange, then, that the Fab Four have traditionally hit a brick wall in *Classic Rock*, with the voice of the reader who argues that Lennon, McCartney, Harrison and Starr should be this magazine's bread-and-butter often drowned out by the admonitory letters that follow the band's fleeting appearances in these pages.

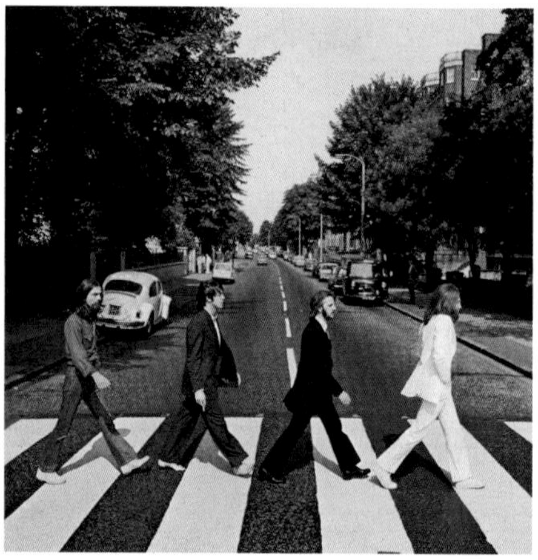

The Beatles, the argument seems to go, are your dad's band, a band that redefined the 60s and rock music itself but who didn't rock hard enough, who weren't part of rock's 70s Marshalls-and-Les-Pauls golden age. But there are plenty more reasons: the crushing ubiquity, or the patronising finality with which Beatles fans declare them the 'best' or, worse still, 'most important' group in history. Or those unbearably twee parts of their back catalogue (*Yellow Submarine*, say, or *Rocky Racoon*), the memories of McCartney mugging through *Yesterday*, and, indeed, the hangdog figure cut by the bassist in modern times. The tailored suits. The whimsical films. Yoko bloody Ono.

But step back from the context, clear your head of the fog of hyperbole and allow yourself to listen to The Beatles as a band rather than as a cultural phenomenon, and you'll remember just how much attitude, wit, sweat, eloquence, melody and – perhaps above all – sheer diversity they packed into their short career. It's reasonable to say you hate some Beatles songs; albums, even. But to claim there's nothing in their staggeringly eclectic catalogue that moves you is tantamount to admitting you're bored with music itself.

At a time when most popular performers were still mouthing the words of the Brill Building writers, The Beatles (along with Bob Dylan) led the way for any band who ever seized the reins of their art, strived to address the physical, spiritual and political world around them, and forced themselves to evolve in the face of commercial pressure to stay the same. The Beatles did all that, in just eight years, and left behind a pile of tunes that simply towers over other artists.

*Abbey Road* is also proof, if any were needed, that they knew how to rock too.

It may have been the final album The Beatles recorded together (although it was released before *Let It Be*) but *Abbey Road* is full of Beatles' firsts: George Harrison's first no.1 single (*Something*), Ringo Starr's first drum solo (*The End*), and the first-ever three-way guitar jam between John, Paul and George (*The End* again).

That it contains some of the group's most enduring melodies and breath-taking harmonies is made more significant when one considers that the four of them were barely on speaking terms just before they went into the studio.

Following the disjointed 'White Album' and the joyless process of recording and filming *Let It Be*, by mid-1969, The Beatles looked finished. The bitter acrimony that was splitting the group apart had even forced George Martin, who had produced all of the band's historic albums, to wash his hands of the *Let It Be* sessions (Phil Spector, for years itching to work with the Beatles, jumped at the chance to sort through the tapes). So the debonair Martin was more than a little surprised to receive phone calls from not one, not two, but all four Beatles begging him to come back to produce the last album.

"You know, like you used to," said Lennon, using all his persuasive charm. "Only if *you're* like you used to be," Martin replied, cautiously. "We will be," Lennon responded quickly. "We promise."

Lennon kept his word and *Abbey Road* brought both the 1960s and The Beatles to a close on the highest of highs. Lennon rocked compellingly on *Come Together* (his thinly-veiled plea to his fractured bandmates) and *I Want You (She's So Heavy)*. McCartney, increasingly the balladeer, growled his way through the larynx-busting *Oh! Darling*. Harrison's *Here Comes The Sun* hinted at the wonders to come a year later with his solo album *All Things Must Pass*. Even Ringo turned in a rare self-written tune, the jaunty *Octopus's Garden*.

The suite that closed *Abbey Road*, meanwhile, is a dizzying display of the group's truly wonderful, matchless talents.

The last song recorded by all four Beatles, *The End* serves as delicious coda to the medley that dominates the second side of *Abbey Road*. Fittingly, each member takes a solo, before a brief piano melody makes way for strings and a celestial harmony asserting that, in the final reckoning, *'the love you take is equal to the love you make'*. It's beautiful, perfect, progressive – with more invention in its 15-or-so minutes than most bands have in their entire careers – and yet never difficult or pretentious. And then, just in case you think they're taking themselves too seriously, they chuck in a daft ditty about the Queen (*'Her Majesty's a pretty nice girl/But she doesn't have a lot to say'*).

Masterful.

year released
**1969**

producer
**George Martin**

# 7 *AC/DC*
# Back In Black

There was a powerful significance in that title, and that none-more-black cover. On February 19, 1980, AC/DC's singer Bon Scott was found dead in a parked car in East Dulwich, south London. The night before, he'd been out in London's Camden, watching bands and drinking himself into oblivion. On the drive home, he'd gotten into such a state that his companion couldn't wake him, so he left him in the car. He never woke again. "Acute alcohol poisoning," said the death certificate. "Death by misadventure." Bon Scott was 33. AC/DC's previous album, *Highway To Hell*, had broken the top 20 in the US. After years of slogging in Australian bars, and then the UK gig circuit, the band had seemed on the verge of breakthrough.

Against the odds, however, they quickly regrouped, deciding that Bon would want it that way. Auditions were quickly held for a new singer (they went for Johnson after someone remembered Bon Scott raving about the singer from one-hit wonders Geordie) and six months later, released *Back In Black*. Guitarist Angus Young described *Back In Black* as "our tribute to Bon", but it became so much more than that. The biggest-selling album of AC/DC's career, and the second-biggest-selling ever (after Michael Jackson's *Thriller*) *Back In Black* is the mother of all comeback records and arguably the greatest *hard rock* album of all time.

The way the band tell it, it was the worst of times and it was the best of times. Bon's death had shook them, but Brian Johnson – seizing the opportunity with both hands – gelled instantly and the ideas came thick and fast.

Recording in the Bahamas, and three songs in to the recording, newbie Johnson worried that he was going to run out of lyrics. Looking for inspiration for *Hells Bells*, a tropical thunderstorm raged outside. "I said: 'That's rolling thunder, that's what they call it in England'," remembered Brian. Producer Mutt Lange told him: "Rolling thunder? Write that down." The rain fell. Brian noted, 'Pourin' rain!' "And the wind whipped up – 'I'm comin' on like a hurricane!' I was gone. The song was ready that night. I hadn't even heard the track..."

It was like it was meant to be. Similarly, his "southern preacher" spoken word intro to *Rock And Roll Ain't Noise Pollution* was done off the cuff in one take: "I never ever thought that it was gonna be on the record," said Brian.

*Back In Black*, Malcolm said later, was AC/DC remembering "the good times" they'd had with Bon. *Have A Drink On Me* had been recorded as a demo with Bon on drums. The lyrics (*'Whisky, gin and brandy/With a glass I'm pretty handy'*) were a drunken toast from Brian to his predecessor. With *You Shook Me All Night Long* Brian proved he had as much of a way with a double-entendre as his predecessor: *'She told me to come but I was already there.'*

On previous album *Highway To Hell*, Mutt Lange had polished up the band's sound and made them more commercial without losing their core identity. *You Shook Me All Night Long* perfectly illustrates Lange's ability to bring an entirely acceptable pop sensibility to a hard rock band as he helps the band deliver a singalong, 'arms around your best mate's shoulder' winner of a tune.

For his part in the lyrics, Brian credits inspiration from beyond the grave. "I remember sitting in my room writing that and I had this blank sheet of paper. And I'll tell you something – and I'm not scared of being called a sissy and I don't believe in spirits and that – but something happened to me that night in that room.

"I don't give a fuck if people believe me or not, but something washed through me and went, 'It's alright son, it's alright'. This kind of calm. I'd like to think it was Bon, but I can't because I'm too cynical and I don't want people getting carried away. But something happened and I just started writing the song."

It has so many classic songs: *Shoot To Thrill, What Do You Do For Money Honey* (a song that dates from sessions for 1978's *Powerage* album), and of course that genius title track, built on a juddering riff that sounds like the blues would if it was deconstructed by Satan and then rebuilt by Tony Stark.

Out of tragedy came AC/DC's greatest triumph. Not only did it go to no.1 in the UK, previous releases *Highway to Hell, Let There Be Rock* and live album *If You Want Blood You've Got It*, joined it in the top 100, as people dug into their back catalogue. In the US, it stayed in the charts for 131 weeks.

Brian Johnson remained AC/DC's singer until March 2016, when he stepped down, citing hearing problems. But back in 1980, his was a fairytale story: he had come from out of nowhere to front the biggest band in the world ("I was completely broke," he once said. "I had nothing. I had two kids and a mortgage to pay. I was driving a VW Beetle that was 14 years old. I was fuckin' skint") and rescued them at a moment when it seemed that all was lost.

"*Back In Black* is not just the best album AC/DC have ever made," *Classic Rock*'s Paul Elliott once wrote. "It's the best album anybody has ever made.".

year released
**1980**

producer
**Mutt Lange**

# 6 *Guns N' Roses*
# Appetite For Destruction

*Appetite For Destruction* is one of the greatest records of all time, and one of the biggest -the biggest-selling debut album, ever - with over 30 million sales worldwide. It revolutionised rock music in the late-80s and transformed Guns N' Roses into superstars, its success all the more amazing given the chaos in which it was created.

Guns N' Roses were so out of control, that the making of their debut album turned into a lengthy and expensive saga. In 1986, Arnold Stiefel's brief tenure as GN'R manager ended after the band's pre-recording sessions at a rented house on the former estate of Hollywood producer Cecil B. DeMille resulted in a $22,000 bill for damage to the property.

Two producers failed to get the record made: Nazareth guitarist Manny Charlton (who couldn't even get the band into the studio at the same time) and Paul Stanley of Kiss (who fell out with Axl Rose after he suggested that one song, *Nightrain*, required an extra hook: Rose never spoke to him again).

What this band needed was a manager and a producer who could exert some form of discipline. Enter Alan Niven, who also managed Great White, and producer Mike Clink, who had engineered UFO's *Strangers In The Night* and Survivor's *Eye Of The Tiger*.

With Clink working 18-hour shifts, *Appetite For Destruction* was recorded in one month over January and February 1987 at Rumbo Recorders studio in the LA suburb of Canoga Park. The total budget was $370,000. Expectations for the album differed. Niven predicted 500,000 sales, Clink two million. But Tom Zutaut, the A&R executive who signed the band to Geffen Records, was more confident. He said five million. In the end, they were all proved wrong. Initial sales were slow, just 200,000 copies in five months. But by July 1988 - a year after its release - *Appetite For Destruction* was Number One on the US Billboard chart.

On one level, the success of *Appetite...* was astonishing. It was the antithesis of corporate rock - raw and obnoxious, full of bad attitude and uncensored swearing. In the PC climate of the mid-80s, this was precisely the kind of record that 'parental advisory' stickers were made for, with nine out of 12 songs making explicit reference to sex, four to drugs, four to drinking.

On the casually misogynistic *It's So Easy*, Axl sneered, '*Turn around bitch, I got a use for you...*' On *Rocket Queen* the singer was taped having sex with stripper Adriana Smith - the then-girlfriend of drummer Steven Adler!

year released
**1987**

producer
**Mike Clink**

But at the heart of the album was a core of truly great songs: In many ways, *Welcome To The Jungle* is the definitive Guns N' Roses song, and an album opener which - from Axl's opening words, 'Oh my God' - warns the listener in no uncertain terms that they better buckle up tight for the road ahead. Detailing Indiana boy Rose's first wide-eyed, open-mouthed impressions of Los Angeles, this was the first song Slash and Axl ever wrote together, and it remains the ultimate statement of Guns' fearless, reckless, last-gang-in-town swagger.

*It's So Easy* was Guns' first UK single, a snarling, seething introduction which double-dared you to get closer to these obnoxious, aggressive, misogynist shitbags. It's hardly the band's most sophisticated tune, but no other early Guns song carries such bad-boy menace.

And if much of *Appetite* declares that Los Angeles is a dirty, depraved, dangerous shithole, *Paradise City* is the album's kicker - an admission that Guns N' Roses wouldn't want to be anywhere else. The quintet's first UK Top 10 single, its simplistic singalong melody is arguably a little too eager to please, though the song may have had less global appeal had the band not changed its original lyric: '*Take me down to the paradise city, where the girls are fat and they got big titties*'. Slash's guitar playing, meanwhile, transforms the whole thing into a sleaze-rock *Born To Run*, all marauding riffs and elegiac solos.

*Mr. Brownstone, You're Crazy, Out Ta Get Me*: the album oozes bad attitude and is littered with great lines ('*I used to do a little, but a little wouldn't do, so the little got more and more*', '*Some people got a chip on their shoulder/An' some would say it was me*', '*Welcome to the jungle it gets worse here everyday/You learn to live like an animal in the jungle where we play*'). And in *Sweet Child O' Mine*, Guns N' Roses had a secret weapon: a beautiful rock ballad inspired by Southern rock icons Lynyrd Skynyrd. Slash didn't much care for the song at first, dismissing it as "sappy" and his own lead guitar melody as "this stupid little riff". But it topped the US chart for two weeks in September 1988, regularly tops polls to find the greatest guitar solo or riff, and it remains the best-loved song of Guns N' Roses' career.

*Appetite For Destruction* arrived at the height of the hair metal era and was born of the LA rock scene, but its roots lay in the great rock music of the 70s - in Aerosmith, Led Zeppelin, AC/DC and the Sex Pistols. It's the newest album album in the top 10 and understandably so - has anybody has made a better rock'n'roll record since its release?

# 5 *Pink Floyd*
# Wish You Were Here

*Wish You Were Here* may have marked the beginning of the end for Pink Floyd but their ninth album remains one of their most loved works and sounds as contemporary now as then.

Its torturous gestation, recorded in increasingly indolent sessions at Abbey Road across half a year, almost broke the band apart, as Roger Waters said in 1999: "The whole thing had fallen to pieces during *Wish You Were Here*." It certainly paved the way for Pink Floyd's third era – the final near-decade when Waters set himself up solely as bandleader, sidelining guitarist and co-writer David Gilmour, alienating drummer Nick Mason and ultimately dismissing founder keyboard player Richard Wright. A critical article in the *NME* by famed rock writer Nick Kent had stung the band, who were already struggling with the fame that *The Dark Side Of The Moon* had brought them. (Gilmour: "It was a very difficult period... All your childhood dreams had been sort of realised and we had the biggest selling records in the world and all the things you got into it for. The girls and the money and the fame and all that stuff it was all... Everything had sort of come our way and you had to reassess what you were in it for...")

Not only that, but *WYWH* was the album on which, as Nicholas Schaffner spelled out so succinctly in his 1991 book *Saucerful Of Secrets*, "the Floyds, whether they realised it or not, were artistically at cross-purposes. Gilmour and Wright were content that Pink Floyd's music should keep transporting listeners into advanced states of REM. Waters was now determined... to wake them up."

The album balanced the two approaches powerfully. Opener *Shine On You Crazy Diamond (Pt. 1-5)*, continues where *Dark Side* left off, moody and beautiful, with Gilmour's defining four-note guitar phrase (which has become known as 'Syd's Theme'), arguably the most recognisable motif of the entire Pink Floyd catalogue.

The theme this time was absence and – Waters in particular feeling that the friendship and camaraderie that had brought them together had gone – and, as if to underline the theme, legend has it that former singer Syd Barrett appeared in the studio just as the band were recording *Shine On...* (Syd definitely appeared – the only dispute is whether it was during that song). Either way, the band, according to backing singer Venetta Fields, "were shocked to see him there, and really shocked at the way he looked and acted."

The resulting track is epic – in the time it takes for Waters' vocals to eventually appear, you could have listened to the opening two-and-a-half tracks from *The Piper At The Gates Of Dawn* – and a profound tribute to an old friend: '*Remember when you were young, you shone like the sun/Shine on you crazy diamond/Now there's a look in your eyes, like black holes in the sky... You were caught in the crossfire of childhood and stardom, blown on the steel breeze/Come on you target for faraway laughter, come on you stranger, you legend, you martyr...*"

On *Welcome To The Machine*, Waters shocks you out of your reverie with cynical take on the treadmill of existence, where even rock'n'roll rebellion is controlled and codified ('*What did you dream? It's alright we told you what to dream/You dreamed of a big star, he played a mean guitar*') while *Have A Cigar* is Waters's cynical take on the music industry, and contains the immortal line: '*Oh by the way, which one's Pink?*' ("We did have people who would say to us: 'Which one's Pink?' and stuff like that," Gilmour recalled. "It was quite genuine.")

With both Waters and Gilmour unable to nail the vocal for *Have A Cigar*, their friend Roy Harper was drafted in to sing. "Roy was recording in the studio anyway," recalled Waters, "and was in and out all the time. I can't remember who suggested it, maybe I did, probably hoping everybody would go: 'Oh no, Rog, you do it'. But they didn't. They all went: 'Oh yeah, that's a good idea.' He did it, and everybody went: 'Oh, terrific!' So that was that." Famously, Harper never got paid.

On title track *Wish You Were Here*, Gilmour's vocal and Waters' lyric provide arguably the greatest illustration of the the salt'n'sweet combination of Waters and Gilmour. Whatever animosity there may have been between them, the balance they brought to Floyd – Waters' caustic sentiments made palatable by Gilmour's majestic guitar playing – provided some of the band's greatest moments. *Wish You Were Here* has become a standard – much covered and beloved of buskers everywhere.

*Wish You Were Here* was released on September 15 and went straight to the top of the album charts on both sides of the Atlantic. It is estimated to have sold more than of 14 million copies worldwide. Richard Wright later said: "I think that's my favourite album that the Floyd ever did. I feel the best material from the Floyd was definitely when two or three of us co-wrote something together. Afterwards we lost that; there wasn't that feeling of interplay of ideas between the band."

It was about loss and the end of friendships in more ways than one.

year released
**1975**

producer
**Pink Floyd**

# 4 *The Beatles*
# Sgt. Pepper's Lonely Hearts Club Band

For the generation who experienced The Beatles first-hand, *Sgt. Pepper's Lonely Hearts Club* Band wasn't just the greatest Beatles album, it was also the greatest album of all time. There had been nothing like it before: a sort of concept album, born of studio experiment, and taking recorded music where it had never gone before. Its reputation dominated the popular and critical view of The Beatles for nearly 20 years, until the arrival of CDs and the renewed popularity of the Fab Four's records such as the White Album and, particularly, *Revolver,* shifted the balance away from *Pepper.* People started to say that with *Penny Lane* and *Strawberry Fields Forever* harvested for singles, *Sgt. Pepper* lacked great songs (apart from *With A Little Help From My Friends* and *A Day In The Life*). They said that there were better tunes and just as much experimentation on *Revolver,* whose conciseness and, well, lack of 1967-ness, endeared it to a more modern audience.

But *Sgt. Pepper's Lonely Hearts Club Band* is now 50, and still a brilliant album. Even without all the experiments, the tapes being thrown in the air, orchestral climaxes and use of Indian musicians, this is (largely) a set of extraordinary songs. The intro to *Lovely Rita* (and Paul McCartney's inspired cry of 'Rita!'); the warmth of *With A Little Help;* the spooky brilliance of *A Day In The Life;* the reprise of the title track; the daring of *Within You, Without You;* the internal rhyming of 'and' and 'grand' in *When I'm Sixty Four.*

This album, like all great albums, has so much for the listener to unpack that you can still find new things in it half a century later. Even its weakest track, *Good Morning Good Morning,* has a strange, basic charm (did the writer of *Meet The Wife,* the now obscure British TV programme name checked in John Lennon's lyric, ever get a thrill from hearing his show name-checked in a Beatles record?). The critics may have other, preferred Beatles albums, but *Sgt. Pepper* is the one that almost a third of you voted for.

Those novelties really did change music. The idea of studio as instrument, the idea that songs could be in any style, could be about anything, and could even (apparently) link up to create a larger whole, all these things were new to the majority of rock fans (let alone the huge pop majority who discovered rock through The Beatles). The gatefold sleeve, the art-school credibility of the cover, the lyric sheet – even the sheer colour of the packaging took the very idea of the album into a new dimension. There is so much new on *Pepper* that it's easier to identify what's old: the Parlophone label, perhaps. Or the fact that The Beatles followed convention and left the single off the album.

Much has been made of the absence of the greatest double A-side of all time from *Sgt. Pepper,* but would *Penny Lane* and *Strawberry Fields* really have fitted? They're epics, almost mini-albums in themselves, and while they would sit neatly alongside wide-eyed visions like *Lucy In The Sky With Diamonds* and *A Day In The Life,* they don't really go with *Pepper's* smaller beauties like *Fixing A Hole* and *Getting Better* (on the other hand, they don't half improve *Magical Mystery Tour,* where they fit extremely well with brilliant nutter butter like *I Am The Walrus*). Still, it's nice to have them here like moons that almost outshine their parent planet.

*Getting Better* is a textbook example of what Lennon brought to McCartney and McCartney brought to Lennon, turning a pair of great songwriters into an exceptional songwriting team. Pared to the bone, a single couplet nails their magic: *'It's getting better, a little better, all the time'* sings thumbs-aloft Paul, while John's instinctive riposte is a characteristically withering: *'It couldn't get no worse'*. It's chalk and cheese, light and dark, fish 'n' chips, Morecambe and Wise – casual, unforced, spontaneous genius. *When I'm Sixty Four,* on the other hand seems the perfect example of everything that helped diminish McCartney's legend, defining him as a counter-revolutionary, backward-looking, anti-rock totem – a Formby amongst Hendrixes. On the other hand: *what a tune.* No matter how much you resist, you will recall these lyrics to your very death bed. Prone to over-sentimentality he might be, but when he pitches it just right, McCartney is peerless. *She's Leaving Home* is beautifully observed, with stark, unflinching, kitchen sink drama detail. As Macca emotes, Lennon inserts apposite, doubtless familiar, Aunt Mimi-isms (*'we never thought of ourselves'*) and there's just enough chalk for the cheese. Mike Leander's string-heavy, harp-led arrangement is a heart-swelling, lush, end-to-end tear-jerk.

Rock music was changed by *Sgt. Pepper* and so were The Beatles. Paul McCartney once said of his solo career that each new album was a reaction to the previous one, and so it was with the rest of the Beatles' career: the White Album is almost a polar opposite to *Pepper,* with its plain cover and half-produced songs. They never did anything like *Pepper* again (although the repackaging of the *Magical Mystery Tour EP* as an album was an attempt to clone it). It'd be unfair to expect them to. This is the album that all others are measured against.

year released
**1967**

producer
**George Martin**

# 3 *Led Zeppelin*
# Led Zeppelin II

On October 22, less than 300 days after their first album, Jimmy Page and co released Led Zeppelin II. Both heavier and more textured than their debut, it far outstripped the success of its predecessor. Their label, Atlantic, received advance orders of 400,000 copies – nearly 10 times as many as Led Zeppelin.

It peaked at No.1 in both the UK and the US. The musical revolution they had started had now officially gone worldwide. "That album captured the energy of being on the road," Page said later. "That's what I like about it. That record and the period around it seems like a tidal wave now."

They had their feet under the table, but now they had to prove themselves. Robert Plant: "That was the album that was going to dictate whether or not we had the staying power and the capacity to stimulate. It was still blues-based, but it was a much more carnal approach to the music and quite flamboyant."

Written on tour and recorded in a variety of far-flung locations (London, NYC, LA, Vancouver), its tapes stowed in a steamer trunk, Zep II comprises the first set of songs Page wrote with the band in mind. Whole Lotta Love wraps blues tradition in boundary-breaking innovation, its 70s-presaging primal riff retains its fundamental power and its effects-laden, free-jazz mid-section still astounds. The song would soon become their onstage anthem – led by Page's distinctive, stuttering guitar riff that would later change the face of rock forever.

Heartbreaker nails fabled Zep immensity and the Pan-like priapism of Plant's Lemon Song ('Squeeze my lemon, 'til the juice runs down my leg') tour de force serves to substantiate an Excess All Areas reputation. They had the songs and they had the sound. For the II sessions Page switched to using a Gibson Les Paul guitar that he bought from The James Gang's Joe Walsh, as opposed to the Telecaster that had dominated his late Yardbirds and early Zeppelin work. The album also marked Page's coming-of-age as a producer. ("Jimmy was an excellent producer," recalled engineer Eddie Kramer. "When he and I mixed Whole Lotta Love we just flayed around the console, twiddling every knob we could. We somehow managed to stretch our limitations and create an effective sound.") His background as a session player who had worked in a variety of studios had made Jimmy Page fascinated in experimenting with sound. A key element was the art of 'distance-mic-ing'. This technique enhanced the sound of John Bonham's straight-from-the-wrist drumming considerably, and also had a huge effect on Plant's wailing vocals. "I discovered that if you moved the microphone away from the drums, the sound would have room to breathe," Page recalled. "I kept exploring and expanding that approach."

II is tightly wound and brilliantly structured. Ramble On teases with a dreamy opening before exploding into life. And if its Tolkien-referencing lyrics about Mordor and Gollum embarrass Plant today, he needn't worry too much. The song is not nerdy or adolescent – it's dipped in raunch and swaggers like The Evil One himself. Bring It On Home, it later turned out, had a loose relation to a Willie Dixon song recorded by Sonny Boy Williamson. Dixon got his credit but only the intro and outro – with the feel of a loose late night jam, all mumbled lyrics and harmonica – bear any relation to the original. It's a bravura ending to one of the greatest rock albums ever made.

Released in the US in late October '69, by the end of the year it had dislodged The Beatles' Abbey Road from the top spot, where it remained for seven weeks. It was clear indication that Zeppelin were set to rule the US chart in the 70s as much as The Beatles had done in the 60s. Despite the millions of units that II has shifted since it was released, perhaps the album's greatest achievement is the influence it has had on so many of the bands that has came along afterwards. From Aerosmith to Def Leppard, to today's guitar bands, Zep's second album has been a hard-rock yardstick. The ferocious riffs, the gentle melodies, the thunderous rhythm section... the record has it all. IV may be the band's biggest-selling record, and Physical Graffiti may be their most diverse work, there is no question that Led Zeppelin II is the record that really established them as a world force.

year released
**1969**
producer
**Jimmy Page**

# 2 *Led Zeppelin*
# Led Zeppelin IV

For sheer impact, immediacy, concision, endurance, influence and intrinsic Zep-ishness, Led Zeppelin IV is unbeatable. Of all their records, Zep's fourth album, released in late 1971, remains their most admired work. From Page's unimpeachable riffs, through Jones musical invention and Plant's clarity of vocal to that titanic John Bonham drum sound, IV (sometimes referred to as "Four Symbols") still emits a freshness that belies its age.

Black Dog's machismo, Rock And Roll's Bonham-propelled brutality, Plant's honeyed, evocative Sandy Denny-complemented vocal on The Battle Of Evermore, Stairway To Heaven's mainstream-slaying production and dynamism – and that's just side one.

And talk about influence: after pretty much defining metal and folk-rock, IV's encore was to unwittingly provide hip-hop with the source of its ultimate breakbeat, When The Levee Breaks.

The almost impossible-to-copy rhythmic swing of opening track Black Dog (4/4 time set against 5/4) was a key indication of how far ahead of the rock game Zep were. Back in the day, bands such as Grand Funk Railroad were touted as being successors to Zep's heavyweight crown, but they were light years behind the grace and timing of something like Black Dog.

Rock And Roll came out of a jam with Rolling Stones' mentor Ian Stewart guesting on piano. Bonzo played the intro of Little Richard's Keep A Knockin', and Page quickly added a suitable 1950s type riff. Fifteen minutes later, the nucleus of Rock And Roll was down on tape and a classic was born...

On Misty Mountain Hop, Jones' electric piano provides the central riff while John Bonham makes an exemplary contribution with some riotous fills, and Plant gets back on the hippie trail, with a tale of being busted in the park ('crowds of people sittin' on the grass with flowers in their hair – hey boy do you wanna score?'), making it a harder-rocking brother to gorgeous hippie anthem Going To California.

California itself continued the acoustic, hippy vibe of Led Zep III, and was evidence of the influence that the likes of Joni Mitchell were having on Plant.

Four Sticks was led by an incessant Page riff and powered by Bonham's literal use of four drumsticks, hence the title. The arrangement was so complex the band only played it live on a couple of occasions.

For The Battle Of Evermore, Plant came up with a set of lyrics inspired by a book about the Celtic wars and then Fairport Convention's folk legend Sandy Denny was brought in for the call and response lyrics. They resisted playing it live until their 1977 US tour with John Paul Jones being handed the vocal duties. Not an easy task.

When The Levee Breaks was a cover of an old Memphis Minnie blues stomper and it's led all the way by that much sampled, pummelling drum sound – echoing in the staircase in Headley Grange where it was recorded. Bonham lets loose with a percussive ferocity which is matched by Page's shimmering guitar work. Thunderous and apocalyptic, it's also a work of fierce beauty.

The epithet 'tight but loose' has always accurately described the band's aesthetic. Squeaks, scrapes and microphone bleed were not errors to be corrected in Page's production ethos, but rather characterful and inherent ingredients of the feel. Combined with the biggest fuck-off drum sound ever committed to tape, IV feels raw and crafted.

Much has been written on the technicalities of this recording – basically two microphones hung above Bonham's kit set up in a three-storey-high hall – and it's not too much of a stretch to venture that Headley Grange, where IV was recorded, is the fifth member here. This ambience positively saturates the none-more-familiar finger-picked figure that introduces Stairway, the band's finest recorded moment, near enough adding delay, such is the size of the reverb.

It's been both loved and loathed in equal measures, but nowhere is Page's supreme understanding of rock dynamics better illustrated than on Stairway To Heaven, with a song that teases and caresses and then climaxes with nothing less than the world's greatest ever guitar solo.

All that glitters is not gold. But this is. This is what we came here for.

**year released**
***1971***

**producer**
**Jimmy Page**

# 1 *Pink Floyd*
# The Dark Side Of The Moon

year released
*1973*

producer
**Pink Floyd**

It's difficult to overstate the influence of Pink Floyd as a defining force in rock culture. And it's not just about the number of records they've sold. You can reel off pages of statistics concerned with the success of The Dark Side Of The Moon, but that doesn't tell you why that album – both the music and the album sleeve itself – from 1973 became an icon for a generation. Or why Pink Floyd became a phenomenon that has affected every generation since. The answer is that they have made some of the most amazing, most singular music in rock.

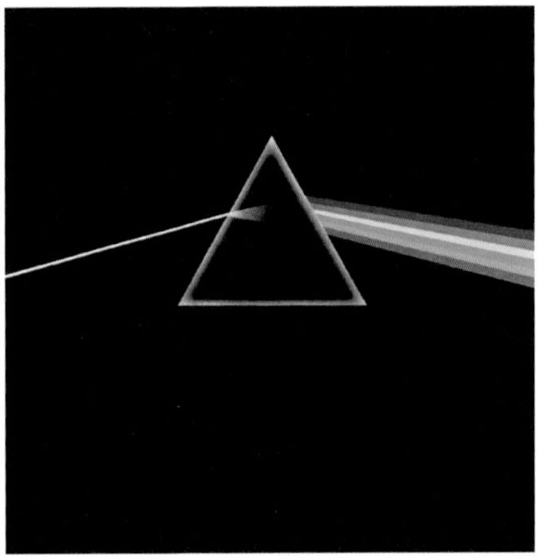

The punks may have hated the band and what they often (wrongly) perceived they stood for, but Pink Floyd's bile against the system was often as venomous as anything the punks could spit out. And through the 80s and 90s, angst-ridden teenagers, including legions who later would also make an impact with their own music – from Axl Rose to Trent Reznor to Billy Corgan to Noel Gallagher – grew up listening to The Wall. Pink Floyd had an impact on them all.

It's an album that brings people together – that metal guys like as much as alternative rockers. "It's the perfect record," says Clutch's Neil Fallon. "I think The Dark Side Of The Moon is one of the albums we've heard so much that we tend to grow a little deaf to it, but it's perfect. The lyrics match the music and the music matches the lyrics. I remember listening to it also at a very young age, and that was one of the very first records I remember closing my eyes to. I still do to this day, which says something."

If more evidence were needed, 42% of everyone who voted in our greatest albums poll, voted for The Dark Side of The Moon among their choices.

One of the most consummate rock albums ever recorded, Dark Side was an ambitious, groundbreaking concept that has become a timeless classic. It's themed around the pressures of modern life and the insanity that can provoke, and the dynamic sound reinforces the songs' contrasting images, from the paranoia of On The Run to the seductive requiem that is The Great Gig In The Sky, a sensitive contemplation of death that ends up in a place you'd never expect given the pretty keyboards that Richard Wright brings to the tune's first minute. Session singer Clare Torry suddenly unleashes a wordless vocal from somewhere uncharted and deep within her soul, well, you're not in Kansas anymore.

Said Torry: "When I arrived they explained the concept of the album to me and played me Rick Wright's chord sequence. They said: 'We want some singing on it,' but didn't know what they wanted. So I suggested going out into the studio and trying a few things. I started off using words, but they said: 'Oh no, we don't want any words.' So the only thing I could think of was to make myself sound like an instrument, a guitar or whatever, and not to think like a vocalist. I did that and they loved it. I remember thinking to myself: 'That will never see the light of day...'"

The impact was heightened by linking sound effects, often integrated into the songs: a heartbeat, the cacophony of clocks at the beginning of Time and the coin-dropping speaker-hopping till-ringing jangle that opens Money. Waters decided that the album needed "an overture" and "I fiddled around with the heartbeat, the sound effects and Clare Torry screaming, until it sounded right". Speak To Me was born. From there to closer Eclipse, the listener is taken on a journey.

Another innovation was the spoken word segments littered throughout the album. Waters hit on the idea of posing questions to Abbey Road staffers, Floyd crew members and other studio visitors – holding up cards with questions printed on them like: 'Have you ever been violent?', 'When was the last time you thumped someone?' – recording their answers and weaving them throughout the album. Abbey Road doorman Gerry said, "There is no dark side of the moon, really, it's all dark". Placed on the album, "it seemed to take on a much more powerful meaning," noted Gilmour.

The sound seems to build, climaxing with Eclipse. "The music grows, it gets bigger," said Rick Wright. "We would lift it up and up. If I ignore the depression of the words, which I tend to do, I think there's hope in it, because of the music."

And there is. To this day, TDSOTM has a beauty and vitality that still has the power to thrill.

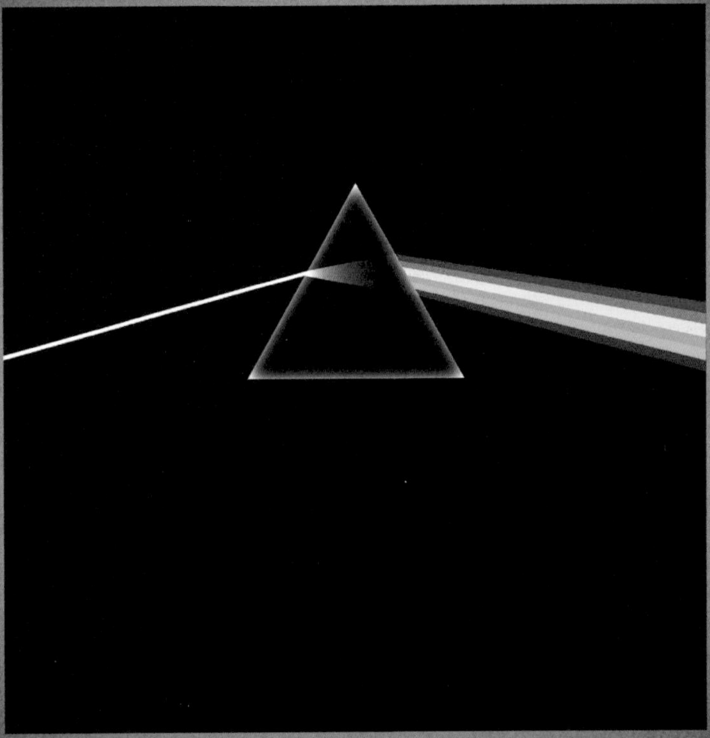

# PINK FLOYD

*The making of*

## THE DARK SIDE OF THE MOON

The story behind the the record that truly defined the sound of Pink Floyd and went on to become the third-biggest-selling album of all time.

# Fly Me To The Moon

The previous eight years had seen Pink Floyd struggling to find their sound. With *The Dark Side Of The Moon* they nailed it and went global.

Pink Floyd's *The Dark Side Of The Moon* is all too often referred to in terms of statistics. Every so often we are reminded of its stature by an anniversary reissue and an article rattling off a string of Wikipedia 'facts' about how it has sold however many millions of copies; that every other person in the western hemisphere owns a copy; that some stoner in America has discovered that it sychronises perfectly alongside *The Wizard Of Oz*.

Ordinarily it would be ridiculous, but the daft thing is most of these 'facts' about *The Dark Side Of The Moon* are largely true (except the bit about *The Wizard Of Oz*). It resided in the US *Billboard* chart for 723 weeks from 1973 to 1988, longer than any other album in history. It has popped in and out of the charts ever since on the back of tours and recurring reissues, and, with an estimated 45 million copies sold, it is Pink Floyd's most commercially successful album and one of the best-selling albums ever.

### But what exactly has made The Dark Side Of The Moon such an enduring success?

"My view," said Floyd drummer Nick Mason in his autobiography *Inside Out*, "is that there was no single reason, but a number of factors working together and multiplying the effect." It had recognisable themes, he said, simple but not simplistic, and a striking and instantly recognisable sleeve, all of which had universal appeal. "The musical quality spearheaded by David's guitar and voice and Rick's keyboards established a fundamental Pink Floyd sound."

And to some extent that really was the key: with *The Dark Side Of The Moon,* Pink Floyd had finally found their sound. It was their eureka moment. They had been slowly rebuilding a career left in tatters following the departure of their errant leader Syd Barrett since early 1968. Not quite headless chickens, but even David Gilmour coming in as Syd's replacement hadn't exactly signalled a sudden sea change. Roger Waters, by now the primary lyricist, lacked focus, and the band, while retaining creativity, lacked consistency.

To most people back then (and to a certain extent even now) Pink Floyd's work ethic conjured an image of four drug-addled individuals working laboriously in a dingy basement day and night to eventually produce a magnificent and definitive piece of work.

The reality, however, was quite different. Pink Floyd were primarily a live experience, and the band had a long-standing history of proving newly written material on the road before it was recorded. *Atom Heart Mother*, the lead track on their 1970 album of the same name, was toured for months as *The Amazing Pudding*. An epic, 24-minute suite was called, variously, *Nothing*, *Son Of Nothing* and *The Return Of The Son Of Nothing* before it finally took shape and eventually became the more familiar *Echoes*.

The problem, however, lay in the group's live repertoire – or rather the lack of it. The Pink Floyd of 1971 was in something of a rut. They'd been on a virtually non-stop tour since 1967, playing every pub, club, university and town hall that would have them, and slotting in recording sessions as

**Pink Floyd in conference with aides circa 1973.**

"It might have been only six weeks before we had to have something to perform."
*Roger Waters on writing for* TDSOTM

and when they could. In those days, David Gilmour recalls, "tours got booked in, and back then they weren't promotional vehicles."

While the band were not exactly idle when it came to recording – turning out the regulation one album per year – most of the songs on their studio recordings didn't lend themselves to the live environment. As a consequence they were still filling up their set with their 60s greatest hits including *A Saucerful Of Secrets, Astronomy Dominé, Careful With That Axe Eugene* and *Set The Controls For The Heart Of The Sun*.

Panicked into writing new material for an already announced UK tour commencing in January, the initial ideas for creating something new were discussed towards the end of 1971 at a band meeting in the usual venue of Nick Mason's kitchen, followed by a period of writing at a rehearsal space in Broadhurst Gardens in West London.

Waters, undoubtedly the main source of inspiration, began furiously writing lyrics. An album's worth of material would also be of convenient length for the first half of a new stage show, the second half of which could be given over to the aforementioned established favourites, which they were still not keen on letting go. As Waters recalled: "It had to be quick, because we had a tour starting. It might have been only six weeks before we had to have something to perform."

Waters came up with the idea of dealing with all the things that

Pink Floyd's post-Syd Barrett line-up: (l to r) Wright, Gilmour, Mason, Waters.

drive people mad, not to mention a link for some unfinished and unused studio pieces. The album would focus on the enormous pressures the band themselves were experiencing on the road: the strains of travelling, the problems of living abroad for great stretches of time, and coping with money. It would also explore violence, social problems and the comforts of religion; this last theme was no doubt prompted by their recent tours through middle America.

It all happened in so short a time it's nigh on unbelievable, as Wright confirmed: "At the start we only had vague ideas about madness being a theme. We rehearsed a lot just putting down ideas, and then in the next rehearsals we used them. It flowed really well. There was a strong thing in it that made it easier to do."

**Lyrically it was Waters's most profound and focused record to date, and for the first time he dominated the creative input, conveying a vision all his own.**

The success of *The Dark Side Of The Moon* is probably attributable to the fact that it was deliberately kept as simple and accessible as possible, with strong dynamics and melodies. It was certainly more focused and down to earth than earlier flights of fancy such as *Echoes*. Indeed Waters gave some hint of what to expect on the forthcoming tour when he spoke to *Sounds* magazine that January under the headline: 'Pink Floyd Have Gone Mental!' "In concept it's more literal, not as abstract as the things we've done before," he offered.

"I think at that time, he [Waters] was finding himself as a lyric writer," Gilmour says. "He was realising that he could get to grips with more serious issues, some political and others that involved him personally. His style had developed and improved. I remember him saying that he wanted to write this album absolutely straight, clear and direct, for nothing to be hidden in mysteries, to get away from all the psychedelic warblings and say exactly what he wanted for the first time."

Finally, it was given the provisional title *The Dark Side Of The Moon*. But, said Gilmour, "at one time it was called *Eclipse*, because Medicine Head did an album called *Dark Side Of The Moon*. But that didn't sell well, so what the hell. I was against *Eclipse,* and we felt a bit annoyed because we had already thought of the title before Medicine Head came out. Not annoyed at them, but because we wanted to use the title."

Both on stage and on record, the music on *The Dark Side Of The Moon* would propel Pink Floyd into the superstar league, severing their underground roots forever. As for Waters, it boosted his confidence as a writer – his skills clearly far outstripped anything any of the others could achieve – and he became the self-appointed lyricist of the band.

With their first nationwide UK tour since 1969 about to commence, the band were still working out the last few details and intricacies of the music, so they booked a few days' rehearsal at a warehouse owned by the Rolling Stones in south London. Final dress rehearsals would take place at the Rainbow Theatre, where they would return to play a show a month later.

To complete the production, the band purchased a brand-new WEM PA with a 28-channel mixing desk and a four-channel, 360-degree quadraphonic sound system. They also had their first complete lighting rig – previously their light show had comprised of a couple of liquid-wheel projectors, built to specification by their newly acquired lighting designer,

**Pink Floyd were renowned for the stunning spectacle of their live show during the DSOTM era and after.**

Arthur Max, who had evidently impressed them as house engineer at their New York Fillmore East show in 1970. (Max remained with the band through to the end of 1977. He now enjoys a lucrative career as a Hollywood production designer.) In addition, specially recorded backing tapes were recorded to accompany the music being played on stage. A total of more than nine tons of equipment, which required assembly by a crew of seven each afternoon before the performance, was put together, and transported by three trucks. Wright himself remarked on the scale of the operation: "Sometimes I look at our huge truck and tons of equipment and think: 'Christ, all I'm doing is playing an organ.'"

> "The piece felt unfinished to me when we were doing it on the road."
> *Roger Waters*

The tour was also the first time Pink Floyd had taken an entire album on the road, and although they were used to previewing material before recording it, *The Dark Side Of The Moon* was a piece that was vastly improved and refined as a result of the decision to tour with it before it was recorded. Live it was performed in exactly the same order as it would appear on the finished album, but the early shows were without synthesisers.

For example, *On The Run,* instead of the now familiar repetitive eight-note synth sequence, was just a keyboard and guitar improvisation, sometimes referred to as *The Travel Sequence*, and concluded not in an explosion but a cacophony of various confusing sound effects. *The Great Gig In The Sky*, on the other hand –widely known to fans at the time as *The Mortality Sequence* – was an electric piano solo backed by pre-recorded tapes of readings from the Book of Ephesians, the Lord's Prayer and other lengthy Biblical discourses, along with recordings of the controversial British broadcaster Malcolm Muggeridge in full rant. *The Sunday Times* described Pink Floyd's show on this tour as "a vision from hell".

Fortunately, Pink Floyd didn't start entirely from scratch. They had already accumulated a bank of rough sketches from previous sessions and out-takes: the music on *Brain Damage*, for example, was written at the time of *Meddle*, but not used; *Breathe* started life as a piece on the Roger Waters/Ron Geesin soundtrack to *The Body* (1970); *Us And Them,* resurrected by Wright, came out of a track called *The Violent Sequence* from the sessions for the soundtrack to the 1970 movie *Zabriskie Point*. Floyd were also prone to influence: a quick listen to the 1971 Beaver & Krause album *Gandharva* will reveal that the whole musical approach is undeniably very similar, which is surely no coincidence. Gilmour has also recently confessed to stealing bit parts such as Eric Clapton's Leslie speaker sound from Cream's *Badge* for *Any Colour You Like*, and, unlikely as it may seem, the echoey and dry sounds on *Money* from Elton John's earlier work.

Despite first-night hitches at the Brighton Dome show on January 20, 1972 caused by an electrical fault that knocked out the tape playback at the start of *Money*, and a total power failure in Manchester, the tour was acclaimed, but certainly not fully comprehended by the public. Proving the value of roadwork, Waters came up with the lyrics for the *Brain Damage/Eclipse* sequence just in time for their show in Leicester on February 10 – eight dates into the tour. "The piece felt unfinished to me when we were doing it on the road," he later said. "I came in one day and said: 'Here, I've just written the ending and this is it.'"

The pivotal performance on the tour was undoubtedly at the Rainbow in London in mid-February, where the world's press sat in attendance to witness *The Dark Side Of The Moon* in all its seemingly well-rehearsed glory. In a series of presentations, and despite some rather stilted performances, Pink Floyd were heralded as a triumph of the imagination and, for the first time, received critical acclaim throughout the national press. Programmes distributed at the show also included the by now complete lyrics for the work (but not the song titles) under the heading 'An Assorted Piece For Lunatics'.

"It was a hell of a good way to develop a record," Nick Mason recalled. "You really get familiar with it; you learn the pieces you like and what you don't like."

There are not many instances where a band begins writing a new album, tours it for a few weeks before going off to write and record a completely different album, tours the original a bit more, goes off and does a ballet, and then carries on recording the original.

In Pink Floyd's case this appeared to be entirely normal procedure. The French director Barbet Schroeder invited them to write music for *La Vallee*, his film about a young woman's spiritual awakening in Papua New Guinea. In two one-week sessions – one before and one after a tour of Japan that March – the band composed and recorded the entire work at Strawberry Studios in the Chateau d'Hérouville near Paris (known as the Honky Chateau, thanks to Elton John). It was released as an album in June as *Obscured By Clouds*.

*Obscured By Clouds* is as striking as it is subtle, with some remarkable music that would be performed on later tours. Perhaps the last true combined effort by the band, it contains some particularly pensive lyrics by Waters. *Free Four*, for example, deals for the first time with the pressures of touring, well before the subject was taken to its conclusion on *The Dark Side Of The Moon*. Waters's father's death is also discussed, perhaps flippantly, but it was a theme that recurred on *The Wall* with greater vehemence. Significantly, *Childhood's End* was Gilmour's last complete lyrical and musical composition in this line-up.

With *Obscured By Clouds* completed, Pink Floyd returned to Abbey Road studios at the end of May to start getting down to the serious business of recording what would become *The Dark Side Of The Moon*. It was an album that benefitted from a vastly improved production from what Floyd had been used to, largely the result of the different textures used but also the appointment of two young and very keen studio technicians: mixing engineer Chris Thomas and recording engineer Alan Parsons. Their collaborative input was invaluable.

*Time*, for example, begins with a recording by Alan Parsons of hundreds of clocks (taken from a quadraphonic sampler he produced for EMI), followed by the abstract use of total silence as a second instrument to Mason's Rototoms.

The first track the band worked on was *Us And Them*, followed by *Money*. Both featured the saxophonist and Cambridge associate Dick Parry, and, for the first time, female backing vocalists. The sound effects on *Money* were cut-and-pasted by Waters. "I made those recordings in the shed at the bottom of the garden, throwing coins into a big industrial food-mixing bowl that my wife used for mixing clay." Waters immersed himself in the whole process with glee. "Roger worked all sorts of hours on the concept, while we went home for our suppers," recalled Gilmour.

Song titles were still very much in the air, as revealed by the running order on a recording sheet from the sessions: *Intro* (*Speak To Me*) / *Travel* (*Breathe*) / *Time* / *Home Again* (*Breathe, Reprise*) / *Religion* (*The Great Gig In The Sky*) / *Money* / *Us And Them* / *Scat* (*Any Colour You Like*) / *Lunatic* (*Brain Damage*) / *End – All That You...* (*Eclipse*).

Pink Floyd also had a unique work ethic: they generally kept businesslike hours, and always had a month off for holidays in August. But there were distractions, as tape engineer Alan Parsons recalled: "The hours we worked depended on which day of the week it was. If it was a football night we would always finish early. Roger was very into any big matches that were going on at the time. He was into playing, as well. There was a Pink Floyd team. And if *Monty Python* was on TV we'd stop."

The band continued their extensive touring of the album with another round of dates in North America and Europe, playing their largest venues to date on both continents. At one spectacular concert at the Hollywood Bowl, eight searchlights beamed skywards from behind the domed stage of the vast amphitheatre into the night sky, and a colourful fireworks display rounded off the evening. Elsewhere, impressive effects included sheets of flame shooting from cauldrons at the back of the stage during Echoes, and a huge gong that burst into flames at the climax of Set The Controls For The Heart Of The Sun.

It was also the year that Floyd delved into other performing arts. They had already provided incidental music for the Ballet Rambert in 1968 and '69, and now approaching fruition were plans to link up with Europe's foremost contemporary ballet school, based in Marseilles and directed by Roland Petit.

**"I don't think you ever come out thinking: 'Bugger me, I've done it this time.'"**
*Roger Waters*

**Drummer Nick Mason feels his way.**

**Four young men poised to become just about the biggest band on the planet.**

The band was brought to the attention of Petit by his daughter, a fan, who had suggested marrying a traditional ballet with modern music. The idea was discussed by the two parties in the middle of their American tours of 1971, when it was suggested that Proust's novel *Remembrance Of Things Past* be adapted for the project. However, this idea floundered almost immediately, having failed to fire anyone's imagination sufficiently, and the project was abandoned.

Waters recalled, with some disbelief, the farcical planning meeting that took place in London that year: "First of all it was Proust, then it was *Aladdin*, then it was something else. We had this great lunch one day - me, Nick [Mason] and [manager] Steve [O'Rourke] - with [Rudolf] Nureyev, Roman Polanski, Roland Petit and some film producer. What a laugh. It was to talk about the projected idea for us doing the music, and Roland choreographing it, and Rudy Bryans being the star, and Roman Polanski directing the film, and making this fantastic ballet film. It was all a complete joke. Nobody had any idea what they wanted to do.

"We all sat around this table until someone thumped the table and said: 'What's the idea, then?' And everyone just sat there drinking wine and getting more and more drunk, until someone suggested *Frankenstein*. And then Nureyev started getting a bit worried. And when Polanski was drunk enough he started to suggest we make the blue movie to end all blue movies. And then it all petered out into cognac and coffee, and we jumped into our cars and split. God knows what happened after we left."

In what seemed like a sensible conclusion to the encounter, it was agreed that the band should compose 40 minutes' worth of original material to which Petit would provide choreography. But, still pushed for recording time, Pink Floyd finally agreed on a 40-minute set of existing material from their current repertoire. The performance was finally staged in Marseilles, at a residency midway through the band's European tour in November 1972. From here it moved to Paris for a series of shows in January and February. But, concluded Gilmour: "the reality of all these people prancing around in tights in front of us didn't feel like what we really wanted to do on a long term basis."

1973 was also the first year that the UK was largely ignored in favour of touring in North America, which received the full-scale sensory assault of a greatly improved *The Dark Side Of The Moon* on two extensive tours. Additional on-stage personnel were also used for the first time, including saxophonist Dick Parry and a string of female backing vocalists who stayed on board for the next two years, including established session singers Liza Strike, Doris Troy, Vicki Brown, Venetta Fields, Carlena Williams and Clydie King.

The album was finally released in March. However, all of Pink Floyd except Wright boycotted the press reception at the London Planetarium because the quadraphonic mix had not been completed in time. Against

"Our music is about neuroses. We are able to see it, and discuss it."
*David Gilmour*

**Bassist Roger Waters's songwriting partnership with David Gilmour was at its zenith on Dark Side Of The Moon.**

the band's wishes, EMI presented a stereo playback through an inferior PA system.

Waters had commented to the *NME* shortly after the release of *Meddle*: "However long you go on working on an album, I don't think you ever come out thinking: 'Bugger me, I've done it this time.' I don't think it's possible to make an album that you think is definitely all right from beginning to end." Nevertheless, *DSOTM* successfully combined every element of Pink Floyd's collective ability, and for the first time was consistent throughout, with strong dynamics and thoughtful lyrics.

It also received enough FM radio-friendly tracks, *Money* in particular, to make a serious dent in the hard-to-crack US market. It exposed Pink Floyd, for the very first time, to a mass audience, propelling them out of the 'weird cult band' bracket and into a solidly mainstream rock market that The Who and Led Zeppelin had been enjoying for some time. But it came at a price, as Gilmour ruefully recalled: "It included an element that wasn't versed in Pink Floyd's ways. It started from the first show in America. People at the front shouting: 'Play *Money*! Gimme something I can shake my ass to!' We had to get used to it, but previously we'd be playing to 10,000-seaters where, in the quiet passages, you could hear a pin drop."

"The thing about *Dark Side...*," commented Nick Mason, "is that I think when it was finished, everyone felt it was the best thing we'd ever done to date, and everyone was very pleased with it. But there's no way that anyone felt it was five times as good as *Meddle*, or eight times as good as *Atom Heart Mother*, or the sort of figures that it has in fact sold. It was something of a phenomenon, and was about not only being a good album, but also about being in the right place at the right time."

Nor could Chris Thomas explain it. Asked some 27 years later if he was surprised by the staying power of *Dark Side...* he replied: "Yeah, cos I didn't like it when I finished it. The album before that was *Meddle*, which had *Echoes* on it, and I had hoped they were going to get into something like that, but *Dark Side...* was just a bunch of songs. And bunches of songs are what I always did, so I thought: 'Great - Pink Floyd. I'll get to do something strange and out of the ordinary.' But that wasn't really the case."

As Wright commented: "We approached the album, I would say, in exactly the same way as any other album we've done. Except that this was a concept album. It was about madness, it was about one's fear, it was about the business, whereas none of the other albums had been about that. They may have been musically tied together, but there hadn't been a theme like that running on both sides."

The album begins and ends with a heartbeat - the simple thread that pulls the whole thing together. "It alludes to the human condition and sets the mood for the music, which describes the emotions experienced during a lifetime," Gilmour explained. "Amid the chaos, there is beauty and hope for mankind. The effects are purely to help the listener understand

The sometimes surreal
experience of Pink Floyd live.

what the whole thing is about."

The sleeve also follows the idea through. A centre-spread gatefold repeats the central theme, showing a cardiograph blip, while the stunning front cover has a simple white light beam that is split into a full spectrum that fans out from a central prism. The mysticism of the prism image continued in the publicity material, which used shots of the Great Pyramids at Giza in Egypt, which Storm Thorgerson and Aubrey 'Po' Powell of Hipgnosis had travelled to Egypt especially to photograph. "It represented both the diversity and the cleanliness of the sound of the music," noted Thorgerson. "It was Roger's idea to turn the light into a heartbeat inside the sleeve – the sound that starts the music."

The material as recorded on the album was significantly different from how it had been previously performed live, and the female backing vocals lent a much softer edge to the overall piece. *On The Run* was developed entirely in the studio to replace the comparatively weak guitar and keyboard jams. It also saw extensive use of their newly acquired EMS VCS3 synthesiser, first used by the band on *Obscured By Clouds*.

The *Mortality Sequence* was perhaps one of the most significant changes from how it had been live to how it appeared on the album, as *The Great Gig In The Sky*. Live it had featured a cacophony of religious discourse, For the album, Alan Parsons tried another idea: "I put some dialogue from a space-walk on it, which I thought worked really well. And they didn't." Instead the band brought in gospel singer Clare Torry to provide a vocal improvisation. It transformed Wright's melancholy piano piece beyond recognition. It became one of the stand-out tracks on *Dark Side*...

"Clare didn't really look the part. She was Alan Parsons's idea," Gilmour recalled. "We wanted to put a girl on there, screaming orgasmically. Alan had worked with her previously, so we gave her try. And she was fantastic. We had to encourage her a little bit, we gave her some dynamic hints: 'Maybe you'd like to do this piece quietly, and this piece louder.' She did maybe half-a-dozen takes, and then afterwards we compiled the final performance out of all the bits."

**Torry was paid a £30 session fee – double the usual rate because it was recorded on a Sunday.**

Another significant aspect of the album is the number of taped voices that can be heard proffering advice and enlightenment on a variety of subjects all loosely fitting into the concept. Interviewees were asked questions about their thoughts on life and death and what 'the dark side of the moon' meant to them. Roger Waters devised a system of questions that were written out on a series of cards and presented in such a way as to prevent anticipation and elicit a definite answer. In all he interviewed about 20 people for this exercise, including Paul and Linda McCartney (although they don't appear on the album, being too well-rehearsed to deliver spontaneous responses), who happened to be recording Red Rose Speedway with Wings in an adjacent studio.

When the cards were mislaid, Waters instead looked at the band's road crew for inspiration. Road-worn technicians are generally a no-nonsense breed who don't mince their words, and Floyd roadies Chris Adamson and Peter Watts were no exception. Adamson delivers the immortal opening line to the album: "I've been mad for fucking years," and Peter Watts's wife Patricia suggests threateningly: "That geezer was cruising for a bruising." But it was the doorman at Abbey Road studios, Irishman Jerry Driscoll, who responded magnificently with: "I've always been mad," "I'm not frightened of dying," and "There is no dark side of the moon, really." All of the questions were delivered on a one-to-one basis, with very little repetition to prevent interviewees having prior warning from others who may have told them what to expect after their own session.

In one amusing exchange Henry McCullough (Wings guitarist) was asked: "When did you last thump someone?" According to Alan Parsons "McCullough's response was: 'New Year's Eve.' The next question was: 'Were you in the right?' And he said: 'I don't know, I was drunk at the time.' His wife was also asked: 'When did you last thump someone?' And she said: 'New Year's Eve' too!"

Very noticeable on the finished album is a stream of manic laughter, which is that of roadie Roger 'The Hat' Manifold, who also delivers the lines: "A short, sharp, shock," in describing a particularly memorable moment of road rage. In response to the question of, as Waters put it, 'peggin' out', The Hat replies: "Death? Wow! Doesn't bovver me in the slightest. Live for today, gone tomorrow, that's me," followed by yet more manic laughter.

Despite the length of time the music had been developing on the road, and the time spent on it in the studio, people still didn't understand the meaning of *The Dark Side Of The Moon*.

"It's amazing," said Gilmour. "At the final mixing stage we thought it was obvious what the album was about, but still a lot of people, including engineers and roadies, when we asked them, didn't know what the LP was about. I really don't know if our things get through, but you have to carry on hoping. Our music is about neuroses. We are able to see it, and discuss it. *The Dark Side Of The Moon* itself is an allusion to the moon and lunacy. The dark side is generally related to what goes on inside people's heads – the subconscious and the unknown."

By the end of 1973, sales of the *Dark Side Of The Moon* showed little signs of tailing off whatsoever. By then, more than 700,000 copies had been sold in the UK alone. From that year onwards, the album would continue to sell and sell and sell. It was later calculated – eventually some 25 years after its release – that the album had sold in excess of 35 million copies worldwide. It is still in the top five best-selling albums of all time. Surprisingly, it never reached the No.1 spot in the UK, at the time being kept from the pinnacle by Alice Cooper's *Billion Dollar Babies*.

Waters recalls this time with great fondness: "They were very happy times. We discovered what we did, each of us, what our contributions were. We had gelled as a group, we were working very well together and we were working very hard, doing lots of gigs.

**"We were in the springtime of Pink Floyd, when it was all good fun and we had a common purpose: we wanted to be popular, we all wanted to be rich and famous, and yet we weren't. And I could express myself within that context, and Dave could play his guitar, Rick could play keyboards and write and Nick could do what he did, and we were all content to be together and it was very jolly. It was a wonderful time."**

ATLANTIC
HIGHWAY TO HELL
LONELY HEARTS
CLUB BAND
BLIZZARD OF OZZ
The Beach Boys Pet Sounds
ALADDIN SANE
NEVER MIND
HERE'S THE
THE ROLLING STONES
LOU REED-TRANSFORME
BOSTON
motörhead
The Clash
MCMLXXXIV
VAN HALEN
MCMLXXXIV
JAILBREAK-THIN LI